WAR STORIES

WAR STORIES

VIETNAM

ROBERT O. BABCOCK

Deeds not Words!

Bob Babcock

DEEDS PUBLISHING | ATLANTA, GEORGIA

Most of the material in this book is a subset of stories previously published in 2006 by Deeds Publishing in *War Stories: Utah Beach to Pleiku* by Robert O. Babcock.

Disclaimer — No claim is made as to the historical accuracy of the stories in this book. They are as accurate as memories faded by thirty to thirty-five years can make them, but this is not intended to be a history book that will stand the test of historical scholars. It is the military experiences of 4th Infantry Division veterans as each GI remembers it.

Published by Deeds Publishing
Athens, GA
www.deedspublishing.com

Printed in the United States of America

Library of Congress Cataloging-in-Publications Data is available upon request

ISBN 978-1-944193-48-5

Books are available in quantity for promotional or premium use. For information, write Deeds Publishing, 220 College Avenue, Suite 606, Athens, GA 30601 or info@deedspublishing.com.

Design and layout by Mark Babcock

First edition 2016

10 9 8 7 6 5 4 3 2 1

This book is dedicated to all past, present, and future veterans of the 4th Infantry Division, especially those who made the supreme sacrifice in defense of our American way of life, and their families.

TABLE OF CONTENTS

January—December 1966   17

Fort Lewis Training Days 18
Another Egg for Breakfast 23
The Flame Thrower 24
Loyal Troops 26
Fort Lewis and the "Boat People" 27
Train, Retain, and Deploy 30
Still Together 31
A Lapse of Military Courtesy 33
Clarence 36
The Naming of Camp Enari 37
Entering the Mouth of the Dragon 39
Tuy Hoa—September 1966 45
Water Supply 47
A Hilarious Sight 48
Ammo Resupply 49
Royal Welcome 50
First Combat Assault 52
Ghosts from the Past 55
Tuy Hoa Shower Point 63
The Kool-Aid Caper 64
The Centipede 65
Hoboes 67
I Wish I'd Asked His Name 69
Chapel Service on the Cambodian Border 70
Christmas in Vietnam 73
New Year's Eve 1966 74

January—December 1967   77

From Knox to the "Nam" 78
Tet 1967 87
What Are Those Ugly Looking Sores? 89
Close Call 91
Cherry Pies 94
Letter from a Hospital Bed February 18, 1967 96
Central Highlands, Vietnam '67 98
Night Listening Post 100
The Pig Lady 102
Grenades 104
Picking on PSG Kay 105
Short Rounds 108

A Memorable Experience in Vietnam 110
Lightning Bug Ambush 111
The Battle of Soui Tre 112
Admiration for the Artillery 117
Chasing the NVA 118
My First Mission 119
The Individual Soldier in Company B, 1st Battalion, 22nd Infantry Regiment, 1966-1967 120
Martha Raye 122
April Fool's Day 1967 124
What Did I Get Myself Into? 127
Breaking In 131
Operation Francis Marion—May 26, 1967 135
Malaria Pills 137
Premonitions 138
Combat Strength Forward 139
Living With Green Plastic Bags 140
Too "Short" for This 143
Unusual Incident 144
Short-Time Ambush Patrols 145
Central Highlands of Vietnam—October 3, 1967 146
A Man I'd Like to Meet 148
Men Called Lurps 150
My Mother, the Patriot 156
Jungle Living—Things to Know 160
How Many Scared GIs Will Fit Behind One Large Rock? 161
Dak To—November 1967 168
Dak To—Hill 724 170
Dak To Debriefing—MG W. Ray Peers—CG 4th Infantry Division 187

January—December 1968   189

A Noel Visit 190
The Dog Bone—February 1968 191
Headline Story from "Ivy Leaves" Newspaper 198
Regulars, by God 199
Chu Mohr Mountain—April 1968 200
Have You Ever Seen a Pink Elephant? 202
Tiger Pulls Switch on Lyrics: Holds That Man! 204
Water Buffalo 205

Saga of a Listening Post 206
The Longest Night 209
Delta Tango 211
Seven Short Stories 213

January—December 1969 219

Vietnam—Arrival and First Patrol 220
Operation 'Clean Up' Sweeps Local Hamlets 226
Rats 227
The Patrol 228
The Birth 230
Following a Tradition 232
Rucksack Packing—An Art Form 233
A Game of Hearts 235
The Oasis—Mother's Day 1969 243
A Man on the Moon 252
A Long Night on FSB Larry 253
The Simple Joys 258
Persistent Sniper 259
The Combat Assault 260

January—December 1970 261

Bad Day in the Punchbowl 262
Lost Ambush Patrol 268
Walking Point 269
The D-Handle Shovel 270
Cambodia 272
Battle Analysis 275
Monkey in the Foxhole 283
The Sniper 285
Absolution 287

Introduction

This book is one of a series of three that are subsets of the book, War Stories: Utah Beach to Pleiku, first published in 2001. That book was my effort to preserve the stories of 4th Infantry Division veterans who had served in World War II, the Cold War, and in Vietnam. Thanks to the input of the 4ID veterans and their family members, that book turned out to be over 725 pages long—much larger than most people want to buy and read.

In 2014, the 70th anniversary year of D-Day, the liberation of Paris, the Battle of the Hurtgen Forest, and the Battle of the Bulge in World War II, we decided to republish that book into two World War II and one Vietnam volumes—available in both paperback and e-book. Although the large version is still available in paperback format, we believe our readers will enjoy these smaller volumes as they read or re-read the exploits of Soldiers of the 4th Infantry Division.

After getting the two World War II volumes out in 2014, we decided to wait until 2016, the 50th anniversary of the 4th Infantry Division's deployment to Vietnam, to publish this volume.

As you read the stories in all three books, you will see that some stories show the author as deceased. That was the status as of 2000 when the book was first written. Since then, sadly, many more, if not most, of the

WWII contributors to these stories are now gone, as are a growing number of Vietnam vets—but their stories live on.

When I first started attending annual reunions of the National 4th Infantry Division Association in 1990, the highlight of each reunion was sitting with WWII vets and listening for hours to the stories of their exploits in Europe. As I anticipated each year sitting down again with a specific veteran whose stories had captivated me the year before, I found that all too often I would ask about where he was, only to find out that he had died, and his stories died with him.

When I became president of the National 4th Infantry Division Association in 1998-2000, one of my primary missions I set for myself was to preserve the stories of 4ID veterans so they would be available long past the time that our veterans went on to their heavenly rewards.

I am currently working on War Stories II, adding more World War II, Cold War, and Vietnam stories, and including sections on the 4th Infantry Division's actions in Iraq and Afghanistan. That book will be published once I have enough stories to make it viable. It is my hope and desire that we will have it available in 2017, the 100th birthday of the 4th Infantry Division.

All who served in any capacity with the 4th Infantry Division are encouraged to send me their stories.

As you read the 70th anniversary WWII commemorative edition, reflect back on those members of "the greatest generation" who cared enough to not only fight and defeat the Nazi threat to the world, but also cared enough to write down their memories so future generations could learn from their experiences. And as you read this 50th anniversary Vietnam commemorative edition, you will find that we Vietnam vets also had great stories to preserve about our time in Vietnam. Each and every one of us Vietnam vets can take pride in stepping up to the call of our country, just as our WWII fathers did.

I challenge all veterans of all eras to send me your stories—and make sure your family, your unit, and others you care about have access to your stories. If you need help doing that, feel free to contact this author at info@deedspublishing.com.

Ten percent of all profits of this book will be donated to the National 4th Infantry Division Association to help perpetuate its almost 100 years helping the veterans and family members of those who served in our great division.

Steadfast and Loyal,

Bob Babcock, July 2016

President and Historian, National 4th Infantry Division Association

Company B, 1st Battalion, 22nd Infantry Regiment

2nd Brigade, 4th Infantry Division, Vietnam 1966-1967

The 4th Infantry Division in Vietnam 1966 to 1970

After having advisors active in South Vietnam since 1959, the Gulf of Tonkin incident in August 1964 propelled the United States into a more active role in Southeast Asia. With the first combat troops introduced into South Vietnam in early 1965, the winds of war were once again threatening for the United States Army. Troop strength escalated, and by the end of 1965 over 184,000 American soldiers, sailors, airmen, and marines were fighting the Communists in a country that few Americans even knew existed a few years earlier.

The 4th Infantry Division was alerted in late 1965 to begin preparations for their future role in Vietnam. With troop strength at a critically low point, the division was infused with fresh recruits to "train and retain" as they prepared for their entry into the Vietnam war in the last half of 1966.

Led by the 2nd Brigade, lead elements of the 4th Infantry Division left Fort Lewis, Washington, and the Port of Tacoma on July 21, 1966, en route to Vietnam. By late October, all three brigades had closed into Vietnam and begun this new chapter of the division's life. By the end of 1966, total American military strength was over 385,000 before reaching its peak of 536,000 at the end of 1968.

Unlike World War I and World War II, there were no front lines and no clear objective to end the war in Vietnam. The 4th Infantry Division's mission was basically to "search and destroy"—find the elusive Viet Cong and North Vietnamese Army and destroy him. This mission was accomplished primarily in the central highlands along the Cambodian border to the west of the last major city of Pleiku (thus the inclusion in the title of this book). From July 1966 until finally returned to Fort Carson, Colorado in December, 1970, the 4th Infantry Division covered the largest area of operation of any division in Vietnam and slowed and damaged the North Vietnamese Army as they infiltrated into South Vietnam from the Ho Chi Minh trail that wound from North Vietnam down through Laos and Cambodia.

No war except for the Cold War was as long and no war was as divisive to our country, (except for the American Civil War), as the Vietnam War was. The role and accomplishments of the American fighting man, however, should always be separated from the political and governmental implementation of the war. These soldiers, sailors, airmen, and marines did the job they were asked to do by their country, and they did it very well. It has often been said that the Vietnam war was not a ten year war, it was a one year war fought ten times as experienced American troops were replaced after a twelve-month tour of duty. In the case of the 4th Infantry Division, their manpower turned over a full five times between 1966 and 1970 before the division was withdrawn from the war. With average division strength of 16,000 men, that meant that over 80,000 American soldiers wore the 4th Infantry Division patch while serving in Vietnam.

Although their mission was not as well defined and the historical results are not as positive—the courage, sacrifice, and patriotism exhibited by the 4th Infantry Division soldiers in Vietnam was every bit as great as their counterparts whose stories make up the first part of this book.

January—December 1966

The highlights of 1966 include the massive training mission conducted at Fort Lewis, Washington, from January until the last brigade departed for Vietnam in September. The deployment started with the 4th Engineer Battalion sailing for Vietnam on July 6, 1966. The entire 2nd Brigade arrived in Vietnam in early August 1966. The 1st Brigade and Division HQ arrived in early September, and the 3rd Brigade in early October. The 3rd Brigade was deployed west of Saigon at Dau Tieng, and worked closely with the 25th Infantry Division. The 2nd Brigade and Division headquarters worked from the base camp that they established south of Pleiku in the central highlands. The 1st Brigade began operations in the area around Tuy Hoa along the coast. Operations participated in included Paul Revere III and IV, Attleboro, and Adams. Hamlet visitation programs began. Major General Arthur S. Collins Jr. commanded the division. The first 4th Infantry Division soldier killed by hostile action in Vietnam was PFC Albert Collins of Company C, 1st Battalion, 22nd Infantry Regiment on September 3, 1966. Total hostile and non-hostile killed in action for 1966 was 106.

Bob Babcock, Marietta, GA

Company B, 1st Battalion, 22nd Infantry Regiment

Fort Lewis Training Days

By the end of January 1966, the rumor that my company commander, Lieutenant Sandy Fiacco, had heard was true. My platoon was filled, overnight, with 48 men—most of them fresh out of basic training and ready for Advanced Individual Training (AIT). Our entire brigade was filled with troops to "train and retain." Even though it was unofficial, we all felt certain we would be in Vietnam before the summer was over.

AIT consisted of weapons training with the M-60 machine gun, .45 caliber pistol, 81mm mortar, M-79 grenade launcher, M-90 rocket launcher, hand grenades, and other specialized weapons. We also did extensive training on small unit tactics at the fire team and squad levels.

Many other subjects, such as map and compass reading, radio procedures, first aid, land navigation, escape and evasion, artillery fire adjustment, and other skills infantrymen needed to survive and perform their mission in combat rounded out the eight weeks of AIT.

Most of the teaching load fell on the four platoon leaders. We tried to share the load as best we could. Even at that, during one week, I was the primary instructor for eighty hours of live fire, day and night squad attack exercises. At the end of the week, I was physically and mentally exhausted. The intense lecture load was tough, but that was nothing compared to the responsibility of teaching troops how to work together under combat conditions, with live ammunition, without shooting each other. And I was still a rookie myself.

After successfully completing the eight weeks of AIT, capped off by a graduation ceremony with all the military pomp and circumstance, we took a deep breath over the weekend, then went into our platoon and company training phase. During that two-month period we really learned to work together as a unit. Feeling certain we would be going into combat together, we leaders made special efforts to learn everything we could about the individual men—their strengths and weaknesses, their quirks, and other important idiosyncrasies.

Every day we learned something new and valuable. During hand grenade training we learned one man could not master the skill of throwing one. Despite repeated attempts at teaching him with dummy grenades, we had to dive for cover behind the protection of the concrete bunkers every time he threw a live grenade and it landed only a few feet in front of his position. We made sure he did not carry hand grenades when we got to Vietnam.

Two men in my platoon showed unique skills at path finding. Ernie Redin and Mark Petrino had grown up playing in the woods of their native Connecticut. They possessed keen skills of observation, alertness, and selecting the best path through the forest. They became the two men I alternated as point man in critical times. Point man was a dangerous and extremely important job—a skilled point man was priceless. He kept the unit from walking into an ambush as well as leading them to their objective. Because of the skills Ernie and Mark demonstrated, I am certain they saved more lives in Vietnam than we will ever know.

A quirk I learned was that Ernie would follow a compass azimuth heading as straight as an arrow. Mark would always drift five degrees to the right. Knowing that, I could compensate for the drift when I gave Mark a heading to follow. Learning habits such as these were invaluable. Too many men went into combat without knowing the capabilities of the men they were depending on to do the job. By training together as a unit, we gained an advantage far too few men in Vietnam had. I have always been thankful we had the advantage of five months training together before we saw actual combat.

It was also during this period that we selected our leaders. Besides Staff Sergeant Frank Roath, my platoon sergeant, I had only three non-commissioned officers in my platoon. In addition to Sergeant Roath, my mission and organization required eleven non-commissioned officers (NCOs) to serve as fire team leaders, machine gun crew chiefs, and squad leaders. Since most of our troops had been drafted, we had a good cross section of America in the company.

Three men quickly distinguished themselves as leaders. Doug Muller was an aeronautical engineer, a college graduate from New York. Aubrey Thomas was a native of the Virgin Islands and had served a short time in the British Army. Willie Cheatham had grown up on the streets of Detroit. All three had been drafted. Aubrey and Willie were African American, Doug was white; all had natural leadership skills. Doug and Aubrey became squad leaders, and Willie became my most reliable fire team leader. All three would be wounded before their tours in Vietnam were over.

Some leaders are born; others have to be trained. We were successful in training some outstanding small unit leaders during those long, rainy days at Fort Lewis. Each day we gave our men the opportunity to show their leadership skills. Soon we had an outstanding group of young leaders, not just in my platoon but across the entire company. Again, we had the advantage of building a team before we came under enemy fire.

As training progressed, formal platoon training tests were conducted. A keen sense of competition permeated the battalion as we all honed our skills to show we could function as a unit. After a day and night of constant challenges, my platoon finished with the second best score in the battalion—second only by a few points to the score of Dick Collins and his platoon. We did not feel so bad being beaten by Lieutenant Collins since he was a West Point graduate and in another company. We had earned our place as the best platoon in our company and one of the best in the battalion and brigade.

Bravo Company developed a unique "esprit de corps" during our Fort Lewis training days. Lieutenant Fiacco insisted the platoon leaders lead by example. We would not ask our troops to do anything we were not willing to do ourselves, and we helped them learn from the experience. Lieutenant Fiacco practiced what he preached and spent most of his time in the field with the troops, as did First Sergeant Bob MacDonald. The officers, NCOs, and troops were quickly learning we were a unique company and took great pride in ourselves. The leadership spark of Lieutenant Fiacco and First Sergeant MacDonald inspired all of us.

Physical conditioning was another element of training in which Lieutenant Fiacco led by example. Before we completed our training day, he led us in daily five-mile runs around the back roads of the training areas. Our men complained, but we knew Bravo Company was better prepared than most for what lay ahead of us.

Towards the end of company training, we got the official word. We were shipping overseas to USARPAC—United States Army, Pacific. Vietnam was not mentioned in the orders, but we all knew our destination would be that Southeast Asian country.

The first of June was the beginning of our final training before we left the States—a 14-day Brigade Field Training Exercise (FTX). After two days of intensive preparation, we were up long before daylight on the first day of the FTX.

Our brigade was assigned to attack a mythical Southeast Asian objective, pacify the natives, and wait for further orders. Our battalion was to lead the attack, Bravo Company would lead the battalion, and my third platoon had the lead for our company—thus, leading the brigade into the FTX.

We had a spring in our step as we entered this "final exam" stage of our training. Soon after we left the line of departure, we came upon a river. A sign reading "Bridge Blown Out" attached to a roadblock kept us from crossing the bridge. Several umpires stood by to insure we followed the rules of the FTX.

Not to be slowed down, we quickly found a spot to ford. Our teeth chattered as the freezing cold water from the spring thaw raced by us on its way from the Cascade Mountains to nearby Puget Sound. We had barely reached the opposite bank after wading through the chest deep water when the "aggressors" opened fire. We spread out and returned fire, forgetting how cold we were. The radio quickly crackled to life as Lieutenant Fiacco called, "Do you want an air strike?"

Without hesitation, I replied, "Affirmative!" as I tried to assess the situation in the confusion of the gunfire.

He told me, "Mark your position with smoke."

In little more than a minute after I threw out a yellow smoke grenade, two F-4 Phantom jets came screaming out of the sky toward us. The noise was deafening as they came to the bottom of their bomb run and turned their nose back skyward and hit their afterburners to make a quick getaway.

I had frequently called for an air strike during our training. Everything was always simulated and no real airplanes ever appeared. You can imagine the shocked look on all of our faces when real airplanes responded to our call. That really brought it home to me—we were about to finish training and go on to the real thing. (The "real thing," we found out, was much more spectacular and awesome than this.) Fortunately, the planes did not drop real bombs or they would have gotten us. We learned from that experience to respect the power of an air strike and to hug the earth and use whatever terrain features were available for protection when we called one in.

The FTX was a success, but it strongly pointed out to us the confusion and chaos that can reign when so many men are involved in an operation. We saw those leaders who responded well under pressure, which ones did stupid things, and the true meaning of SNAFU. (Situation Normal, All

Fouled Up). We were all sobered with the knowledge our next operation would be for real, and mistakes would be paid for in American lives—potentially our own.

Our five months of training at Fort Lewis were very eventful. I was transformed from a green, broken legged "shavetail" to a qualified, confident infantry leader. During that time, I also gained the confidence and respect of Sergeant Roath. He was always true to his tradition of looking down his nose at second lieutenants, never failing to point out he was a "senior" NCO and I was a "junior" officer, only slightly more intelligent than dirt. But he showed me in subtle ways he thought I was doing OK.

Donald Brady, (Deceased)
Company C, 2nd Battalion, 22nd Infantry Regiment

Another Egg for Breakfast

As told to his daughter, Suzanne Bullock

My dad, Private Donald Brady, was in basic training at Fort Lewis, Washington in January 1966. One day while in the field for training, the Commanding General, Major General Arthur S. Collins, came to see how his new troops were doing. They were heading for Vietnam soon, and he wanted to see if they were learning how to be soldiers. The general approached a private by the name of Polhan and asked him how things were going.

The private responded, "Sir, not bad with one exception!" General Collins asked what that exception was.

Private Polhan's response was, "Well, sir, I'm from Iowa. In farm country, breakfast is a very important meal for us, and I'm not getting enough to eat in the morning here."

General Collins, not wanting to have one of his hungry troops writing a letter to his congressman to complain, said, "Well, Private, tomorrow morning you tell the mess sergeant that I said you could have another egg for breakfast."

The next morning, Polhan was in the chow line, just a few guys ahead of my dad—close enough that Dad heard the following exchange.

The mess sergeant was frying eggs as Polhan approached the grill. The private repeated what General Collins had said to tell him. The sergeant looked at Polhan and after careful consideration placed another egg on his plate and said, "Move on, troop."

At that moment, there was a lot of commotion at the back door. Someone announced "AT EASE!"

In walked General Collins. The General walked through the kitchen area to the chow line where Polhan and the mess sergeant were still standing.

General Collins approached the Private and said, "I thought I would stop by and see if you got that extra egg this morning."

The sergeant had beads of sweat on his forehead, which could have been from standing over the hot grill, or...

Private Polhan replied, "YES SIR, THANK YOU, SIR!"

The troops were put at ease and continued with their morning meal.

Roger Hill, Lena, IL
Recon, 1st Battalion, 12th Infantry Regiment

The Flame Thrower

Another pre-departure preparation, as we trained at Fort Lewis, included training a selected few within the battalion in the maintenance and use of the flame thrower. I was designated along with about five others to receive this training. The program lasted one day and consisted of classes and a live "fire" exercise on the range.

We were all surprised at the kick when the weapon was fired. We had to lean well forward to compensate for the recoil. There was a tendency to lunge forward slightly when the trigger was released and the pressure of the discharge was stopped. The heat was another surprise.

There was an incident on the range during live firing that scared us all. We were taught how to mix our fuel, load the two fuel tanks, close the valves, pressurize the air tank, and put it on and prepare to fire. Once a soldier was ready to fire, he was to reach behind him, find the air tank knob and open it, light his igniter, and point the nozzle down range at the target and squeeze the trigger for about a three to five second burst. All of these steps were to be followed under the assumption that the flamethrower had been placed properly into operation. We all took turns on the firing line to demonstrate our skill and proficiency.

It must have been close to the last couple of firers when an incident occurred. It seems that when one soldier filled his fuel tanks, he failed to close the small vent caps on top of the tank caps. This allowed the fuel to be sprayed out under high pressure up and over his head when he opened his air tank valve when he was ready to shoot. We were all standing back behind the firing line when we saw what was happening. It was as if everything was in slow motion. We were all yelling at him to stop, but for some reason he kept right on going through the firing steps. With dual streams of jellied gas spewing up over his head, he ignited his striker and attempted to fire the gun. With most of the pressure gone, only a short stream of burning fuel shot out from the nozzle. As it hit the ground in front of him, it began to burn back toward him.

Realizing that something was wrong, he looked back at us to notice that we were screaming at him to drop the unit and run for his life. At about the same second he finally understood, the fuel spewing out of the top of his tanks began to rain back down on him. He must have gotten about ten feet away when the flames reached the tanks lying on the ground. With a loud and hot, "Whoomp," the fire ball shot up in the air where he had been standing just a moment before. We all got a lesson in safety that day. Luckily, the only damage done was the loss of a flame thrower unit and the soldier's dignity.

Our biggest concern was that we would actually have to carry one of these weapons into combat. Nobody wanted to have one strapped to his back and take a tracer round through a pressurized tank of jellied gas. Like so many other things, we never heard about them again after we got to Nam. Nobody asked, either.

Judson Miller, Tacoma, WA
Brigade Commander, 2nd Brigade, 4th Infantry Division

Loyal Troops

I am sure that many of you will recall that just before the 2nd Brigade shipped out in July, 1966, virtually all five thousand men of the brigade task force were given leave. Just after everyone went on leave, there was a nationwide airline strike and some predicted that hundreds of our soldiers would miss shipment to Vietnam. (President Johnson even went on TV and said we would not be considered AWOL if we missed shipment). To the contrary, all but five or ten soldiers made it back on time by hitchhiking, taking the bus, using Canadian airlines, or other means to overcome the lack of air transportation in the U.S.

Bill Matz, Chicago, IL

HQ Company, 2nd Battalion, 22nd Infantry Regiment and Gary Krek,
Phoenix, AZ

Recon, 2nd Battalion, 22nd Infantry Regiment

Fort Lewis and the "Boat People"

*Most of the Vietnam guys who served with the 4th Infantry Division got to
Vietnam via a fast airplane ride from the West Coast. For the original group
who trained together at Fort Lewis, and fought together during our unit's first
year in Vietnam, we experienced a memorable boat ride during the late summer or early fall of 1966, prior to getting to Vietnam. In late November of
1999, Bill Matz, medic with HQ Company, 2nd Battalion, 22nd Infantry
Regiment, and Gary Krek, Recon, 2nd Battalion, 22nd Infantry Regiment,
started swapping memories over the Internet of their experiences as "boat people." It expanded to include training at Fort Lewis and early days in Vietnam.
I entered into the ongoing discussion, which continued to build on the Internet
over about four months. Here are some excerpts from the dialogue, covering the
last days at Fort Lewis.—Bob Babcock*

Gary Krek: Bill, You may not remember this, but you and I worked together at Fort Lewis, Washington. You guys (medics) were bringing the
whole battalion up to date on our shots for Vietnam. I was in line towards
the beginning, and, after finishing, I remember hearing one of the medics
state they didn't have enough help to finish on time. I stepped forward
and volunteered to help in any way I could. One of you, I don't remember who, asked if I could help with the shots. I said Yes, but added that I
had no experience doing this. With that, I was handed an orange, given
some instructions, and told to practice for a few minutes. I remember that
after a couple of dozen shots, I was starting to get pretty good. No more

complaints, except for a few guys I didn't particularly care for. I also made a bunch of new friends that day: "Hey Gary, what are you doing giving shots, BUDDY?"

Bill Matz: Gary, You're not a real medic until you can hit someone in the arm by throwing the syringe across the room like a dart. I do remember giving out the shots before Vietnam. Some of the guys got pretty sick in reaction to the plague vaccine. You caught on to a dirty little medic's secret. The shots always seemed to hurt people you didn't like.

Gary Krek: I also volunteered to help out over at the chapel, where the allotments were being made out. I interviewed and typed a bunch of those up, and never heard a complaint while in Vietnam about someone not getting his allotment checks sent to the right address or bank. Could be they forgot that I helped.

Bill Matz: I was trying to remember something about packing our equipment and getting the tracks ready to ship, but all I can remember is that I used to sneak away to the "Donut Hut" a lot when we were supposed to be packing. I must have been one lazy S.O.B.

Gary Krek: The Donut Hut. Boy, this is getting scary. I remember that place.

Bill Matz: Around the time we were packing our gear, they had us all go over to the Brigade HQ, where a bunch of "legal affairs" types were set up at tables. We proceeded to make out our Last Will and Testament. I remember someone asking, "Do you suppose they're trying to tell us something?"

The PX was also doing a "land office" business in green dye. At the laundromat, we were dyeing our white underwear green. The 6th Army personnel (Permanent Party at Fort Lewis) were all pretty upset about this. It seems our guys were running so much dye through the washers that everything the permanent party washed was coming out green. We didn't have much sympathy for them.

Bob Babcock: When I first checked in to Fort Benning as a Second Lieutenant, fresh out of ROTC, the First Cavalry Division was just ready to leave for Vietnam (August 1965). The local Columbus, Georgia newspaper was warning everyone to stay away from the washers and dryers in the laundromats because of the green dye that was everywhere. It was the identical problem—different location and division.

Bill Matz: I guess it's time to "own up" about the paint shed at Fort Lewis. Remember? It was right across the street from the battalion area, on the edge of the depression where the PX was located. The night before our ship left, I was heading back to our company area feeling no pain. (Well lubricated, so to speak). I ran into Bill Sanders (B Company), who was from my old neighborhood in Chicago. We got the idea into our heads that the shed should be rolled down the hill into the depression. We tipped it over and started it rolling, and then we walked away. The next day, as we got ready to leave, I saw my buddy, Farrell (medic HHQ). His fatigues were covered with paint down the front.

I said, "Farrell! What happened to you?"

He said, "Last night, I was heading back to the barracks with a couple of guys, when we saw two guys try to roll the paint shed down the hill. But the #@%$&'s didn't finish the job, and it only rolled half way. We rolled it the rest of the way to the bottom. The colonel caught us and made us roll it back up the hill where it belonged!"

I didn't tell Farrell who the #@%$&'s were.

Gary Krek: Our last night at Fort Lewis was a bit on the crazy side. I recall that most of the battalion was down the hill, trying to drain the state of

Washington of its last can of beer. Olympia, Black Label, Rainier, it didn't matter. I do recall the teamwork on rolling the old paint shed, and I was part of your cheering section. I also remember that the tables we were gathered at became instant firewood to help light up the festivities. The military police had been cruising the area, but not confronting anyone until the benches went up. Remember the MP with the loud speaker? I don't know what was said, but the next thing I saw were GIs and MPs going at it—bad move on the MPs part.

Bill Matz: When we were shipboard at the Port of Tacoma, we were at the railing watching the 6th Army Band perform patriotic tunes. A small crowd of civilians was also milling around, waiting to see friends or relatives depart. A young woman on the dock shouted up to a loved one, "Don't forget to take your pills," apparently referring to seasickness pills.

Some GI down the rail shouted back, "And don't you forget to take your pills!"—obviously referring to "The Pill" (birth control), which was just becoming popular in the mid-sixties.

Jim Stapleton, Atlanta, GA
Companies A and C, 1st Battalion, 22nd Infantry Regiment

Train, Retain, and Deploy

At Fort Lewis we considered ourselves fortunate that we were designated a train, retain, and deploy division. That meant we would receive soldiers right out of basic training and with our officer and NCO cadre provide Advanced Individual Training (AIT), Basic Unit Training, and Advanced Unit Training. After a brigade-qualifying Field Training Exercise in the National Rain Forests, we deployed as a unit. It was the best way to go to war—with a chain of command you were familiar with, soldiers who knew each other, and, we were at one hundred percent of our authorized strength. It was a successful twelve-month tour (army policy in the Vietnam war was for soldiers to have an twelve-month tour in the combat zone and then redeploy to the States and be replaced with new troops); however, at the end of our tour, the majority of the company was scheduled to rotate out at the same time.

Departure dates from the field were spread out over several weeks. The dates were not announced until the day that the evacuation helicopter was scheduled to come in to the company LZ. This was very tough on morale. Everyone wanted to be the first out, but some of the best soldiers were not necessarily the first out. It was tough to watch others get on the chopper, while good men stayed out in the jungle and continued their exposure to combat.

Roger S. Barton, Walkersville, MD
4th S&T Battalion

Still Together

My story starts shortly after graduation from high school in 1965, but it actually began in the eighth grade when I met my best friend, Norman Lilley. Norman was a couple of years older than I was, but we hit it off right away and soon were the very best of friends. We went to school together, played sports together, and were soon more like brothers than friends. There was a "game" that we played in our neighborhood woods called, simply, "Army." We would choose teams of two or more on a side and head for the local woods after dark. One team would enter the woods and hide. The other team would wait ten minutes or so and enter the woods from another point. The object of the game was to move silently through the woods until you located one of the enemy and "killed" him. Little did we know that we were already training for our tour in Vietnam.

When I graduated from high school in 1965, I was seventeen years old. Norman was nineteen and we knew that he would soon be drafted into the army. We decided that we would enlist together so that we would have a better chance of staying together. We did not enlist on any type of "buddy plan," and there were no guarantees that we would stay together. We enlisted for Airborne Infantry, and on August 18, 1965, we were in Baltimore, Maryland, boarding a train for Fort Jackson, South Carolina. We stayed at the reception station in Fort Jackson for several days where we were issued uniforms and such. Then it was on to Fort Gordon, Georgia, for basic training. It was no surprise that we were still together.

Shortly before our eight weeks of basic training were over, five members of our company were selected to go to Leadership School. This was a two-week course that trained us to be squad leaders in Advanced Infantry Training (AIT). Two of those five were Norman and I. After Leadership School, we stayed at Fort Gordon for eight weeks of Advanced Infantry Training. Norman and I were still together. During AIT, we took and passed our physical tests for Parachute Jump School. When AIT ended, we boarded buses and were off to Fort Benning, Georgia, and Parachute Jump School. Norman and I were still together. During Jump School, we were approached and offered Parachute Rigger School to learn parachute packing, maintenance, and air delivery. At first we were not interested until we learned that the school was three months long and was at Fort Lee, Virginia, only three hours from home. We immediately signed up. Norman and I were still together. We spent our three months learning how to become riggers. Boy, were we surprised when we learned that the final test for parachute packing was to pack a chute and them jump with it. We passed.

Towards the end of Rigger School, everyone was ripe with anticipation about where they would be stationed. Most of us had been in training of one sort or another for ten months or so and this would be our first permanent assignment. When the orders finally came down, two people out of the entire class got orders for the 4th Infantry Division. Norman and I—we were still together. How ironic! To this day we don't know how we managed to stay together. Only two out of the entire class? Why us, Barton and Lilley?

Upon our arrival at Fort Lewis, Washington, we were assigned to the 4th S&T Battalion. Everyone was busy packing the unit for the move to Vietnam and we spent most of our time dodging details. One day we were called into the Orderly Room to see the CO. We figured that we had been "busted" for dodging all those details. It ended up that two other riggers had arrived, and the C.O. had called all of us to the Orderly Room. He said that he needed two volunteers and Norman and I stepped forward right away. He then told us that we would be going to Vietnam first with the 2nd Brigade of the 4th Infantry Division, and the other two riggers would go later. We were still together.

Needless to say, we went to Vietnam with the 4th ID, spent our year there, and then upon our return to the States we were both assigned to the same Company at Fort Bragg, North Carolina, where we finished our enlistments. Norman and I were still together. To this day, Norman and I remain the best of friends. Norman and I are still together.

Bill Saling, Big Canoe, GA
HQ Company, 1st Battalion, 22nd Infantry Regiment

A Lapse of Military Courtesy

I reported to the 4th Infantry Division at Fort Lewis, Washington, in early June 1965, and was assigned to the 1st Battalion, 22nd Infantry. Having just graduated from the Infantry Officer Basic Course at Fort Benning, I was anxious to begin my military service.

I was first assigned as a platoon leader of the third platoon, Company A, and later as Executive Officer of Company A. During the latter half of 1965, our battalion was operating at approximately fifty percent of its authorized strength because we were being tasked with sending replacement personnel to Vietnam. This was especially true of our NCO cadre.

At the beginning of 1966 our division was notified that it would be deployed to Vietnam the following summer. Almost immediately we began receiving new recruits and were responsible for conducting advanced individual training and small unit training in preparation for deployment. About this time I was transferred to Battalion Headquarters as the support platoon leader to begin the training process along with everyone else in the battalion.

During the initial training cycle we identified individuals who did not appear to be suitable for deployment. As we completed that phase of training, our commanding officer, Lieutenant Colonel Len Morley, called an officers' meeting one Friday afternoon and requested each platoon leader to submit the names of those individuals we would like to have removed from our platoon. Many of the individuals listed simply did not want to be in the army and were a constant source of problems for our NCOs.

After the meeting we all were pleased to have finalized our platoon roster. Now our life as junior officers would be much easier. I vividly remember going to the Officers Club at North Beach and drinking more than one beer to our good fortune.

However, on the following Monday, I was summoned to Colonel Morley's office and informed that the personnel that we identified as unsuitable for deployment were being transferred to my platoon.

As time for deployment was rapidly approaching, we worked around the clock to complete our training and create a functioning unit. Sergeant

Gary Miller, my platoon sergeant, did a magnificent job of pulling everyone together although his methods were rather harsh at times.

We had a particularly hard time instilling military courtesy among our newly formed unit. Saluting was a real problem. I would be called on the carpet almost daily for some infraction that dealt with a failure to salute some officer within the battalion.

Each time I was summoned regarding this shortcoming, Sergeant Miller and I would discuss the need to improve military courtesy. I couldn't help but notice the number of abrasions and black eyes that would appear after Sergeant Miller's counseling sessions, but slowly we achieved a modicum of military courtesy.

In fact, when we arrived in Vietnam, it seemed every member of the platoon was eager to render a hand salute and yell, "Yes, Sir!" whenever I was in the field and in an exposed position. They thought it was hilarious that the VC would make a real effort to eliminate our officers.

During the period from July 1966 to June 1967, this platoon, composed of individuals deemed unsuitable for military service and discarded by others, accomplished every mission assigned in a professional, if not sometimes an unorthodox manner. We participated in every air assault during that period, often being the first on the ground to facilitate the necessary resupply function. We successfully operated the forward firebase resupply operation during the eleven months we were deployed in the field. All members of our platoon returned home to their families in July 1967. It was a great honor to work with and learn from men like Sergeant Miller. It provided me with a sense of accomplishment that I value to this day.

Dick Donnelly, Martinez, GA
HQ, 1st Battalion, 22nd Infantry Regiment

Clarence

Once upon a time, a long time ago, there was an old ship named the USNS Nelson M. Walker. In July of 1966, she loaded aboard the first contingent of the 4th United States Army Infantry Division. Many of the brave young soldiers who embarked on the USNS Walker were assigned to the 1st Battalion, 22nd Infantry Regiment. In addition, some of these were in a subordinate unit, which was known as Charlie Company, nicknamed "Charging Charlie." Their leader was a young infantry captain named Chris Keuker. Before leaving their homeland, some of his lieutenants, wishing to have company on the long voyage across the Pacific to a land called Vietnam, decided to purchase a mascot for "Charging Charlie" to bolster their morale. They thought that a dog, cat, or bird would not be allowed aboard the ship because some sailors harbor superstitions about animals aboard ship, and they would not be able to smuggle it aboard ship. They thought about a fish, but this did not really meet the needs of what they thought a mascot should be. They talked and thought and then decided to get an animal that symbolized strength. They selected a boa constrictor and named him Clarence.

Clarence would fit very nicely in a small suitcase called an AWOL bag. Clarence would not require much food because he only ate once a month. His last meal before being smuggled aboard ship was a nice big juicy rat. The lieutenants did not have any problems getting Clarence aboard ship. All of "Charging Charlie's" lieutenants were assigned the same stateroom. As long as they were in the room, Clarence was free to roam about, investigating the pipes and vents in the ceiling. Before they left the stateroom, the lieutenants would put Clarence back in his bag and he would settle in for a nice nap; in fact, he rather enjoyed being in the bag because it was warm and cozy. The long voyage across the ocean took about two weeks, and everyone was enjoying the trip—until an accident happened.

Shortly before arriving in Qui Nhon, the lieutenants left their room, but forgot about Clarence up in the overhead. It so happened that the room steward went into the room to give it its daily cleaning. While the steward was bending over to make one of the beds, Clarence became curious about this newcomer and coiled down from the overhead to have a look-see, stretching almost his entire length of about six feet to look the steward right in the eye. Clarence was just curious.

The steward, startled by Clarence's face that was almost in his, stood straight up. His eyes bulged out of his head like two large ping-pong balls and his hair stood out at right angles to his scalp. His voice could be heard all over the ship. He did not bother to use the door to the stateroom, but made his own, right through the thin steel bulkhead. The steward never went back into that stateroom again during the trip and the lieutenants were forced to make their own beds. I do not recall whether Clarence was allowed to go ashore in Vietnam, or whether he even made the rest of the trip.

Bob Babcock, Marietta, GA
Company B, 1st Battalion, 22nd Infantry Regiment

The Naming of Camp Enari

Anyone who served with the 4th Infantry Division in Vietnam after early 1967 knows that the base camp was called "Camp Enari." Most, however, do not know about Private First Class Albert Collins, Company C, 1st Battalion, 22nd Infantry Regiment and First Lieutenant Richard Collins, Company A, 1st Battalion, 22nd Infantry Regiment, and their role in the naming of the base camp.

As Colonel Jud Miller, commanding officer of the 2nd Brigade of the 4th Infantry Division, completed preparations for leading his brigade from Fort Lewis, Washington, to Vietnam, Major General Arthur Collins, Division Commander, called him to his headquarters to wish him luck and give him final instructions. Among other things, Colonel Miller was to establish the base camp that the division would occupy when they arrived later in the year.

"Jud, I want you to name the base camp after the first man killed by hostile fire after you get to Vietnam. That would be a fitting tribute to a brave soldier," said General Collins in his parting instructions.

Colonel Miller left that day in July 1966 to board the plane taking the advance party to establish the division's new home, south of Pleiku, Vietnam. On September 3, 1966, while operating on a search and destroy mission with Charlie Company, 1st Battalion, 22nd Infantry Regiment, Private First Class Albert Collins became the first Ivy Division soldier killed in action when he was cut down by heavy fire from a Viet Cong unit.

Knowing General Collins would not want it to be perceived that the base camp was named after him, Colonel Miller sent a back-channel message to General Collins at Fort Lewis, explaining his proposed alternative plan for naming the base camp.

"Since the first enlisted man killed in action was named Collins, I recommend we name the base camp after the first officer killed in action."

General Collins agreed with Colonel Miller's recommendation.

On November 5, 1966, while participating in Operation Paul Revere IV with Alpha Company, 1st Battalion, 22nd Infantry, First Lieutenant Richard Collins, graduate of the West Point class of 1965, became the first "Ivy" officer killed in Vietnam when a dug-in North Vietnamese force shot him. By now, General Collins had arrived in Vietnam and discussed the dilemma with Colonel Miller.

"We'll name the base camp after the first posthumous recipient of the Silver Star, regardless of his name or rank," they agreed.

First Lieutenant Mark N. Enari had worked on the 2nd Brigade staff and was constantly prodding Colonel Miller to let him go to a line company to lead a rifle platoon. As a replacement was needed in the 1st Battalion, 12th Infantry Regiment, Lieutenant Enari received his wish and was sent to take over a rifle platoon. On December 2, 1966, Lieutenant Mark N. Enari earned the Silver Star while fighting the North Vietnamese regulars during Operation Paul Revere IV in the central highlands of Vietnam. Lieutenant Enari died as a result of the wounds received during that battle.

Early in 1967, the 4th Infantry Division's base camp, sitting at the foot of Dragon Mountain in the central highlands of Vietnam, was named Camp Enari in honor of Lieutenant Mark N. Enari and retained the name as long as American forces were in Vietnam.

PFC Albert Collins' name is engraved on Panel 10E, line 66 on the Vietnam Memorial Wall in Washington, D.C. Lieutenant Richard G. Collins' name is engraved on Panel 12E, line 27 on the Wall, and Lieutenant Mark N. Enari's name is on Panel 13E, line 4 on the Wall.

This story was told to me by BG (Ret) Jud Miller when I met him at a reunion at Fort Lewis in 1992. I found it fascinating to hear stories from the viewpoint of a brigade commander. My views were always from the rifle company perspective.

Frank Camper, Hueytown, AL
Company C, 2nd Battalion, 8th Infantry Regiment

Entering the Mouth of the Dragon

I took a few moments off my work detail to get to a porthole and look out. It was early Saturday morning, and the sun was just up. I saw a coast of green hills and jungles. I was transfixed by it, knowing this was a turning point of my life. Vietnam was the dragon sleeping placid in the dawn, and we had to go into the mouth of the dragon.

I pulled on my helmet and combat equipment, shouldered my ruck-sack, grabbed my M16, and joined the groups of milling soldiers on deck as we boarded the landing craft. U.S. Navy warships protected us, their guns and rocket racks aimed ashore, and we climbed down into barge-like landing craft, infantry (LCI), not using ropes, but through hatches low in the hull of our ship.

We did not have ammunition for our rifles or food in our packs. This was not a beach assault; it was just a movement ashore so we could organize and prepare to move again. We were near the coastal city of Qui Nhon, and transport to the airstrip there was waiting so we could be flown to Pleiku.

My LCI steered us past the curious Vietnamese on sampans to the beach. I couldn't see anything from where I stood except worried faces and steel helmets. Soon, the LCI's engines reversed; we bumped a sandbar and lurched to a halt, and the LCI's ramp fell.

We struggled through the soft sand, helping each other. Beachmasters barked orders and directed us through the palm trees to clearings beyond. Trucks stood ready to take us immediately to the Qui Nhon airstrip. I climbed into a dump truck and squeezed between other soldiers. The driv-er clashed the gears, and we bounced away with landing craft still coming ashore behind us.

We drove through the city of Qui Nhon, and I saw South Vietnam-ese soldiers carting old U.S. World War II carbines, M-1 Garands, and Browning automatic rifles. There were sandbag bunkers on every street corner and barbed wire strung along the sides of roads and across the tops of walls of the low stucco and brick buildings.

As we jumped off our trucks at the airstrip, Air Force personnel hand-ed us several boxes each of ammunition for our M16s, but there was no time to load rifle magazines. We were assembled and quickly loaded into big, camouflage painted, four engine C-130 transport planes for the flight to Pleiku. We filled the C-130s, sitting anywhere we could. The tailgate of our aircraft closed as we taxied down the strip and lifted off into the air. I couldn't get to a window to look out or down.

I tore open my cartridge boxes like everyone else and clipped ammunition into my magazine. We soon landed at New Pleiku Airport where more trucks waited for us. We left our C-130 and boarded the trucks, gawking at the remote airstrip with its aluminum huts and buildings, rows of cargo and combat aircraft, heavily armed perimeter defense bunkers, and barbed wire entanglements.

The sky had been clear over Qui Nhon. Pleiku was overcast, and it began to rain on us as we drove in convoy along isolated dirt roads into the countryside.

Machine gun jeeps and M113 armored personnel carriers of the 25th Infantry Division escorted us. The 3rd Brigade of the 25th Division had a base camp several miles from where we would establish our own. There were also some elements of the 1st Air Cavalry Division nearby for our security.

It was the beginning of the monsoon season in the central highlands, and rain began pouring down on us, making visibility impossible. The road turned into serious mud. I saw our big, "all wheel drive" trucks sliding and swaying over the road, some of them sticking in ditches, abandoned until they could be pulled out by other vehicles.

When we finally reached the end of the trip, we seemed to be in the classical "middle of nowhere." Before us lay a vast, grassy plateau. Off to the immediate west was a small mountain that rose out of the flatland, and the first thing I noticed about it was the complete tail section of a cargo plane sticking out of the trees on the mountainside—remains of an accident that should have been removed. It was bad for morale...at least my morale.

On the plateau were a few GP (general purpose) medium tents such as I had lived in back at Fort Jackson. It was our advance party from brigade, existing out in the grass like settlers in the American west.

We dismounted the trucks and slogged through standing water, trying to locate our pre-marked areas. There were wooden stakes in the earth with our unit designations written on them. The rain had not stopped, but it had slackened, and, dripping wet, we began to form into lines so we could pair off and set up shelter halves.

Base Camp—August 8, 1966

One of the men, Specialist 4th Class Richard Ives, in the 1st Battalion, 22nd Infantry Regiment, my old outfit, was killed when his buddy accidentally shot him in the head with a .45 pistol. It was the 4th Infantry Division's first casualty. I was soaking wet and tired. We worked all day to unpack the trucks that made it through the mud to the plateau and lay in water all night either trying to sleep or performing guard duty. We ate cold C-rations and drank only the water brought to us from water trailers, and even that was in short supply. Trying to erect the big GP medium tents in the rain and mud was exhausting. The support poles sank, it was difficult to make the ropes tight, and most of our tents looked as if drunks had set them up.

Incredibly, it was cold and foggy. We had to wear our field jackets. I had never considered that a tropical country could be as chilly as a cold day in the States. The fog usually lifted before noon, but the cold and wet stayed. I shivered in my soggy, clammy, cotton fatigues. I realized that there was a lot about this place we had to learn.

There was all-night firing from distant places beyond our perimeter that was a crude barbed wire circle around a rain-saturated dump of supplies and frustrated men. Sometimes our own perimeter would open fire at noises and have to be brought under control. Several mortar rounds sailed in and exploded inside our perimeter, but we didn't know if they were "theirs"—and therefore intentional— or "ours" and just the result of a unit out there getting their coordinates wrong.

Jungle Boots—August 10, 1966

A big Skycrane helicopter crashed during the night two miles away from us, but we didn't know it until one of the crew staggered in the next morning. He was badly injured. One of our Headquarters Company officers was almost killed when a heavy CONEX container fell on him as it was being unloaded from a truck bed. He was evacuated to Japan with crushed ribs.

Fighting broke out southwest of us between the Viet Cong and a unit of the 1st Cavalry Division. Many of our trucks from Qui Nhon, with most of our equipment and several of our men, still had not arrived; but the afternoon of the tenth, we got a treat.

From the back of the truck, we were each issued two pairs of jungle boots. The boots had deep-cleated soles and canvas "uppers" so they would dry more quickly than leather combat boots. As I stood in the line behind the boot truck, a patrol from the 1st Cavalry Division walked past. All of the infantrymen were muddy, and they were loaded with ammunition and equipment.

A tall black soldier turned to us, looking at me as I reached for my boots. "Get 'em big, man, so they don't hurt your feet," he said.

Our trucks were at a standstill. Only helicopters were bringing in food and supplies to us within the perimeter. The rain was perpetual. We finally got the brigade tactical operations tent up and equipped the way we had it in Fort Lewis—but this place was another world from Fort Lewis. The fighting holes we had scraped out of the mud were full of water. If we had had to take cover in them, we would have drowned.

One wet morning as I trudged through the mud between the head-quarters bunker to the briefing tent to post the latest position reports on the "war board," I saw an M-60 tank swimming and plowing along one of the muddy river "roads" between the tents. It was heading for a spot where at least two other tanks had been stuck before and had been pulled out by bulldozers. Each tank had left the hole deeper. Right before my eyes, the M-60 tank submerged. The crew scrambled out of it, bubbling brown water rushing into their hatches. They stood on top of the turret. If it had not been for the cannon muzzle and antennas sticking up out of the mud, no one would know there was a tank there.

When the mud was the worst, the trucks could not move, the tanks and armored personnel carriers could not move, and finally the D7 dozers were stuck. The only vehicles able to travel anywhere were the huge truck-like "goers" with massive flotation tires and boat-like cargo beds. The mud had our modern army stuck like a fly in glue. The mud had almost got me killed. Division headquarters had arrived and was being set up a few hundred meters from brigade. They had nice new prefabricated buildings. House trailers had been flown in and placed intact by Skycrane helicopters.

Until they arrived, the 2nd Brigade had been in command of the base camp. The loss of status was felt at my headquarters. We had to send documents to division every day, and this was done by messenger, with much difficulty, because of the sea of mud and general flooding. When I was told to take some papers to division, I left with my rifle and helmet, and stepped out of the briefing tent into the rain. I was up to my knees in muddy water in no time and began to track toward a path that might get me to my destination.

Some places were over my head in mud and water. I had to make it from island to island on high ground, holding onto barbed wire, posts, anything. I could see the division area ahead, uphill slightly and out of the liquid morass that I fought through. My major obstacle was a road, or more accurately, a rutted canyon about eight feet deep in places and running with sluice water.

Crossing it was necessary. I found a place and slipped down the mud sides to the water, splashing along and looking for a way out. Then I heard the rumble of a diesel engine. I looked right and saw the blade of a bulldozer coming my way, collapsing the mud, grading it into something usable. The operator of the machine was high above me. I could see his face, but he wasn't looking down.

Some places were over my head in mud and water. I had to make it from island to island on high ground, holding onto barbed wire, posts, anything.

I ran from the dozer, my feet sticking in the mud. The jelly-like walls of ruts were trembling with the vibration of the big machine. I knew I could shoot at the driver if I had to—or I thought I could—but I had to do something quickly. I could imagine talk about me the following day: "He was only going to division, and he just vanished."

The dozer was going to plow me under six feet of base camp mud. I saw a spot along the mud wall that I thought would support me, and I hit it with all fours, digging like a cat. I went up the wall and onto the surface as the dozer passed. The driver never looked my way. I washed off in a pool of rainwater to make myself more presentable before I handed the documents to division.

Jim Liles, Edgewood, KY
Company C, 1st Battalion, 22nd Infantry Regiment

Tuy Hoa—September 1966

This story, about some of the first enemy action of the 22nd Infantry in Vietnam, took place a few days after Private First Class Albert Collins became the first KIA of the 4th Infantry Division and 22nd Infantry Regiment in the Vietnam war. I was a gunner on a 106mm recoilless rifle and our first mission was in Tuy Hoa. Our 106mm recoilless rifle squad was assigned to guard a water purification plant run by several engineers. They were set up under a bridge that ran across Highway 1. Approximately a mile or so away was a large mountain. We already had several of our guys shot, and one killed, at the base of the mountain.

One day several of the rifle platoons were on patrol near the mountain base. They started taking fire and were pinned down. I was watching through the binoculars from the water purification point. Near the middle and top of the mountain I could see three or four VC come out of a cave with a machine gun on a wheeled platform and fire at our guys. They called in helicopters to take out the machine gun but the VC would just wheel it back into the cave. After the helicopters fired and flew off, the VC would come back and fire at our guys again. The GIs called in jets, but they were unable to take out the machine gun.

I told my squad leader, Sergeant Johnson, that I thought I could raise the 106mm recoilless rifle up and could fire a WP (white phosphorous) shell right into the cave. Sergeant Johnson called the CO, Captain Bill Kerans, and advised him we would take out the machine gun. A 106mm recoilless rifle is an anti-tank weapon meant to fire in a straight line directly at a target. I was going to use it like a mortar or artillery piece. I elevated the rifle and was able to exactly judge the windage from my scope, but I could not judge the elevation and had to guess at it. I waited until the VC ran back into the cave. I lined the 106 up and fired the first round of WP. It went right over the top of the mountain. I dropped the elevation by several clicks and fired the second round. That round went right into the cave. I sat and watched through the scope and did not see the VC come back out. I watched as our guys moved up the mountain to the cave.

The next day I talked to several of the guys from second platoon who had been in that firefight, and they told me they got up to the cave but due to the WP and smoke and fumes were unable to go very far inside. They stated there was a strong smell of burnt flesh and were sure the VC were eliminated. It was an unusual way to use a 106mm recoilless rifle, but on that day it did the job.

When we moved back to Pleiku and on to the Cambodian border, I had to give up the 106, as there were no roads to drive on.

Ray Dunkel, Irving, NY
Command Sergeant Major, 4th Engineer Battalion

Water Supply

When I arrived at the Dragon Mountain Base Camp, the battalion water purification units were set up and operating within the base camp. The monsoon rains provided an adequate source of water to meet the requirements for potable drinking water. With the approach of the dry season, it became apparent that our water source would soon be depleted and a new source would have to be found quickly. As there were no streams running through the base camp, the new source of water would have to be found outside the camp. Engineer reconnaissance revealed that a good-sized lake existed not too far from Dragon Mountain and that it could provide the source of the needed water.

Operating a water point at the lake would require resources to secure the site and special equipment to transport the potable water back to the base camp for distribution, thereby exposing personnel and equipment to danger. Additionally, an access road would have to be constructed and maintained. With all these considerations, it was determined that the water point would remain within the base camp where units could receive water in relative safety and with a minimum of travel. This challenge was met by installing a large water pump at the edge of the lake, constructing a pipeline from the pump to a large, raw water holding tank that was located within the base camp. (Where and how these items were procured remains a mystery.) When the system was completed and in operation, there were relatively few problems encountered with providing potable drinking water and non-potable water for bathing and laundry operations. It should be noted, however, that initially the pipeline was not buried, which was a mistake. Each morning an engineer work party would have to go out and patch the bullet holes in it. (It was buried shortly thereafter.)

Ray Dunkel, Irving, NY
Command Sergeant Major, 4th Engineer Battalion

A Hilarious Sight

As most early 4th Infantry Division men will remember that during the monsoon season, vehicles moving on the roads of the base camp made a quagmire of mud, and the roads became virtually impassible to vehicles and foot traffic. To get to division headquarters, we had to cross the road running parallel to the 4th Engineer Battalion (one of the worst). My battalion commander, who was slight in stature, being summoned to a meeting at division, made several attempts to walk across this road but kept getting stuck in the mud because of its consistency and depth. Seeing he was frustrated by not being able to cross, I said to him, "Let's go." Being considerably larger than him, I picked him up under my arm and carried him to the other side. I have been told it was a hilarious sight, as I am sure it was. Mission accomplished.

Bill Saling, Big Canoe, GA
HQ Company, 1st Battalion, 22nd Infantry Regiment

Ammo Resupply

Our battalion, the 1st Battalion, 22nd Infantry Regiment, was located just south of Tuy Hoa during September 1966. Our mission was to protect the rice harvest from the local VC. We occupied a position on the beach near Highway 1, and mainly conducted search and destroy missions in that region. On September 6, Companies B and C were dispatched to check out a village that reportedly was hiding approximately fifty VC. Our 4.2 mortars were mounted on tracks and were dispersed to support the "search and destroy" mission. That evening, around 2200 hours, the VC probed Recon platoon. Their platoon leader, Paul Protzman called for illumination flares. Our XO, Major Cliff High, tried to contact the Air Force to secure airborne flares, but none was available. Shortly before midnight Major High called me into his tent and explained that we would need to make an ammo re-supply run to Lieutenant Ron Czepiel since he was just about out of illumination rounds (4.2 in. mortar) and could no longer support Recon platoon.

I rounded up my platoon, and we loaded a deuce and a half with one hundred rounds of HE and one hundred rounds of illumination. Before departing, I reviewed the exact location of the mortar platoon with Major High, and we agreed on a series of radio checkpoints en route. Major High, one of the most decorated combat soldiers of the Korean War, indicated that he thought the midnight resupply mission was a setup for a probable ambush. He said he was concerned for our safety and insisted that we radio in after passing each agreedupon checkpoint. During this period in our AO (Area of Operations), Charlie would routinely mine the roads every night and ambush anyone foolish enough to be caught traveling after dark. Needless to say, our "pucker factor" was at an all-time high as we set out on this mission. Our convoy was made up of two vehicles, my jeep and a deuce and a half with a ring-mounted .50-caliber machine gun.

We were driving with blackout lights, going about forty miles an hour down an unsecured road, when the machine gunner manning the .50 caliber on the truck right behind me chambered a round and fired a burst over my head. I damned near had a heart attack, thinking that we were under attack.

We arrived later that evening at the mortar platoon's position and delivered the ammo. We spent the rest of the night telling our "war story" about our near ambush. It was only later that the gunner "fessed" up that he had fired the machine gun by mistake. It was just one of those memorable moments that bring a smile to your face when remembering the many varied experiences of being in Vietnam.

Al Fuller, Wilmington, DE
Company B, 2nd Battalion, 22nd Infantry Regiment

Royal Welcome

There were about ten or twelve of us Philadelphia guys who all got drafted in December of 1965. A few of us knew one another from high school or just hanging around on the same street corners. We did our basic training at Fort Lewis, Washington, and then our AIT. We had Basic Unit and Advanced Unit training after which we were informed we would be going to Vietnam.

The army sent us home on leave and we reported back to Fort Lewis in August of 1966. We sailed out of Puget Sound, near Seattle. The voyage was twenty-one or twenty-two days, but at least it counted as time in country. It took most of the three thousand or so soldiers about three or four days to get their sea legs and stomachs together. Sleeping quarters were about four or five decks below and there were five cots in a stack. For obvious reasons, you avoided the bottom one.

I remember one of the first things we all were wondering about once we got on board was why there were handles on the sides of the johns. Well, once we got away from the mainland and out to the open sea, it became pretty obvious. If you had to go when the seas were rough, without those handles to anchor you down, there was no way to imagine where you might have ended up. Looking out of a porthole while doing your business; one minute there would be nothing but sky and the next, nothing but ocean.

After about nineteen or twenty days of being at sea, we got word we were getting close to the Philippines and would probably be allowed off the ship. We all figured we would do a little R&R, check out the place, get a few drinks, etc. We docked in the Philippines, but were marched right off the ship and made to do PT for about an hour or two then right back on the ship again. I think the stopover was for the benefit of the crew.

That wasn't the biggest surprise, however. As we got closer to the coast of Vietnam—it was only about two or three days from the Philippines—and you could see the flashes of light at night, we all started to get a little more serious. Then, when we got within a mile or so from the beach, they started loading us into the landing craft—for what we thought would be like the D-Day landings. But something was not quite right. We had our M-16s, but no ammunition, and we had our duffel bags so I figured this could hardly be a combat assault. The landing craft hit the beach, dropped their ramps and what do we see? No enemy, but a female captain or major leading a military band in the Star Spangled Banner. As it turned out, we landed in Vung Tau. It was a secure area and they gave us a royal welcome.

Roger Hill, Lena, IL
Recon, 1st Battalion, 12th Infantry Regiment

First Combat Assault

Our first combat assault was an event to remember. On October 16, we got word that we were going to move into a new area of operation west of Plei Djereng that wasn't safe. We got excited and figured this was it—finally, real combat.

On October 17, the day before the operation began, we were given a briefing by our platoon leader and were told this would be a jump into a "hot" landing zone. This meant that the S-2 (Intelligence Officer) had intelligence that there was a strong possibility that the LZ would be occupied by the NVA when we got there, and we would have to fight and take it from them. As the lieutenant's briefing continued, we found out that shortly before our insertion time, the LZ was to be saturated with artillery. The way he made it sound, we had nothing to worry about because everything would be destroyed by the time we got there.

Then the gunships were to follow, making strafing runs while looking for any targets that the artillery may have scared out or missed. We were to be on the first stick (a group of helicopters) flying in and following the gunships. The lead elements of the Tactical Operations Center (TOC) was going in with us, and our mission was to provide security for them. A squad of combat engineers, with their bangalore torpedoes, was also squeezed in with us and the TOC communication vehicle (an M-37 truck with a box body) was to be sling loaded in by a Chinook (a CH-47 cargo helicopter) as soon as we hit the ground. That was the plan. On paper it sounded good, but as we were to find out, a few things had been overlooked.

The next morning, October 18, we tore down our bunkers, packed our equipment, and organized ourselves by aircraft loading sequence along the edges of the LZ. It seemed as if we waited for hours. In reality it was only thirty or forty minutes. I don't remember what we talked about while waiting, but I bet some of us asked our buddies to make sure our families got word if something happened to us. We didn't say it, but most of us were scared and had visions of bullets flying around us as we exited the aircraft. Ha! Boy, were we green...too many movies.

Finally, the aircraft arrived. Loading a helicopter is an art. You crawl in with all your gear, find a comfortable position, and then get squeezed into a mess by the crew chief as he shoves in more gear you didn't expect. I was lucky that I got a seat in the middle. Some of the other guys had to sit on the floor facing the door. Once we (the first stick) were loaded, we had to wait some more.

I had no idea that helicopters had weight restrictions and normally didn't taxi down the runway like an airplane until I heard the crew chief start to talk to the pilot about throwing some baggage out so we could get off the ground. Way down at the end of the LZ, we finally cleared the treetops and slowly gained altitude. As we got up to cruising height, I could see other aircraft ahead of us and a couple off to one side. The view was great: blue sky, no clouds, and rolling green hills passing by beneath us. I had no idea how far away the new LZ was, but I hoped it would be a while yet, as I was beginning to enjoy the flight.

No sooner had that thought entered my mind than the aircraft began to bank sharply and begin a steep descent. The door gunners stood up behind their machine guns and began looking out and ahead. We strained to look out the cabin doors and windows for any signs of incoming fire of the enemy. All we could see was a small, low hill mass to our front that was covered with green vegetation. No artillery, no smoke, nothing.

In the next instant, the aircraft was hovering above the ground, and the crew chief was screaming for us to get out as he fired his machine gun into the nearby brush. If you didn't jump, you got pushed. I was surprised to find the grass and bushes way over my head. As I hit the ground with my rucksack, I looked around for the rest of my squad and found only two guys.

Over the roar of the helicopter and the blasting of the machine guns, I tried to ask the two guys where everyone else was and if they had taken any fire yet. Both questions got an "I don't know" answer. As soon as the aircraft departed and the noise level dropped, we began looking for the other members of the platoon. I soon found the platoon sergeant, who was trying to get us all organized into the security perimeter for the TOC.

As soon as I heard the Chinook coming, I looked up to see the commo truck being dropped down almost next to me. It landed on a stump about five feet away and sat at an angle. I remember thinking that the S-3 was going to be really angry when he saw that. The next thing I heard was, "Fire in the hole! Fire in the hole! Fire in the hole!" which was followed by a terrific explosion on the other side of the commo truck and by a shower of dirt, dust, and vegetation.

It seems they forgot to tell us what the engineers were going to do and when. Had it not been for the truck, I probably would have been wounded right then and there. As it was, the truck shielded me and had several holes punched into it by the shrapnel from the bangalores. For about the next five minutes, there followed a series of sharp explosions as the engineers cleared out the vegetation all around us. Every time they yelled, "Fire in the hole!" we dived for cover.

The next stick inbound was the battalion mortar platoon. They were supposed to land in the LZ, but because the ground wasn't clear enough yet, they made a few passes dropping their equipment and ammo. When we realized that the helicopter door gunners were pushing the 4.2-inch mortar rounds out as if they were on a bombing run, we ran for our lives. We couldn't believe what we were seeing; our own people trying to bomb us. Eventually we began to settle down.

After determining there were no enemy forces in the LZ, the command group was brought in along with the line companies. One company stayed in the new LZ for perimeter security, while the other two moved out to provide security on some neighboring hills that overlooked the new LZ.

Then the real mission for the Recon platoon became apparent: we were to fill all the sandbags needed to build the bunker for the battalion command post as well as what we would need for our own bunkers. Talk about a raw deal. I have no idea how many bags it took to complete that bunker, but more than thirty of us dug for two days to get the job done. When it was finally time to go out on patrol, we couldn't wait to get going, anything to get away from battalion and that damned LZ. And, once the precedence of the Recon platoon building the TOC was set, it became the norm for all future battalion moves.

Dave Gehr, Sheboygan, WI
Company C, 3rd Battalion, 22nd Infantry Regiment

Ghosts from the Past

As 4th Division troops embarked to Vietnam, the 1st and 2nd Brigades were sent to the North, and were camped in Pleiku. The 3rd Brigade arrived in October of 1966. Many disembarked the USNS Nelson M. Walker troop ship on the shores of Vung Tau. As time passed, members of Charlie Company, 3rd Battalion, 22nd Infantry, found themselves sleeping in squad tents just east of the little village of Nha Be. The village is located near the shores of Song Nha Be, a portion of the Saigon River, southeast of Saigon.

On November 21, 1966, during Operation Bremerton, Company C boarded helicopters and headed southeast to the Rung Sat Special Zone.

When the drop zone was reached, Charlie Company quickly unloaded and received incoming fire from the Viet Cong. The enemy pulled back quickly and Captain David Jablonsky from Washington, D.C., ordered his platoons to make a huge swing out to the left while the fourth platoon would make a huge swing to the right. The second platoon would move up the left middle, several hundred meters from the first platoon, while the command group would move middle-right, between the second and the fourth platoons.

The movement was difficult because of the numerous rivers we had to cross. During low tide these crossings were made through armpit-deep mud that took enormous amounts of time and energy. The jungle canopy allowed little sunshine to trickle through; the heat was unbearable and the insects took their normal toll.

The enemy was definitely using the area. Several vacant bunkers were found along with small huts, water jugs and rice. We took sniper fire again, but luckily, no casualties were reported. As the third platoon moved between two small rivers, they unknowingly walked into a well-fortified and concealed VC base camp. It was nearly 1430 hours when the VC opened fire on the unsuspecting American troops. The jungle roared as machine gun and small arms fire ripped into the third platoon. They were pinned down and took casualties.

The other platoons halted in their tracks. Our fourth platoon made a small perimeter and prepared for the unknown. We were the weapons platoon but unable to carry our mortars in this mud-filled terrain. The twenty-five of us huddled up, hoping and praying that the VC did not decide to retreat in our direction. We prepared for battle by stacking up magazines, unhooking grenades from our web gear, fixing bayonets and putting together our cleaning rods. The jamming of our M-16s seemed inevitable so the rods were prepared to push out the usual ruptured cartridges.

Small arms fire roared on as the artillery started descending to the front of the third platoon. Shrapnel filled the air as scores of 105mm and 155mm artillery rounds pounded the area. The high explosives were brought to within fifty meters of the third platoon. Shortly, helicopter gunships arrived, filling the jungle with machine gun and rocket fire. The VC still did not back off, and the battle raged on. Captain Jablonsky radioed to Lieutenant Colonel John Bender, the battalion commander that he was in need of reinforcements. The call for "medic" sounded throughout the third platoon area.

As we listened to the turmoil of war, our eyes kept a constant surveillance for the approach of the enemy. Suddenly, F-4 phantom jets started a strafing run directly over our position. The scream of the 20mm cannons made me think we were receiving incoming fire. It was our first experience with jet support, and we were all quite thankful they were on our side. When they dropped their 500-and 750-pound bombs, the earth just shuttered. With the small arms fire finally winding down, the VC ultimately decided to move on.

The call for reinforcements was answered by Company A, led by Captain George C. Shoemaker. They were airlifted in on choppers and dropped into a landing zone a few hundred meters from the main action. The PRC-25 radios called out to the other Charlie Company platoons to move in to help the battered third platoon. So the fourth platoon moved out through the mud and thick jungle to try to reach them.

Our boys used machetes to chop and cut their way while daylight became darkness. The whole platoon struggled to stay together. It was nearly impossible to see your hand in front of your own face much less the guy you were supposed to be following. I was not sure which of my fears had top priority—the fear of getting lost in the jungle or the fear of running into the unfriendly group of VC that had ripped into the third platoon.

Eventually we arrived at the site of the battle. One could sense an eerie feeling. Company A had secured a perimeter, and other Charlie Company platoons were drifting in, finding a place to settle in the mire. Dustoff choppers came in and out of the landing zone, taking loads of third platoon wounded and some heat exhaustion cases to hospitals. Every member of my platoon was totally exhausted. When the word came down for "shuteye," it was a matter of seconds and our lights were out. The company enjoyed nearly five hours of uninterrupted sleep.

Our wakeup call was before dawn, as the men in higher places had made plans. Our platoon leader, Lieutenant Gonzales, came back and gave us the scoop. Our platoon along with the remnants of the third, would move out on a search and destroy mission. The second and first platoons would do the same with ambush patrols planned for that evening. I think Company A stayed behind and checked out the bunker complex and also searched for the enemy.

As we moved out, the devastation of the previous-day's battle was clear. Many trees had been blown down; sampans had been torn apart; mangled bunker positions were everywhere as were numerous bomb craters. The trudge through the mud-laden jungle floor was at a snail's pace. The enemy retreat was evident by the trail of blood-stained bandages, marks where the VC had dragged their wounded or dead comrades, plus hundreds of sandal prints. Our movement was deliberate and silent. We all realized that we were in the "badlands," and that there were hundreds of VC who would enjoy nothing more than to end our career as soldiers. You could sense the fear in the entire group.

In my estimation, trailing a battalion of pissed-off enemy soldiers with a slightly oversized platoon was quite asinine. I knew my feelings were shared by most of my comrades, but onward we trudged. Unbelievably, our forced march was uneventful. The heat, mud, numerous river crossings, bugs, and snakes were definitely the least of our problems.

We reached a small river and planned our night's ambush. Twelve grunts would climb four trees that overlooked the river. The rest would form security to the rear. Our newly acquired experience with the ocean's tides made us realize that those on the ground would eventually be sleeping, or trying to sleep, in nearly a foot of water. Our squad was chosen as the tree dwellers. Our plan was finalized, and up we climbed. My group was in the second position (tree) with each position about seven to ten meters apart. I found myself low man on the totem pole about five feet above the river. My squad leader, Bob Duplechin of Mamou, Louisiana, was directly above me with someone else above him. We tied ourselves into position and strung a communication line between all the middle men in the trees.

Now the idea was to hope an unsuspecting sampan would try to maneuver down the river. Our threesome was to take turns on watch and try to get some sleep. That was a laugh! Ever try to sleep crammed between a couple of branches? As darkness fell, the fourth platoon was in place and at the ready. The chirp of frogs and other nighttime critters was welcome. It meant that two-legged creatures were not disturbing their activities. The bountiful jungle canopy made the world black. As the tide came in the water crept up over the banks. I knew our comrades in the ground positions were getting wet and uncomfortable. I had to smile knowing that at least I was dry for this night. Then I started to feel the creeping of a huge variety of insect life crawling over many portions of my body. As the tide moved up the banks, the bugs moved their residence to the trees. I was literally pouring bug juice across the branches to try to discourage the little critters from crossing into my area. It didn't work, and I was being eaten alive.

I tried to doze off, and between the slapping of bugs, the resident of the apartment above me was suddenly stepping on my helmet. "Dup" was whispering that a sampan was coming and I should get ready. My heart started beating at triple speed, and I could hear a Vietnamese singing as he poled a sampan in our direction.

Our plan was to let any sampan pass the first and second positions so that our machine gun team could spring the ambush. The plan was working like we hoped. As the sampan approached, I realized that the VC doing the poling was in a standing position and would be less than three feet away from this dumb grunt at the low end of the totem pole. He would be so close I feared he would hear my heart beating. Using the river current, the sampan slid past rather quickly, and the action was about to begin. I felt it was payback time for our third platoon. My rifle was aimed and at the ready, and my distance from the sampan was be about fifteen feet. I had confidence in my squad and couldn't help thinking that this could be like shooting fish in a barrel.

Suddenly, the war was on! Charlie Shepherd from Gatesville, Texas, and Larry Belew from Yukon, Oklahoma, sprung the ambush at exactly the right moment. The M-60 machine gun expended numerous shells into the sampan and a chorus of M-16s joined in from each of the positions. In a ten-second time span more than two hundred rounds were fired. It was over as quickly as it began. The disabled sampan drifted toward the machine gun position and someone yelled to pull it to shore. Larry Belew and Charlie Shepherd would check out our prize. Charlie would climb on board with his flashlight and .45 caliber pistol at the ready. He told Larry to cover him with his M-79 grenade launcher loaded with buckshot. As Charlie made his move, the rest of the platoon held tensely in their positions. The clamor of small arms was replaced with a hush. Charlie's first step into the craft was answered with a groan from inside.

Charlie yelled, "Belew! Shoot, there's someone alive in here!" Larry answered quickly with a blast from his M-79.

Now Charlie really gave a scream: "You dumb jerk, you shot me!"

Charlie got a couple of pellets in the back of his shoulder, but it didn't stop him from shooting three or four rounds from his pistol. The groaning had stopped so the two troops continued their inspection. A few documents and weapons were found along with a single dead Viet Cong.

Things settled down, and a couple of grenades were dropped into the river to discourage any VC from hanging around. I remember this distinctly because the grenade I tossed never exploded. I had carried it for a month and it turned out to be a dud. I was relieved that I did not have to depend on that grenade to possibly save my life.

We renewed our vigil of waiting for more unsuspecting visitors. It was my turn for watch so I tried to get comfortable between the offshoot of branches, and I continued to swat the pesky bugs. As I surveyed the area, I noticed an unfamiliar shape on the bank between our position and the machine gun team. The blurry shape had not been there before. What was it?

I rubbed my eyes and tried to look from a few different angles, but whatever I tried, the disturbing shape remained. I could not make it out, and my fear was making my patience run thin. I reached up and grabbed the pant leg of Bob Duplechin. I whispered my predicament and asked if he could see the strange silhouette. His location was six feet higher up in the tree, and he said he couldn't make anything out because of the darkness. I was pleading with him, considering the form was only ten feet away. He said I should shoot it. Throughout my military training, I was instructed to make sure of your target. Maybe it was one of our ground sleepers who moved his position. Maybe one of them had to use the bathroom. (We didn't really call it that.) That must be it!…must be one of our guys out of his position. I didn't shoot.

As I pulled my guard duty, I was continually scanning in the direction of the mysterious figure. The hour slowly passed and anxiously I wakened Duplechin again. Although my shift was over, I could not stop pondering over the predicament I had just gone through. I tried to sleep, but one eye or the other kept opening to check on my riddle. I finally got in a few winks and was rudely awakened with a boot tapping on my helmet again. It would be light shortly, and we were going to regroup and move out.

Our troops started to mingle around, but I had to resolve my situation. I tried to escape the trees, but the heel of my boot had jammed between two limbs. I forced it out, and the heel came right off my boot. The nails pushed into my heel as I walked, bewildered, toward the mystery location. Finally arriving, the pieces of the puzzle came into place. I discovered a drag mark from the river on the bank where the wounded VC must have pulled himself out of the river. But the size of the pool of blood on the ground meant he must have lain there for quite some time. He had retreated into the river as evidenced by a second drag mark. I shudder to think that there was an enemy soldier within a few feet of our positions.

After we chowed down it was time to move out. The PRC-25 radios screeched, and communications checks were accomplished. Someone bellowed, "Saddle up!" and we were off again, trudging trough the muck and mire of the jungle. Our trek lasted only until mid-afternoon when I believe we were airlifted out by groups of choppers. We were always relieved when we heard the "Whoomp, whoomp, whoomp" of the blades and saw those lovely machines coming in to pick us up. This incredible mission was finally over!

Although this particular assignment was long over, the memories lasted for years. Most grunts probably had a few ghosts that they brought home from their experiences in Vietnam. This one is mine. The nightmares that kept me awake for years was of this wounded VC ghost that crept out of the river and through the mud. The dreams were never quite the same, but he was always there. I could see him tossing a grenade toward our position, crawling up my tree with a knife and cutting my throat, or pulling out a rifle or pistol and killing us all. Waking up in cold sweats, searching the dark room for ghosts from the past happened often the first years back. After many years, the ghosts have finally diminished. My Vietnam comrades and I have talked away the demons of the past. Thanks, guys!

Bill Saling, Big Canoe, GA
HQ Company, 1st Battalion, 22nd Infantry Regiment

Tuy Hoa Shower Point

During the fall of 1966, our battalion was located in an AO (Area of Operations) just south of Tuy Hoa on the coast of Vietnam to protect the rice harvest. The battalion headquarters section was located on the beach, and the rifle companies were located at various points along Highway 1.

Our XO (Executive Officer) was Major Cliff High, a decorated veteran of the Korean War and a dynamic leader. Major High had a very low threshold of boredom. He was very effective in his role as XO, but preferred being in the field.

One day, Major High called our S-4 (Supply Officer), Captain Larry Kinchelow, and I to a meeting where he told us he had decided that we needed to have a shower point on the beach. We had a combat engineer platoon attached to our battalion, and they began digging a hole on the beach. If you ever tried digging in sand, you know how frustrating it is to watch the sand fall back into the hole you just dug. To correct that problem, the engineers began welding 55-gallon drums together end to end. It became apparent that you could reach only so far into the hole to excavate the sand.

We obtained the services of some local Vietnamese to assist in this project. We lowered them into the well, and they dug out the sand. Finally, we reached the water table. We now had a well dug but had no way to get the water pumped out of it. Major High called me into a meeting and said he wanted a gasoline powered pump delivered to the well site—within two hours. I asked him where to obtain a pump and he told me to "get creative." I called in my ever-resourceful platoon sergeant, Sergeant Gary

Miller, and explained the problem. He said not to worry, he would get a pump. Two hours later, we had a gasoline powered pump.

It seems Sergeant Miller and a couple of guys from my platoon took a truck and drove to the nearby Air Force base at Tuy Hoa. They found a pump and told the Air Force personnel that he was there to service the pump. He asked them to help load it into his truck. They did, and voila! we had our pump.

All identification numbers were covered on our truck, so it was impossible to identify our unit. Several days later we heard that the Air Force Police were looking for a stolen pump but had no leads on who took it.

Within twenty-four hours, our shower point was complete. We pumped water into 55-gallon drums from our well and let the water sit all day in the sun. In the evening, our troops had a warm shower. Our showerheads were made of softdrink cans with nail holes punched in the bottom. Our battalion was the only infantry unit on the beach with their own shower point, thanks to Major High and members of the support platoon.

William Moen, Fort Pierce, FL – HQ and Company C, 3rd Battalion, 12th Infantry Regiment

The Kool-Aid Caper

After several weeks out in the field, returning to base camp filled my mind with three thoughts: a shower, clean clothes, and a hot meal. With these three accomplished, the next event was mail call. What a surprise it was. Not only did I receive letters from home, but I also received a package from mom. This time she outdid herself. The package was full of homemade chocolate chip cookie crumbs. They started out as cookies, but by the time I received them, they were mostly crumbs. Also in the package was the ever-present Kool-Aid packages and a quart of Bacardi Rum. As any grunt will tell you, Kool-Aid in Nam was necessary if you wanted to drink the water.

With the cookies gone and the rum disappearing as fast as the cookies, my thoughts turned toward the approximately fifty packages of Kool-Aid. I would need two hundred gallons of water to use it properly. Where would I find that much water in one location? Someone suggested our showers. They were 55-gallon drums cut lengthwise and welded together. So off I went, packages in hand, to climb up the shower tower. It all made sense to me—or was the rum doing my thinking?

Soon I was up on the tower mixing two hundred gallons of Kool-Aid. But what were we going to do with it? I'd worry about that decision the next day.

Little did I realize that someone wanted to take a shower. Who should want to use it but a fresh new captain? To make matters worse, he had a new white towel. Anyone who ever has had Kool-Aid spilled on them knows how sticky it can get from all that sugar. Well, in went our captain to shower. When he tried to dry himself off, he realizes something is wrong. There he stood, completely naked, looking like a six-foot plucked chicken.

The next morning, I was informed that a certain captain was looking for me. At this moment I realized I must get out of there. I immediately volunteered to return to the field as soon as possible.

Roger Hill, Lena, IL
Recon, 1st Battalion, 12th Infantry Regiment

The Centipede

The NCOs had gotten into the habit of taking their ponchos and snapping them together into one long tent. I was invited to add mine to the end and join them. After settling down and blowing up our air mattresses and a few minutes of talking, most quickly fell asleep except for me. As the new guy, I was still somewhat excited and wasn't ready to call it a day, so I just lay there and went over the day's events and wondered about tomorrow.

After a moment or two I became aware of a soft scratching noise next to the head of my air mattress. My first thought was that there was a small field mouse looking for something to eat. As the sound got louder, I decided to investigate. Grabbing my flashlight and shielding the lens with my hand, I pointed the flashlight at the noise and turned it on.

What appeared in the circle of light was something out of a bad science fiction movie. Digging in the grass, no more than three or four inches from where my head had been, was a reddish-colored centipede as thick as my thumb and eight to ten inches long. My immediate reaction was to recoil, right up through the top of the tent. They say that for every action there is an opposite and equal reaction. Well, whoever "they" are, they're right. On the way up through the collapsing tent, I let out a blood-curdling yell and managed to grab my machete and chop this monster into three pieces.

The reaction on the part of the NCOs trapped under the collapsed tent was pure pandemonium. They were trying to figure out who had yelled and why. The next ten or fifteen seconds were chaotic as I tried to explain what had happened while hunting for the three pieces to prove I hadn't imagined the whole thing. As luck would have it, nothing was found of the centipede. I didn't realize until years later that all three pieces literally just ran away!

As soon as the tent was repaired and everyone began to settle down again, there was some discussion about what would happen to me if I saw anything else for the rest of the night. The general consensus of the occupants of the tent was that I was crazy after being in country for only a few days. I must have told the story a dozen times the next day and nobody believed me. It wasn't until several months later that I saw another one of these giant red centipedes, but by then everyone had all but forgotten the incident.

- -

Bob Babcock, Marietta, GA
Company B, 1st Battalion, 22nd Infantry Regiment

Hoboes

Our trained reaction to the first crack of a rifle shot brought us all to the ground. The sound was followed by intense gunfire as we responded to the enemy fire with our own. My heart was pounding. Adrenalin pumped through my body at an ear-throbbing rate. I had tried to overcome the initial mass confusion, assess the situation, and determine what to do next.

We had found a number of abandoned enemy bunkers earlier in the afternoon. As I observed where the gunfire had started, it appeared there was a line of bunkers on the small rise in front of us. From where we were it was impossible to tell how many there were and how many people were occupying them. The sound of the radio interrupted my thoughts.

"Oscar 61, this is Oscar 6. What's the situation? Over."

I responded, "We have a line of bunkers in front of us and have received fire. We need a fire mission, over." It took no time to get our supporting 105mm howitzers from Charlie Battery, 4th Battalion, 42nd Field Artillery, called into action.

The jungle soon shook from the exploding artillery blasts.

As we lay watching the area and continued to direct our rifle and machine gun fire at the bunker line, we got another radio call:

"Oscar 6, this is Birddog 19. I have a flight of Hoboes on station. Do you need them? Over."

"Hobo" was the radio call sign of the 1950s vintage, propeller driven, Douglas A1E Skyraiders stationed at Pleiku Air Force Base. "Birddog 19" was the Air Force Forward Air Controller (FAC) whose job it was to direct the fire of all airplanes in the area.

"Roger," I replied. "We'll lift the artillery, and you can come in on target."

As soon as I called to adjust the artillery fire to the rear of the target area, we could hear the first Hobo screaming toward us from right to left.

The FAC had marked the target with a white phosphorus marking rocket, and the A1E released his bomb load right on target. His bombs were Cluster Bomb Units (CBUs) that exploded before they hit the ground, throwing thousands of tiny BB sized projectiles across the target area.

Our position was scarcely seventy-five yards from where the CBUs were hitting. The shrapnel was ricocheting through the trees above us as well as on the target area. The sound of the metal ripping through the trees gave the saying, "make myself one with Mother Earth" new meaning. The first Hobo was followed closely by a second, and then a third, as they saturated the bunker line with their CBUs. I had never heard anything like the clatter made as the bombs ricocheted through the trees.

As quickly as they came, they were gone. While we were getting up to move across the bunker line, we got another call from Birddog 19.

"The Hoboes have some 20mm cannons they can help you with. Do you want them to strafe the area before you go in? Over."

Again, "Roger," was my reply. (No one ever accused me of not using all the firepower I had at my disposal.)

This time the Hoboes came from our rear and flew directly overhead as they peppered the area to our front with their 20mm cannons. Another reality of war hit me as a hail of spent 20mm cartridge hulls came raining down on our heads. Training had never included being pelted with the four-inch long brass cartridge hulls that fell through the trees. I pulled my helmet down tightly. Those things hurt and were still hot as hell.

As the third Hobo completed its strafing run, we got up and quickly swept across the bunker line, firing into each bunker as we advanced. We moved through without stopping and took up defensive positions fifty yards past the bunkers, waiting for the rest of the company to join us.

As was so frequently the case, all we found were blood trails leading away from the bunker complex. We never knew whether we had killed any of the NVA. Fortunately, none of us was hurt.

We gained a better appreciation for the Hoboes. We knew they were usually on station to come to our aid when we needed them. They were slow and ugly in comparison to the sleek jets, but they had more staying power and could fly in much nastier weather.

Bill Bukovec, New Braunfels, TX
Company B, 1st Battalion, 22nd Infantry Regiment

I Wish I'd Asked His Name

As a "grunt" stationed in Vietnam, my days were never usual or common. A particular incident happened during the time I was on one of many missions.

Some mornings after breakfast, time permitting; I would take a short walk while eating my ration of canned fruit (usually peaches). I would go along a path, up a small hill or around the perimeter from my area and foxhole.

On most of these morning walks I would see and talk with one particular guy. He was a "grunt" too, but he was in the company headquarters section and one of the Commanding Officer's RTOs. He would be eating his canned fruit (usually fruit cocktail). I didn't know his name but he seemed a nice fellow, and we always found things to discuss.

We talked a lot those mornings, but I can't recall exactly what we discussed. Perhaps it was sports, the weather, or whatever. We never exchanged names or talked about where we were from in the states. This was not uncommon for those times because we learned not to get too friendly or too close to another GI, especially in a combat environment. All either of us knew was that we were both "grunts" from the United States, in the United States Army, stationed in Vietnam. I didn't particularly care for my usual canned fruit ration of peaches. This guy wasn't particularly fond of his usual canned fruit ration of fruit cocktail. We discussed this and decided to trade. It became sort of a morning ritual. When time allowed, I usually walked to meet him and ask how he was doing.

He would say, "Fine," and then ask how I was doing.

I'd say, "Fine," then we'd trade our canned fruits, sit and chat a few minutes while eating them. I would then leave and we'd both go about our daily duties.

One morning I took my canned peaches and walked to exchange fruits. When I arrived at the company CP, he wasn't there. I asked his whereabouts and learned the guy had been killed the night before, during a mortar attack. To this day, I wish I had asked his name, or at least where he was from.

Bob Babcock, Marietta, GA
Company B, 1st Battalion, 22nd Infantry Regiment

Chapel Service on the Cambodian Border

It was mid December 1966. We had been on a constant search and destroy mission since November 3. On this day we were as close to Cambodia as anyone was supposed to be. A rule had been established by II Corps Headquarters that no American unit could set up overnight defensive positions any closer than three kilometers from the border.

The day before, as we cautiously followed a well-traveled, high-speed trail through the jungle, we had found a large NVA base camp. Moving into it, we had killed one NVA soldier and were sure many more had heard us and fled. Small fires were burning, pots of water still boiled. The latrines were littered with fresh human waste.

With relish we started the "destroy" part of our mission. After leaving the base camp in ruins, we moved west trying to find the NVA that seemed to always stay just beyond our reach. Before long, as I read the terrain features on my map, I knew we had crossed over the border and were in Cambodia. There were no signs that said, "Welcome to Cambodia," or "You are now leaving Vietnam." It all looked the same—dense jungle.

We patrolled another hour deeper into Cambodia. Our senses stayed razor sharp as we probed further and further into this known NVA sanctuary. Trails were numerous, but we found no sign of the NVA. When we called our position back to battalion HQ, they became irate when they heard where we were. Our orders were to turn around and get out of there, "Right now!"

We retraced our steps and found a small hill about three kilometers inside Vietnam. The terrain suited Captain Fiacco, so he ordered us to stop and build our nightly triangular defensive position.

After a tense night, the first light of the new day brought a sigh of relief. Rather than move out again, we decided to stick around, send out some patrols, and see what we could find. By cutting down only a few trees, we cleared a spot that allowed a helicopter to come in to resupply us.

When the helicopter arrived, Captain Walt Sauer, our battalion chaplain, jumped off. We were as happy to see Chaplain Sauer as we were to see the yellow mail sacks and other resupply items. "Chapel" was held whenever and wherever we could do it. (All infantrymen know there are no atheists in foxholes.)

Chapel services in the jungle were always well attended. That day, with Cambodia and who knows how many NVA not too far away (and probably listening), the service was a little better attended than normal. As usual, we maintained listening posts and security around the perimeter. If more people wanted to go to church than could be accommodated without taking too many men off security, the chaplain would always hold two services.

We were sitting on the side of the hill about ten minutes into the service, singing to the accompaniment of the organ on a tape recorder, when the sound of a single rifle shot rang through the jungle. As we all hit the ground, the chaplain calmly said, as if he had rehearsed it many times before, "Men, go to your posts!"

You never saw so many men scatter to the safety of their bunkers so fast. I do not know what the chaplain did; none of us looked back to see.

As we sprinted the short distance to our bunkers, we heard one of the men on the line shout out, "As you were! False alarm! Take it easy!"

As we investigated the source of the shot, one of the men admitted sheepishly what he had done. While cleaning his rifle, he had forgotten to take the round out of the chamber and it went off. Fortunately, neither he nor anyone else was hurt.

Chapel service resumed, but the attendance fell off. Some of the men decided it made more sense to stay close to their bunkers and listen from a safer location. When the helicopter came back early that afternoon to pick up the chaplain, I think he was more relieved than normal to be getting out of there and heading back to the relative safety of the battalion fire support base. We resumed our search for the elusive NVA.

Joe Dietz, Naples, FL
Company C, 2nd Battalion, 22nd Infantry Regiment

Christmas in Vietnam

Holiday time in 1966 found me and a few hundred others looking at Dau Tieng for the first time and being told this was our new home. What a mess the place was—nothing but dirt, brush, and more dirt. We were faced with building it from the jungle up. This was not at all how I had spent my holidays in Portland, Oregon. Every day it was dig, cut, build, fill sandbags—lots of sandbags. The only tent we had was a mess tent. We were living on the perimeter.

My mom kept me and, I swear, half the platoon supplied with Christmas goodies. I was always getting cookies and the like from home. She was big on sending clean white cotton socks, too. One can of cookies I especially remember because she wrapped each one in a different holiday wrap, so they would be a surprise when opened. No one knew what the flavor of the cookie was until the wrapping was removed. These were a big hit with the squad. She even sent a small tree and a Santa. I hung the Santa off the barrel of the .50 caliber machine gun, put the tree on the trim vane, set some of the items around it, took a picture with the squad, and sent it home.

I remember thinking about the great dinner everyone would be enjoying at home, the laughter and good times. Then I looked around me and where we were, what we were doing, and what we were about to be doing…a sad time for sure. The bright side was that I was not alone, and we all made do with what we had, managing some laughs along the way.

Our cooks really outdid themselves at Christmas. There was no lack of food, and it was actually good—at least at the time. They were making up for Thanksgiving when we were in the field, and food for the holiday went to some other unit. Turkey loaf never tasted so good.

As I sit here at the picnic table enjoying my gin and tonic with lots of ice, I remember back when we would go to any means to get ice and not waste a bit of it. I think the commanders missed the best motivator they had. If we had been told that behind the enemy positions was an unlimited supply of ice, there would have been no holding us back. So I raise my frosty glass and make a toast to all my fellow soldiers who have had to serve on foreign soil at this time of year, and wish everyone a (belated) Merry Christmas.

Ray Dunkel, Irving, NY
Command Sergeant Major, 4th Engineer Battalion

New Year's Eve 1966

While watching the festivities welcoming the new millennium on New Year's Eve, December 31, 1999, I was especially fascinated by the fireworks displays. I was reminded of New Year's Eve 1966, spent in Vietnam as a member of the 4th Engineer Battalion. As I remember it, New Year's Day was a usual workday and spirits were high with everyone wishing each other a "Happy New Year" and wishing they were back in the "World." Just inside the perimeter wire surrounding the camp, there were bunkers spaced fifty to seventy-five meters apart. Each unit was assigned a number of these bunkers, which they would man to provide security for the base camp. Well, on New Year's Eve 1966, the normal security force was in place fully armed and ready for any eventuality. The troops inside the perimeter were trying their best to celebrate the incoming New Year.

As midnight approached, I was with the first sergeant of Headquarters Company. At the stroke of midnight, a shot rang out from the bunker line, then another shot, and in a very short time, it appeared everyone on the perimeter was firing. Tracers were leaving a trail from the bunker line into "no-man's" land, creating the illusion that the firing was to welcome in the new year. In our battalion area, our troops poured out of their tents hooting and hollering wishing everyone a "Happy New Year!"

After about five minutes of firing and hearing the call for "Cease fire!" the firing stopped and things returned to normal. It was one "hell of a fireworks display" and provided a great morale booster for a group of young red-blooded Americans a long way from home. To my knowledge, no one was called to task for this unannounced celebration welcoming in 1967 by the troops of the 4th Infantry (Ivy) Division, serving in Vietnam.

January—December 1967

Highlights of 1967 include movement of the 1st Brigade to the central highlands, officially naming the base camp "Camp Enari," after First Lieutenant Mark N. Enari, and the switching of the 3rd Brigade of the 4th Infantry Division with the 3rd Brigade of the 25th Infantry Division on August 1, 1967. With that switch, the 4th Infantry Division took control of the 1st and 2nd Battalions, 35th Infantry Regiment and 1st Battalion, 14th Infantry Regiment (with supporting units) and gave up the 2nd and 3rd Battalions, 22nd Infantry Regiment and 2nd Battalion, 12th Infantry Regiment (with supporting units). Operations participated in included Sam Houston, Francis Marion, Junction City, and McArthur. Among many others, the major battles included the Battle of Soui Tre, "Nine Days in May," and Dak To. Hamlet visitation programs continued. Major General W. Raymond Peers commanded the division. Eight 4th Infantry Division soldiers earned the Medal of Honor in 1967. The largest number of hostile and non-hostile killed in action occurred in 1967, with 824 soldiers making the ultimate sacrifice.

Albert "Swede" Ekstrom, Dekalb, IL
Company A, 4th Aviation Battalion

From Knox to the "Nam"

Entering the U.S. Army in November of 1965, I was sent to Fort Knox, Kentucky, for basic training. One of the first things I was taught that I still remember was A-14-4, second platoon's "Every man's a Tiger," motto. At the end of that saying we all yelled and then took our seats, usually during a training session. That was the way basic training started.

Fort Knox was a cold place during the winter of 1965 and 1966, but our clothing was adequate for the job. Once, we marched to a location about ten miles from post where we were supposed to bivouac for the night. Mother Nature was the enemy, however, and the ground was so frozen that we could not dig a trench around our tents, nor could we even pound the tent stakes into the dirt. Guess what? That's right! We marched all the way back to Knox! Some of my other recollections include standing in the rain in the middle of our company area, waiting my turn to call home to Illinois, being awakened each morning to the sound of tanks heading for the tank range, and our drill sergeant yelling cadence as we marched throughout the surrounding hills.

Without a doubt the dumbest thing I did in basic training was volunteering to be a fireman. I thought that a fireman fought fires. No, not in basic. A fireman stays up all night while the others sleep and keeps the fires stoked to provide heat in the barracks. What made it worse was being told that if I got the fire too hot, the grates might break, and I would have to pay for them myself. What a great way to start an army career!

Well, most of us made it through, and although I had wanted to be a tanker, I qualified for helicopter maintenance school and was sent to Fort Rucker, Alabama. This was a bit of a cultural shock for a farm boy from Illinois, but the training was interesting and the times that we got to fly were a lot of fun. We were all young then, so very little thought was given to our personal safety. Learning to "sling load" and chasing cows in a farmer's field was our daily fare.

One may wonder how this prepared us for later service in Vietnam. It was documented on more than one occasion that an irate farmer would shoot at our helicopters because of us scaring the cows. Some of the local people didn't really seem to care for us a whole lot, which also helped us later in Vietnam, since they didn't like us much either!

At Rucker we were in old World War II barracks that had to be redone for our use. I think the place was called "Tank Hill." Each morning after chow, we would march to a training site for lecture or hands-on work concerning "Huey" helicopters. Usually, on the way to training we would encounter a number of snakes attempting to cross the road ahead of the column. Some of the snakes were a type of water moccasin that up north we referred to as cottonmouths. Nasty looking things! We would break ranks and kill the snakes by hitting them with limbs and rocks. The dead snakes were gathered up and hung on the outside wall of our mess hall. I have no idea why we did that, but many of us would one day encounter similar creatures in Vietnam, and we hung those up also.

One of the strangest things I remember from Rucker was once seeing a soldier sleeping while he was standing. We were on break from one of our classes, and we had gone outside the building for a smoke. All of a sudden, I heard what sounded like snoring coming from one of our classmates. We checked him out, and sure enough, he was asleep. He awoke before falling to the ground.

After graduating from advanced training at Rucker, we were spread to the wind like so many pieces of winnowed husks of wheat. I ended up with orders for Fort Lewis, Washington, in the great Northwest. I'll never forget my flight from Chicago's O'Hare Field to Seattle. Soon after boarding the plane, I fell asleep. Some time during the flight, I was offered something to eat by the stewardess. I declined and went back to sleep. The next thing I know, we're flying over Mt. Ranier. Good Lord! What a sight for the farm boy from Illinois. I had never seen a large hill before, let alone a mountain! I remember seeing the snow-capped peaks. It was breathtaking!

At Fort Lewis I was assigned to what was called the USAG. This stood for United States Army Garrison. It was where they put all the people who didn't have specific orders for anywhere else. The USAG was a huge red brick building that looked just like all the other big red brick buildings. Without orders, we went out each day to different jobs such as mowing the lawns near the airport, and painting details. The worst was yet to come. Some of us were moved to what was called 3rd Company, where we worked off post on an afternoon shift washing clothes at the quartermaster laundry. We were all PFCs and had less than a year in the Army. We all thought that Uncle Sam had forgotten about us.

One day a major came to the company area and asked if anyone was interested in joining up with a unit that was going to Vietnam as replacements for those already serving with the 4th Infantry Division.

Several of us jumped in the air, and said, "Yes!"

After all, many of us had a helicopter MOS (Military Occupational Specialty), and we were washing fatigues for God's sake!

Well, when the Army decides to move, you had better move with it or get the hell out of the way! We quickly joined together with the other troops and many of us were promoted to Specialist 4th Class. Wow! We're really going up the ranks now.

Soon we were flying in the Yakima Mountains and shooting our M-60 machine guns from different altitudes in order to prepare us for combat assaults and other missions in Vietnam. Once I remember being at a training location where the rainfall was so great it washed my eggs right out of my mess kit as I was walking out from inside a tent. Funny, how we remember the goofy things. After training, I got to go home to see family and friends for Christmas of 1966.

During the first week of January, 1967, we flew aboard a C-141 transport from Lewis to Pleiku Air Force Base near the 4th Infantry Division base camp at Dragon Mountain. This would be my home for the next year. As the plane was touching down, we were issued .38 caliber bullets for our Smith and Wesson Model 10 pistols, which were standard issue for flight crew members.

We were told before we left Washington that our company area was being prepared for our arrival by the engineers. When we got off the truck in the base camp, however, we found a muddy area with a few trenches dug for sewage. We set up tents and made a quick trip to Pleiku for supplies such as shaving gear and the like. We had only been in the base camp for a couple of days when we had a tragedy. A couple of our guys went to Pleiku and got drunk. When they returned to the company area they played quick draw and one of them was shot, which left him somewhat paralyzed, as I recall. Someone came and took them both away. We never saw either of them again. So we had our first casualty before even leaving the camp.

We didn't have our own helicopters when we first arrived, so we went to the coast and trained with some AHCs (Assault Helicopter Companies) at Qui Nhon. A couple of weeks later our birds had arrived from the states on ships, and we were ready to go on our own. Our company was designated Company A, while our gun company was Company B. We used the call sign of Blackjack, with the gunship boys calling themselves Gamblers. We were blessed with some of the finest, most experienced pilots anyone could ever hope to fly with! Some of our pilots were sent out to other units since we were a bit top-heavy.

We had a number of high ranking officers who were flying where a warrant officer or lieutenant might normally be filling that slot. I remember one pilot in particular. His name was Mr. Peppers, and I believe that he was a W-4. He and I would sometimes team up—he being the aircraft commander and me being the crew chief and gunner. At the end of a day of flying we often would fly over a small island in a river somewhere and try to hit a target with a smoke grenade. Peppers had a way of sighting the target through the chin bubble, maintaining a certain airspeed and altitude, then telling me when to throw the smoke. We won more than our share of beer using that method.

It wasn't all fun and games, however, and we learned early on that we were facing an enemy that was bent on killing every damn one of us if they could. In the first few months we lost a "slick" from our company with a buddy from North Dakota named Buckey. I don't know if I ever knew his real name, since we most always used nicknames or first names only. There have been many times since that I thought of trying to find Buckey's real name in the Wall book, but I've never done so. About the only thing recovered from the crash site was a belt buckle and some teeth, since most everything burned. Another time, some guys and I visited the hospital where one of our pilots had been taken following his chopper being downed. I remember seeing him sleeping in the bed in a cradled position and looking so very young. I don't know what happened to him.

Many other sights and sounds come to mind as I mentally return there for this article. Like the time we slung loaded two horses out to a FSB (fire support base). Some of our artillery buddies had purchased a male and female horse from a village. The FSB was moved to a different location, and the guys were without their animals. We flew to the village with an old sergeant who had been with the army in Italy. He had experience with pack animals and knew what to do. We stood the horses up in the center of a cargo net, one at a time, blindfolded them, tied their legs together, and laid them down. We then drew up the corners of the net and attached it to the cargo hook beneath the chopper. We flew each horse at a slow speed and low altitude out to the FSB. The pilot showed great skill and set those horses down nice and easy. The artillery boys cheered our crew.

And I must say that I was proud to have been able to give those guys that kind of feeling.

Another time we were moving a company and all their gear to a new location. We were flying quite low over a forested area. Slung beneath my helicopter was the company toilet! All of a sudden, I heard a loud explosion behind my chopper. I looked out the door and saw a cloud of blue smoke some distance behind us. Charlie was firing some big stuff at us but he missed. A couple of gunships went down on the deck to see if they could locate the source but were unable to do so. We all joked about almost getting shot down while flying an outhouse.

There were many other events in Nam that will forever be a part of me. Of the three that stand out the most, one was an attempt to bring back the body of a downed fixed wing pilot that had crashed in the jungle some miles from Dragon Mountain. We had been returning from a day's flying when the word was received by the pilots concerning the downed plane. We flew directly to the site near dusk. As we approached we could see where his plane had gone in and had taken off the tops of some of the trees before striking the ground. We had no support with us, but the pilot put down on a small hilltop some distance from the plane. The crew chief and I left the chopper and made our way down the hill. As we walked by the plane I remember seeing small fires nearby, but the plane was largely intact. The pilot lay ahead of the plane with his chute partially opened. We tried to carry his body but were unable to do so in the rugged terrain. We ran back to the ship and rejoined our pilots. Others soon arrived, and people were put on the ground. I have always felt as though I let that guy down, even though the enemy did not get him. The second incident took place on March 22 at Polei Doc. Company A, 1st Battalion, 8th Infantry, was attacked by a North Vietnamese battalion. We were flying back from a staged combat assault with NBC television cameramen on board. The camera guys had two large heavy motion picture cameras with tripods. The call came out that the 8th Infantry needed help. Materials were needed to clear a landing zone to extract wounded. Unknown to us in the air, First Sergeant David McNerney was on the ground and was distinguishing himself by acts of heroism. McNerney's commander and his forward observer had both been killed, so he took charge and for his actions was later awarded the Medal of Honor.

Meanwhile, we had taken on fuel and had gotten some items to bring to the fight. When we arrived in the area, there was no available landing zone. In fact, there wasn't any area that even remotely looked like an LZ. But our pilots were 4th Infantry, and they had a plan. We were directed to hover down through a hole in the tree line that had been created by a bomb blast from an earlier time. The hovering down part went pretty easy. As the ship lowered, I could see that there were grunts lying in a circle around the bomb crater. They were firing their weapons into the surrounding trees to provide cover for us. We went into a stationary hover, and I started to throw the supplies into the crater so they could be retrieved. What happened next scared the crap out of this Illinois farm boy!

We tried to hover up back through the canopy, but were unable to rise high enough due to our weight. We fell back toward the crater, and our rotor blades started to make contact with the tree limbs. After one or two more failed efforts, the aircraft commander ordered that some additional items be thrown from the helicopter in an effort to reduce weight. We had been trained to accept a pilot's order without any questioning, and that training proved itself in the next couple of minutes! The gunner and I were told to throw the NBC cameras out the door. We did so, and they landed on the inside slope of the bomb crater. We made another try at rising through the treetops but again sank down. The pilots had to pull in all the collective power that bird had to keep from crashing. I can remember looking down at some of the infantry guys, and they were looking back up at me. Had we gone down, many would have been killed. Things were looking pretty crappy. The next order made the day. We grabbed the cameramen and escorted them out the door. They landed right beside their cameras and took cover as best they could.

Our next attempt was successful, and we were able to clear enough to hit transitional lift and get the hell out of there. I don't remember hearing what happened to the NBC guys. They're probably still cussing.

Years later, in 1984, I had the honor of meeting Sergeant McNerney at a hotel in Washington, D.C. He had spoken at a meeting of Ivymen who were in town to attend the dedication of the three-soldier statue at the Wall. McNerney handed me a small printed card that detailed his heroic actions on that day so long ago. I read the card and gave it back to McNerney. I remembered the date (March 22, 1967) and told David that I was there that day. He looked at me with suspicion and doubt! He quizzed me by asking what was thrown from the helicopter that had come to help him. I told him we had tossed out two cameramen and their cameras. McNerney bought me a beer. I don't know if I have ever felt so proud.

The third event that I will never forget was the battle for Dak To, which took place in the fall of 1967. Several NVA regiments and division size units had come into the area in October. They were intent on destroying the Special Forces camp at Ben Het. In previous months the 173rd Airborne Brigade and the 1st Cavalry Division had several encounters with the enemy. "The Herd" (173rd Airborne) as they were called, had lost some 76 men on June 2. Hill 875 was to become a number that many of us will always remember. The second battalion of the 503rd was given the job of taking the hill after contact with the enemy. A couple of mistakes were made early on that would prove to be biggies. The enemy troop strength was underestimated, and there were no LZs made in advance for resupply and medical evacuation.

As the battle raged, several helicopters were lost to fire in an attempt to help the Herd. For several days we flew food to the Dak To landing strip and carried bodies and wounded back to Pleiku. Not much, if any, of the food reached the Herd. On November 23, after being joined by Ivymen, the combined force took the hill. Enemy losses were reported at over seven hundred, while our casualties ran as high as seventy-five percent in some of the companies. Thirty to forty helicopters were reported lost during the action.

Years later I again stood on that Dak To airstrip as part of a group visiting Vietnam. I thought of the irony of the whole effort. Since it was Thanksgiving, we had flown things like turkey and eggnog north from the base camp. We would land briefly while these items were stacked on the end of the runway. I remember seeing 175mm howitzers lined up alongside the strip, firing into the mountains for support. I don't know if anyone ever got any of the food; there wasn't time for eating for the guys on the hill, and no way to get it to them.

In December I was a short-timer with only a couple of weeks left in my tour. I think I was assigned to pull guard on the perimeter on Christmas and New Years Eve, but paid someone else to do it. At least on one of those nights I got drunk with one of our pilots.

Then came the day to go home. I flew in my short-sleeved khakis aboard a civilian airliner from Vietnam, back to Seattle-Tacoma (SeaT-ac) Airfield in Washington State. It was early January and cold and rainy when we deplaned. We rushed through the return process and that night I found myself in a Tacoma hotel room lying in bed staring out the window. I never felt so alone in all my life. I was headed home, but this Illinois farm boy would never be the same.

Gary Krek, Phoenix, AZ
Recon, 2nd Battalion, 22nd Infantry Regiment

Tet 1967

Just what were you doing on "Tet 68" (the "Big One")? I can tell you what I was doing on Tet 67, not as noteworthy as Tet 68. The day before Tet, we (recon platoon) were convoying down a dusty road and stopped at a small village along the dirt road. Immediately, the "Coke kids" were out and about selling their warm Cokes to whoever would buy them. There were a few "mama sans" about just watching and talking to the troops.

One approached me and asked, "Where you go, GI?" I answered, "I don't know, you tell me."

She responded with, "you go to Soui Tre, GI."

I ignored her and she finally left. As she was walking away I thought, "where the hell is Soui Tre and how in the hell did she get this information?" (They were usually correct.)

We made our way down the road until we came to an ARVN (Army of the Republic of Vietnam) Ranger Camp where we would stay for the night. It had been announced over Armed Forces Radio network that President Lyndon Johnson and the North Vietnamese government had come to an agreement for a cease-fire during the Vietnam Tet holiday. We stayed alert all night; you couldn't trust the NVA (North Vietnamese Army). There was some light small-arms fire from the enemy and return fire from the ARVN—not much to get excited about.

The next morning, just before we were to leave the ARVN camp, the platoon sergeant approached me and said he was short an M-60 gunner and wanted me on his APC (Armored Personnel Carrier) to gun for him. No problem, I answered, and went to my APC to get my M-79 and M-16. As we pulled out of the ARVN camp, I thought to myself, "This isn't bad, riding third track back." A couple of miles down the road, the lead APC (my former APC) hit a land mine. It blew the turret off with the TC (Track Commander) in it. He and the driver were the only men who were really hurt and medivaced out. The rest of the crew was dispersed through-out the platoon. As a few of the guys were setting off C4 (explosive) on my former track, I remembered that some of my clothing and personal effects were still on it. Too late…Oh well. Just another day in the Nam.

Later in the day we came to a small river and swam the tracks over it. On the other side was a small, steep hill. When we pulled over the hill to the top of a small clearing, all of a sudden we were getting small arms fire from the tree line. Immediately, an RPG (Rocket Propelled Grenade) was fired at the lead track. The RPG missed the track and hit both gunners square on with shrapnel, also hitting the TC in the head and neck. At the time, we were in a diamond formation, which meant I was right in line with the lead track and the RPG. After taking a few seconds to clean parts of my friend and former gunner off me, I heard my platoon sergeant screaming to fire into the tree line, and I did. The TC in the lead track had jumped out—holding onto his neck to slow the bleeding—trying to get the driver to back the track towards the rear of the formation. (He was in complete shock.) All the time, a firefight was in full progress.

When we saw the TC of the lead track out in the open, everyone laid down a line of fire to cover him from the enemy.

The medic was in my track and as he started out he turned to me and said, "Gary, you cover me and don't let them get me, OK?"

I answered, "No problem, just get going and keep your head down because the bullets you hear whizzing over your head will be mine."

As it turned out, we hit back with such force and accuracy that the enemy split sooner than they had planned, leaving behind a blood trail and eighteen command detonated anti-tank mines that were sitting right on top of the ground (whew!).

After everything settled down and the perimeter was secured, the wounded and the bodies of those who had died in battle were medivaced. When our medic got back to our track and looked at my hands, arms, and face and saw the blood, I told him it wasn't mine. He started to clean me off and I realized that some of it was indeed mine.

He laughed at me and said, "You weren't kidding about keeping my head down. Thanks."

This was the start of Tet 67 for the Recon platoon, 2nd Battalion, 22nd Infantry Regiment Recon platoon.

There were to be many more days like this one before March 21, 1967, and the Battle of Soui Tre. I was patched up two more times by a grateful medic.

Bill Matz, Chicago, IL
HQ Company, 2nd Battalion, 22nd Infantry Regiment

What Are Those Ugly Looking Sores?

I was attached as medic to third platoon, Company A, 2nd Battalion, 22nd Infantry Regiment on an operation when we were working out of Dau Tieng. We were moving on foot against a suspected VC base camp. We encountered opposition and had a sharp little firefight. As I recall, artillery fire was called in from a fire support base. The third platoon was fortunate that day. I only had to treat one flesh wound among our men. After the artillery lifted, we moved in and found the camp abandoned. There were three dead VC in a trench. Our platoon leader called in the situation and then looked at me.

"Doc, Brigade S-2 wants the Viet Cong uniforms," he said. "What?" I asked.

"Strip 'em, Doc!"

Good old Army Intelligence. The enemy were wearing black pajamas, black bush hats, and rubber tire sandals, and they had been shooting at us. "Duh, do you suppose they might be Viet Cong?"

A friend of mine, Charlie "Tuna" Raas, offered to assist me in this unpleasant job. Tuna had what could be called a dark sense of humor. I don't recall exactly what he said, but it helped to get us through a distasteful chore. We tied commo wire to the ankles of the dead Viet Cong and dragged them a short distance to make sure they weren't lying on grenades. Then we cut the clothes off with the shears from my aid bag. From what I heard later, the S-2 didn't like this. I guess it made it difficult to identify the tailor.

While Tuna and I were engaged in this, a couple of other men discovered someone curled up in the bottom of a bunker. They went down and carried him out. A short while later, the platoon leader called me over.

"What do you make of this, Doc?"

I saw what looked like an old man covered with open, running sores. I asked the lieutenant to step a little off to the side with me.

"Sir, I'm not a doctor and I've only read descriptions of it; but I think that looks like smallpox."

"Are you sure?"

"No, Sir. Like I said, it wasn't something covered in detail at Fort Sam."

I can't remember if there was any more discussion on the subject, but the old man was air evacuated out. Later, the word came back. Unfortunately, my diagnosis was correct. It was smallpox. We were brought, briefly, back to Dau Tieng to be re-vaccinated. Then the whole company was sent back to "the boonies." I think we were quarantined in the field for at least a month. Fortunately no one showed up positive, and we were eventually allowed to return to the "civilization" of base camp.

I've heard on PBS type television programs that smallpox has been eradicated from the world. I may have seen one of the last cases.

Dave Gehr, Sheboygan, WI
Company C, 3rd Battalion, 22nd Infantry Regiment

Close Call

As the years slip away the events from my service days are still strong in my mind although, unfortunately, the details of many incidents are quite sketchy. Portions of the following story were written by SP4 Richard Linneman for the Pacific Stars and Stripes, but I don't know if it ever made it to publication. The story was titled "Looked Right Down the Barrel."

Close calls were common in Vietnam where the average distance between opposing forces in a firefight had dropped from hundreds of meters (common in World War II), to less than twenty meters. None, however, can claim a closer call than SP4 Danny Copeland, Mishawaka, Indiana, and Dave Gehr, Sheboygan, Wisconsin, whose Charlie Company, 3rd Battalion, 22nd Infantry was operating in the Michelin rubber plantation. This was near the 3rd Brigade, 4th Infantry Division's base camp at Dau Tieng during "Operation Diamondhead."

Company C was sweeping through thick underbrush in a jungle area adjacent to the rubber plantation. The "Michelin" was well known as a sanctuary for the Viet Cong and received constant patrolling from the 3rd Brigade. The sweep formation was unusual because we had six columns abreast moving through the gloom of the double canopy jungle. The first platoon had two columns on the left flank; the third platoon, two columns down the center, and the 4th platoon had two columns on the right flank. The headquarters command group trailed the third platoon, with the second platoon following for security and to act as our reaction force.

As usual, the weather was extremely hot, and the air was stifling. The going was tough as the point men from the six columns needed to chop their way with machetes. Staying on line was always a problem because visibility between the columns was only three to five meters. By noon the company had worked their way up to a small bicycle trail. We had been moving without incident for several hours and it was time to break for chow. The CO halted in order to regroup and he gave orders to set security personnel in place. These measures were automatic and happened quickly. A group from the third platoon was sent across the trail. Two lookouts from the first and fourth platoons moved forward, and rear and flank security was put in place.

During the movement, Copeland and Gehr were taking turns on point and leading the inside (left) column of the fourth platoon. As the break took place they found themselves completely surrounded by friendly forces—a column of the 4th platoon to their right, two lookouts to the front, third and first platoons to their left and the command group with the second platoon to their rear. In the middle of the bubble and feeling exhausted and safe, the two kicked back for a meal of the finest C-rations the army could offer. They undid their olive drab socks, which contained the cans of C-rations. As visions of cheeseburgers and T-bone steak danced through their heads, they saw that their real choices were between beans and weenies and turkey loaf. Neither choice would fill the hungry void. The P-38s (can openers) dug into the cans, and the two began to chow down. With a few sips of water to wash it down, their meal ended as quickly as it began, and they kicked back for a few minutes of precious shuteye.

Abruptly the silence erupted with rifle fire. Rounds were ripping through the jungle as figures advanced down the trail. Sitting up and grabbing their weapons, Gehr and Copeland could see two people hot-footing towards them, but identification was impossible even though they were only fifteen feet away.

Their immediate thoughts were that it must be their own GIs who had been sent to the front (Ruben Golding of Mount Airy, North Carolina, and Harold Key from Spanaway, Washington). In seconds, this speculation proved to be completely false as two black pajama-clad VC turned almost on top of Copeland and Gehr.

Weapons were raised to the hip and Gehr opened fire on the first unsuspecting enemy soldier. The soldier was hit with numerous rounds as Sergeant Wayne Knowles of Columbus, Georgia, sitting behind Gehr, joined in. With the action fast and furious, Gehr noticed the second VC pivoting and pointing his rifle toward Copeland. Copeland sat holding his M-79 grenade launcher, unable to fire at this close range. Gehr quickly took on the second VC with a heavy volley of rounds and stopped him in his tracks. Both of the enemy met their fate within six feet of the Americans.

The action was over in a matter of seconds. The VC were checked over, and it was discovered that they both carried M-1 rifles in addition to other weapons. They had escaped their earlier confrontation with Sergeant Eugene Hahaj, South Bend, Indiana, as his M-16 jammed. Copeland helped check the enemy soldiers and was shocked to discover that one of the enemy's M-1s was jammed.

"He must have fired once before he tried to shoot me," Copeland said. "The extractor didn't work…that's all that saved me." He took out the M-1 shell casing and put it in his pocket.

The situation was similar in many firefights in Vietnam. Troops could hump for hours, days, or even weeks with not even a hint of action. But when the action did start, it was hot and heavy. Firefights often did not last much longer than a few seconds or minutes, but the rush of war left an indelible mark on my soul. I will never forget those few exhilarating seconds of my life, and I know Danny Copeland won't either.

E. Q. "Skip" Fahel, Sarasota, FL
Company B, 2nd Battalion, 22nd Infantry Regiment

Cherry Pies

At one time Company B was providing security on the supply routes between Dau Tieng, Tay Ninh, and Cu Chi. It had not been a good mission because of all the mines that the tracks were hitting. Our base camps were being hit with rockets and mortars day and night. The Dau Tieng base camp had the distinction of being the first one to be hit with 107mm rockets. Several men had been wounded, and the company had eight tracks damaged. As Executive Officer for the Company, I was responsible for insuring that the company had the supplies needed to properly support their mission in the field. Every day I would run a supply convoy and deliver the needed materials to the company. The most important item I delivered was the mail.

The company was scheduled to come in to the base camp at Dau Tieng for a one-day maintenance standdown. The company commander requested that we prepare a good meal during the time the company was in. As a special treat for the company, he wanted fruit pies. He especially wanted a cherry pie. I tasked the mess sergeant to prepare the meal and make the pies.

The mess sergeant was able to find the ingredients for the pies and was prepared to make over thirty pies for the company. The company returned to the base camp and began pulling maintenance on the tracks. The dinner was schedule for 1600 hours. The company would have its dinner and then depart the base camp at 2000 hours to get back in position for security.

At approximately 1500 hours, I was driving in my jeep checking the perimeter bunkers of the battalion when I heard the sound of rockets being fired at the base camp. I pulled off the perimeter road at the next bunker, got out of the jeep, and ran into the bunker. The VC/NVA fired a total of six rounds at the base camp. After the rockets hit, I waited for another two to three minutes, then ran back to the jeep and got on the radio to find out where the rockets had hit. I contacted the battalion operations center and found out that two of the rockets had hit in the B Company area. I hit the gas pedal and made my way to the company area.

The first of the two rockets hit in an open area and caused little damage, but the other rocket hit the mess hall right over the kitchen area. The six men in the kitchen were injured, but none in a serious way. The company was lucky that most of the men were in the maintenance area with the tracks and were able to take cover inside of them.

However, the company did suffer a great loss. All of the pies the mess team had made for the company were destroyed, as was most of the dinner that was being prepared. It was upsetting for the men, but it was also funny that they were looking forward to the pies so much. The VC/NVA had no idea that they had hit us so hard by taking out our pies. The company would not be able to get any more pies because it was going back out to the field. The men had to settle for a meal of C-rations.

With no reason to stay in the base camp, the company departed the area earlier than planned for their security mission. The mess sergeant was later able to get the supplies for the pies, but the company did not get back into base camp until May.

However, the company did suffer a great loss. All of the pies the mess team had made for the company were destroyed, as was most of the dinner that was being prepared. The men had to settle for a meal of C-rations.

Jim Liles, Edgewood, KY
Company C, 1st Battalion, 22nd Infantry Regiment

Letter from a Hospital Bed February 18, 1967

Dear Mom and Family,

I guess the Army or Red Cross has already notified you that your son (me) was wounded in the leg. I don't know what they told you, but I got shot through the leg, by the calf. I was really lucky—it didn't hit a bone, but it put a big hole in my leg.

Here is what happened. Our company was on a "company-sized" mission near the Cambodian border. We moved out from our firebase around 0900 hours on February 16. We were moving through the jungle about 1430 hours in the afternoon when we got word on our radio that Company A was getting hit real bad.

We were about two miles from Company A, so we started tearing through the jungle to help them out. It was really rough moving. It was so thick I didn't think I could ever go that fast with a 50-pound pack on my back. Around 1830 hours, we first made contact with the enemy. I was about the fifth or sixth man from the front of our company. We were moving out in file, using trails whenever we came upon one. We shot a couple rounds at the bushes and then moved on up the trail a little further. Another sergeant and I spotted three NVA moving through the bushes and opened up on them. We then moved on down the trail and were about a hundred yards from where Company A had set up their defensive perimeter.

We were opened up on by automatic weapons from the NVA who were in trees. Our captain (company commander) got shot in the neck and was lying out in the open. I was about fifteen or twenty feet from him and our lieutenant yelled, "Somebody get him out of the line of fire!" Nobody moved, and the shots were still coming from the trees so I threw off my pack, dropped my weapon, and took off from behind the tree where I had taken cover. I got over to the captain and there was another GI trying to get him out. The captain was about six feet three inches tall and big, so he was heavy. I was on my knees when the enemy opened up on us with a machine gun.

The other guy got it through the foot, the captain got it again in the back, and I felt a pain in my leg. It didn't really hurt. I felt like my whole leg just fell asleep in a split second. I was still trying to pull the captain away when I looked back and saw the blood on my leg. I ripped off the leg of my pants and there was a huge hole in my calf where the bullet had come out. I started putting on my first aid bandage to stop the bleeding when the medic came up and put another field bandage on my leg. They knocked out the machine gun so I leaned on a guy's shoulder and we started out to get into the perimeter of Company A. We had five wounded and the captain (Captain Colin McManus) was dead. On the way in, I passed over at least eight guys from Company A who had been killed.

We got inside the perimeter, and they got all the wounded in a big group in the middle. There were about twenty-nine of us wounded in the two companies. About 2130 hours a big helicopter, called a Chinook, got about fifteen of the real bad wounded out. The way they did this was they got a group of guys and started clearing out an area by chopping down trees with machetes. After they had an area about thirty feet in diameter, they called in the Chinook, which hovered over the area and let down a cable with a type of stretcher on it. The guys below would strap a wounded guy on it and they would pull him up—the cable was run by electricity.

They only took out fifteen so I had to stay all night. My leg didn't hurt too bad and I didn't take any morphine, only two penicillin shots to fight infection. The NVA didn't hit us that night and early the next morning, I was pulled up into the Chinook with about ten other guys. They took us to the 18th Surgical Hospital in Pleiku where my leg was operated on. Today, they took me by stretcher and flew me to Qui Nhon, Vietnam. They haven't closed the wound yet; they will wait for about three days to see if infection sets in. Don't worry too much; I am doing fine and will still be coming home in June. I won't have to go back out in the field again, so no sweat about getting hit again. Write soon— I will write again when I get to Japan. Write soon, Love, Your Son, Jimmy.

Lou Talley, LaVerne, CA
Company A, 1st Battalion, 22nd Infantry Regiment

Central Highlands, Vietnam '67

From Lou's diary

Captain said we were going on a mission to locate a battalion of NVA who had been wasting base camps. Something does not look right since we have been given an azimuth to follow. Seems as if they were looking for them, but they would not tell us the direction to go.

Heard the point men on the radio say they saw boot prints with water still seeping in them so they know we are here and are going to be set up. We better be taking up position. It doesn't make any sense to keep going if we are where their outpost was; it means they are close.

Captain said to set up a perimeter. I've got that same gut feeling that we are as close as we had better get. Not much daylight left.

Bringing the artillery in close...got a "hot dog" Forward Observer who says he can turn around and call it in backwards. No need for that, the dummy hit a foxhole. Don't need the NVA when we are doing a job on ourselves. Last night, it was mistaken identity when they cut loose with those 20mm; it almost feels like this is the Little Bighorn.

Here come the mortars, amazing nobody got hit, really raked our perimeter good. Captain said to brace for an attack since that is how it goes, first the mortars then it all cuts loose. Heard the outpost say to get ready, they are coming and there are lots of them. Lost radio contact. Hear our other outpost cut loose with the machine gun. Sergeant Reed went into shock, all he can say is, "Oh no, oh no."

Got the artillery going. Something wrong as it is going farther out instead of coming in closer. Captain has started calling it in himself. Almost had it, hitting us from all sides, some hand-to-hand stuff. Heard a pilot on the radio asking what was going on, says he is off course and saw us by accident, has a full load and can buy us some time, has an accent, Australian, not even our own air support. Had to call off the artillery since he is coming in low.

Heard our air support, need our location to get layout of battle area, had somebody fire tracers from the center of the perimeter to see where we are, never so glad to see those guys. Almost all of us are out of ammo and could not have held out two minutes longer. Really did a job on those dudes, everything on fire from the napalm, cooked many of them in front of us, no more enemy fire coming in.

Attack seems to be over, said they will keep the perimeter lit up all night with illumination and want a body count at first light.

Man hit by our artillery is bleeding to death, captain trying to get him evacuated but no choppers will come in, action too hot and heavy. Captain said forget it since he just died.

Never prayed like that before in my life, plumb scared to death. Told God I was not going to promise anything since he knows what happened the last time. Please help us, please help us. Had to be honest, may not deserve anything good, just asking for help and can only promise I will try to play it straight.

Kind of strange that all that stuff reminded me of something in the Bible. Israel against the world and don't stand a chance and that is when God steps in the scene so they know who delivered them and kept His Word to do that, kind of like when God used the enemy to punish His own house because of idolatry and stuff and then He proceeded to restore it.

Captain agreed that we almost had it, seems to have taken the starch out of a lot of hot dogs, bet I ain't the only one who cut through all the stuff and got connected. Wonder how long I will straighten up this time, makes me mad that it don't last very long....

James Frost, Saginaw, MI
Company C, 2nd Battalion, 22nd Infantry Regiment

Night Listening Post

The time was 1967 in Vietnam. The place was near the Hobo Woods in War Zone C. I was an infantryman with Company C, 2nd Battalion, 22nd Infantry Regiment (Mechanized). I had many job assignments that I didn't care for during my tour. One job that stands out was going out on a night listening post (LP). Two or more men would usually be picked to go out beyond our perimeter and act as a forward observer. Duties included calling in situation reports back to the command center once an hour. You were not to engage in military force, but to keep eyes and ears open if enemy soldiers tried to infiltrate the perimeter.

The job was always very dangerous. The Viet Cong were constantly trying to penetrate. Many times the VC would crawl close to our outside perimeter and cut wires from our claymore mines, then use those same claymore mines on us during a firefight.

There was this one night while on LP that I could actually smell the VC; they were that close to our position. I do not remember who I was with, but we were all very nervous. I remember getting our assignment and walking to the LP location in the woods. It was another hot night, and I was sweating so badly that my clothes were completely wet by the time we finally got into our LP position in front of our laager perimeter. The mosquitoes were terrible because we were in the monsoon season.

One night while on LP duty, we noticed a small light near our position. The best we could figure out it might be a VC scout shining the light looking for a trail in the woods. I knew there was a bike trail near our location because I had been briefed earlier by our platoon sergeant. It appeared someone was holding a flashlight in his hand, but had the back of the hand facing the perimeter. We watched this light for quite a while until it was gone.

Later that night, we heard footsteps of men going by our position. In a whisper, we said that we suspected VC. We lay flat on our backs so as not to be seen. It was very dark but by lying flat on our backs, we could see the open sky give off some light. As we lay quietly, we could see silhouettes of men going by our position. Our time for a sitrep (situation report) had come, but we were unable to call back and give a report. There was just no way we could call back so we stayed still and quiet. There was one point where I could smell an orange. I figured one of the VC was peeling an orange to eat. I could not make out the man because he must have stooped down to eat it, but the smell of that orange I will never forget.

It was a very tense time with the VC that close to our position. Once the VC moved out of our LP area, we called back our report on what was happening. The laager position was put on alert. The remainder of the night we heard nothing. When our LP came back into the company perimeter the next morning, we were happy to be back. I was told to report to our company commander on what had happened. I told him the entire story and he said we were fortunate and lucky to have made it out alive.

Dick Donnelly, Martinez, GA
HQ, 1st Battalion, 22nd Infantry Regiment

The Pig Lady

It was in the spring of 1967 and the 1st Battalion, 22nd Infantry "Regulars" were operating out of the 1st Brigade command post in a place called Jackson's Hole, not to be confused with Jackson Hole, Wyoming. It was towards the end of the dry season, and everything that did not move collected a thin coat of red dust. In fact, even if you did move you looked a little rusty from the dust. In addition to the operations of the line companies, the battalion sent out routine patrols and medcaps in and around the local Montagnard hamlets. A medcap was an operation designed to help the "friendly civilians" by giving them medical care and "goodies" which consisted of C-rations and excess sundry packs.

A sundry pack contained cigarettes, soap, shaving materials and the GIs favorite, tropical chocolate bars. These chocolate bars would not melt in a 350-degree oven and were mostly used for restoring the leather on worn jungle boots.

One bright morning a medcap composed of the S-5 (Civil Affairs Officers) Dick Donnelly, battalion surgeon Doc Howie Shiele, a couple of medics and a squad of infantry set out for a hamlet about six kilometers from the Brigade CP. On arrival, they set up shop and began tending to the Montagnards. We dispensed all of the goodies, which had filled the back of a three-quarter-ton truck. Dr. Shiele examined a large number of children while the medics cleaned up minor cuts, abrasions, and skin infections. A couple tetracycline tablets and liberal amounts of bacitracian ointment worked miracles.

The team would inspect the hamlet for signs of MVC (Montagnard Viet Cong) activities and question the villagers, who always feigned ignorance of their presence. Just before leaving, one of the men taking pictures of the hamlet said that he had found an old woman who looked to be living with the hogs in the pig sty. It turned out that this lady, although a member of the hamlet, had no relatives to take care of her. She looked to be quite old, which for a Montagnard would be between forty and fifty years old. She had built herself a small "hooch" inside the sty fence and lived off the scraps that were fed to the hogs.

A quick examination by Doc Shiele revealed a very large and deep infectious wound in her right buttock. This poor human being was filthy, her hair matted with dirt. She wore the standard Montagnard female dress, which consisted of an ankle length black skirt and not much else. Dr. Shiele and the medics took her to a nearby stream and gave her a bath. Montagnards are very modest people and naturally she protested violently, but what can a four and a half foot tall woman do against two six foot medics? After she was cleaned up, she was given an antibiotic shot and the wound was packed with bacitracian ointment. As a reward, she was given a large GI tee shirt and all the tropical chocolate bars she could eat.

The S-5 and Dr. Shiele cut a deal with the hamlet chief to care for the woman. In exchange for ten cases of C-rations and sundry packs, he would make sure that she had a hut to live in and somebody would care for her. The chief was given a bottle of tetracycline pills and told to give the woman one pill when the sun rose, one when it was high in the sky, and one when it went down. He was also promised more C-rations and clothing.

The Regulars operated in that area for three more weeks, then returned to the Oasis. During the remainder of their stay the "Pig Lady," as she became known, was checked frequently. She gained weight, and her infection healed. The people of the hamlet were given a lot of discarded clothing and jungle boots and became very friendly with the medcap team when it was in their area. They also passed on a lot of intelligence on VMC and NVA activity, a small bit of which was useful. A short while before his DEROS, the S-5 had a chance to get back to the hamlet and found the woman to be much improved and enjoying life. Medcap operations did not receive the publicity of combat operations but did show the people the kinder gentler side of the American GI.

James E. Hardin, Columbia, PA
Company C, 2nd Battalion, 22nd Infantry Regiment

Grenades

Never being good at throwing things, I had a concern about grenades. I always had a few lined up for use in ambush, but doubts remained. I look back on the times they were used and wonder how I survived.

In February or March 1967, Company C, 2nd Battalion, 22nd Infantry Regiment was clearing a VC base camp that been vacated without a fight. I came across a small opening that had a trail leading to it from several directions. I looked into it but couldn't see anything. I reached into it, but couldn't touch anything. I believe it was the platoon sergeant who suggested dropping a grenade into it. I located a nearby tree to hide behind and let one go. In four to five seconds, several things crossed my mind. Was it a mine or booby trap in the handy 'cover' I had picked, or was my grenade lying on a million pounds of explosives? When it went off, a brown liquid stream shot into the air. One whiff and I knew I had located and destroyed their latrine. Some guys find Piasters, I find....

At another base camp (only this one was being contested), there was a small bunker where the VC lived about ten yards to the side of our PC

(Personnel Carrier). I handed a grenade to one squad member who was not the bravest man on board. He went out the back door and threw the grenade with all his might. Of course, he missed the entrance. I was sadistically enjoying this and met him coming through the door with another grenade. Again, he threw with all he had. It probably would have gone two hundred yards if it hadn't hit a tree and rolled back to our PC. I got everyone down, and we rocked when it went off. I gave him a third and told him to close in and drop it down the entrance. I also reminded him we had two cases of them. I was distracted on the other side of the PC when the grenade went off. I asked him if he got it and he assured me he hit it this time. Confidently, I grabbed a flashlight and a .45 caliber pistol and walked into the bunker. It was a neat little two-man dwelling. They had Uncle Ho's picture on the wall, raised bunks, a table, and a straw mat on the floor. I was surprised at how little damage the grenade had done until I realized there wasn't even the smell of burnt powder in there. That idiot had missed again and lied to me. I was a fool to believe him, but my luck held; the VC had left.

James E. Hardin, Columbia, PA
Company C, 2nd Battalion, 22nd Infantry Regiment

Picking on PSG Kay

Platoon Sergeant Sammy Kay was platoon sergeant for third platoon, Company C, 2nd Battalion, 22nd Infantry Regiment while I was there. He spent most of the time acting as our platoon leader, since our regular platoon leader was a junior officer and was always being called away to base camp for some thankless duty. Sometimes Platoon Sergeant Kay would say or do something funny, but, as often as not, we were the ones who were thinking up something to pull on him. We were starting an operation one day and had to cross a river. The VC had blown the bridge. Although Recon platoon crossed the sunken bridge, we had an Armor Launched Vehicular Bridge (ALVB) with us. The ALVB didn't reach across the river, so a bulldozer was prepping the approach for it when our recon platoon was ambushed. We were in the depression of the river—securing the bulldozer, thus out of direct fire, but preventing us from supporting Recon a mere one hundred meters away. One of Recon's Personnel Carriers (PC) was burning with all the colored smoke grenades adding to the surreal scene.

We were going nuts, wanting to help our buddies and ordered to stay put! Platoon Sergeant Kay finally got us released, so he and his RTO (Radio Telephone Operator) climbed on board and we started to cross. The PC in front of us stopped, so we were forced to halt about halfway across the sunken bridge. It was deep and we had about a foot of freeboard. It was also too crowded in the cargo hatch, so I sat down. Just as I sat down, everything went black as a concussion hit us. Platoon Sergeant Kay fell to the floor in pain, holding his arm. I jumped up and saw a PC well behind us on its side with pieces still falling, some of which were men. Platoon Sergeant Kay was hit in the elbow by a rock from the blast. Not serious, but it hurt badly. We were still sitting on the sunken bridge in the middle of the river when my dark sense of humor lit up.

I turned to Platoon Sergeant Kay and told him that the VC must have also mined the bridge. It is just what I would have done if I were them. He started climbing out of the hatch, calling to his RTO to follow. Poor Platoon Sergeant Kay slipped over the side and completely disappeared. Just his helmet was floating back to the PC on the current. We must have been very close to the left side of the bridge. He popped back up to the surface, found his footing, took his helmet and headed off to the front. It was a dirty trick—I hope he forgives me.

About a week or so later, we had an air strike. We were operating with a cavalry platoon in the jungle. The Air Force spotted something to bomb and knew we were close, so the cavalry platoon leader was notified and he marked his position with smoke. I was inside my PC when I smelled the smoke. As I came up to see what was going on, a B-57 Canberra bomber dropped some bombs ahead and to the right of us. A large piece of high trajectory shrapnel went through a five-gallon can of motor oil that was sitting on the roof of the PC. It was messy but not serious. The next run brought the bombs much closer. This time, a three-foot long chunk came flying out of the woods horizontally and stuck in the side of a PC.

Throughout this, Platoon Sergeant Kay was talking to the cavalry platoon leader, who assured Kay that the bombs weren't that close. I don't think the lieutenant realized that the column was about a kilometer long. At that point, Platoon Sergeant Kay pulled our platoon out and passed the column. He stopped aside the cavalry platoon leader's PC and waved a large chunk of shrapnel at him while emphatically stating, "Maybe they weren't close to you!"

March 21, 1967, found us running at full throttle to Fire Support Base Gold. It was located in a clearing near Soui Tre. We knew they were in trouble. We had listened to the roar of their battle for some time before we were finally ordered to go there. Any semblance of tactical integrity was abandoned. It you were slow, you were passed. With all those V8 Chryslers turning at redline, it must have been quite a howl as we approached the clearing. The jungle was getting thinner, and we could see light ahead when Platoon Sergeant Kay came on the radio to caution us.

His voice was steady, almost monotone. "We have friendlies in front of us. Do not use your .50 calibers. Return fire only with M-16s or M-79s. I say again..."

At this point, a burst of green tracers went roaring down our left side and Kay's voice goes up an octave or two as he blurts out, "Fire everything you've got!"

We fired some to the flanks, but ignored the incoming and just swept on through. I brought up that transmission to Platoon Sergeant Kay later, but he didn't remember it. I should point out that Platoon Sergeant Kay earned a Bronze Star that day.

James E. Hardin, Columbia, PA
Company C, 2nd Battalion, 22nd Infantry Regiment

Short Rounds

Most of us know the fear of all infantrymen—short rounds or "friendly" fire. Some of the stories are tragic, some are comical, all are part of our heritage.

In Company C, 2nd Battalion, 22nd Infantry, sometime in March 1967, we had set up a perimeter for the night in a large clearing. I was inside the Personnel Carrier (PC) eating, when an artillery round came in. It wasn't the usual roar of one passing overhead, but a real sizzle as it passed by our PC and exploded in front of the PC beside us. There were three fellows outside our PC, and I still laugh remembering seeing the two of them scrambling up the ramp on hands and knees, with a third one going right over both of them. The picture was all eyeballs and elbows as they came up the ramp over me. I don't think they stopped until they overran the driver!

The medic ran over to the next PC, and they evacuated one man. When the medic came back, he told the story. The .50 caliber machine gunner took a small piece of shrapnel in the temple. Not serious, but it bled well. In addition to that, he was almost knocked unconscious by the blast and couldn't hear. While the medic checked him out, his buddies were standing over him assuming he was dead and each was giving an informal eulogy. The medic swears that if he could have heard them he probably would have gone into shock and died. Artillery said one gun had set the wrong deflection.

James' second "short round" story

One time we created our own short round. We were moving in heavy jungle in a column, around February 1967, when we ran into some VC who opened up on us. We had formed on line beside our PCs, but this meant our fires were masked by the squad in front of us. I was near a PC and could hear the radio calls. Artillery was in front of us, so it was a new experience. Artillery would call "Splash!" and the rounds would explode. As the noise died away, we would hear the roar of another flight inbound, then the boom of the firing. The rounds were close!

The shrapnel was sizzling by horizontally, dropping twigs and leaves on us as it cut through the jungle. I was behind an ant hill, resigned to thinking that as long as we had one or two squads in front of me, I wouldn't be directly involved. Someone announced a fifty-meter drop, bringing the next round closer to us. A few seconds later I heard people running at me from ahead. All I could think of was that the VC were charging.

The M16 switched to automatic; I raised up to fire. No VC. Instead I saw the leading squad coming at us at a full run. The squad leader took a dive over my anthill and slid about five meters on his belly.

He quickly crawled back and started shaking me while gasping, "Drop fifty, drop fifty, do you know where that would put it? About twenty-five meters behind my men!"

SPLASH! We could see those flashes even though we were trying to become earthworms. At that point, I believe we asked for a small correction, probably in the add category.

Walt Sauer, Spokane, WA
Chaplain, 1st Battalion, 22nd Infantry Regiment

A Memorable Experience in Vietnam

What kind of day was it? The choppers (UH1D) were flying. It was the monsoon season. The "Regulars" of the 1st Battalion, 22nd Infantry Regiment were out in the boonies. I grabbed my chaplain's kit, an ammo box stuffed with field hymnals and letter writing materials, crawled on the chopper and arrived out in the field in about twenty minutes. The troops with their "as is" appearance were happy to prepare for a service. The chaplain's kit altar was set up, communion elements were prepared, hymn books were distributed, soldiers were sitting on their steel pots, and we were ready to begin.

Suddenly, one of those dark monsoon clouds appeared in the distance. The men said that we could get the service completed before the cloud arrived. We had just finished the opening prayer when we experienced a drenching baptism of rain. In fifteen seconds, water was running down my neck, body and into my boots. The entire congregation laughed at—and with—me. In a few minutes, the rain stopped and we completed the service—never to be forgotten. I picked up the hymnals, closed the chaplain's kit, distributed the letter writing material, collected letters to be mailed, said good-bye, crawled on the chopper, and flew on to the Fire Support Base for another service. What kind of a day was it? A full, busy, wet, inspirational day, and I'm glad I was there.

Bill Saling, Big Canoe, GA

HQ Company, 1st Battalion, 22nd Infantry Regiment

Lightning Bug Ambush

During March 1967, our battalion was located at a firebase along the Cambodian border. The battalion mission was to stop the flow of the NVA into the central highlands. My platoon was responsible for all aerial resupply to our forward infantry companies and to defend our section of the fire base perimeter. Part of our defensive strategy was to conduct ambush patrols in the area surrounding our firebase. One afternoon around 1600 hours, Captain Russ Zink, CO of Headquarters Company, arrived in the firebase from our rear area and wanted to go along on an ambush patrol. During our briefing, we were informed that the NVA were using a certain road network at night and had been observed on bicycles and on foot, and using flashlights. We left the firebase before dark and were moving into position to set up our ambush. By then it had become quite dark. Suddenly, we heard something ahead, and everyone dropped to the ground. At that moment, you tried to become invisible and almost stopped breathing. All you could hear was your heart pounding in your chest so loudly that you were sure everyone around could hear it.

As I was looking around, I noticed what appeared to be lights coming through the foliage. Oh my God! The NVA were coming into our patrol from the side and nobody had seen them but me! I blinked a couple of times to be sure that I was not seeing things, but there was no mistaking it. Somebody was approaching with flashlights, and nobody else seemed to notice. The way I was lying, my M-16 was located just short of Captain Zink's crotch. As I began to swing my weapon around to engage the enemy, Captain Zink turned and asked what was going on. I told him about the flashlights approaching from the side. We both looked again, only to realize that the "flashlights" I thought I saw were lightning bugs.

The rest of the patrol was uneventful, but when we got back to the firebase, Captain Zink told everyone who would listen about my attack on the "lightning bug" enemy. He even threatened to send the story to the Stars and Stripes newspaper. The next time you are walking on a summer evening and see lightning bugs among the trees, you see if they don't look like flashlights!

Author Unknown (Submitted by Dave Gehr, Company C, 3rd Battalion, 22nd Infantry Regiment)

The Battle of Soui Tre

This is one of many after-action reports on the Battle of Soui Tre or LZ Gold.

On March 21, 1967, the 2nd and 3rd Battalions, 22nd Infantry Regiment, the 2nd Battalion, 12th Infantry Regiment, along with the 2nd Battalion, 77th Field Artillery and 2nd Battalion, 34th Armor (plus supporting units), earned the Presidential Unit Citation for their actions that resulted in over six hundred North Vietnamese Army (NVA) and Viet Cong (VC) killed in action. Every battle has many different perspectives. The following is one.

On March 18, 1967, while participating in Operation Junction City, Phase II, the 3rd Battalion, 22nd Infantry, made an air assault landing into LZ Gold to secure a forward support base for the 2nd Battalion, 77th Field Artillery. A perimeter defense was established with Company A assuming responsibility for the western sector and Company B assuming responsibility for the eastern sector.

Three batteries of 2nd Battalion, 77th Field Artillery occupied eighteen firing positions in the center of the perimeter to support the 4th Infantry Division's 3rd Brigade Task Force.

Between March 18 and 20, 1967, the battalion's elements constructed defensive bunkers, planned and rehearsed contingency defensive actions, conducted aggressive daylight patrolling within the defensive tactical area of responsibility, and established night ambushes.

On March 20, while scouting the area in his command helicopter, Colonel Marshall Garth, Brigade Commander, saw at least thirty Viet Cong in an open area. He quickly radioed this information to Lieutenant Colonel John Bender at Fire Support Base (FSB) Gold. This was the first sign that trouble might be at hand.

0635 hours. March 21. The defensive perimeter came under heavy enemy ground and mortar attack. The first indication of the impending attack came when elements of the approaching VC assault force were engaged by an eleven-man ambush patrol from Company B, 3rd Battalion, 22nd Infantry.

A four-man listening post (LP) also engaged the enemy about one hundred meters from the eastern side of the perimeter. The enemy walked past the men in the listening post. The guys in the LP finally realized they were VC and opened fire. The VC went back to get them. Seeing how many enemy they had opened fire on, the men decided to surrender. One man had been wounded and was lying in the bottom of the foxhole. The other three climbed out of the foxhole, dropped their weapons and raised their arms. The VC summarily executed all three by shooting them through the back of their heads at point blank range. One of the executed GIs fell into the foxhole atop the wounded man in the bottom. The wounded soldier didn't dare move. The VC didn't bother to check to see if he was dead. He lived to tell this story. When asked how the VC got past the LP before they saw them, he replied, "We apparently had fallen asleep."

Simultaneously, FSB Gold began receiving heavy mortar fire from VC 60mm and 82mm mortars located in firing positions to the northwest and southeast.

0635 hours. The Recon platoon, 3rd Battalion, 22nd Infantry, which was located on the southeastern portion of the perimeter, engaged a large VC force, which had approached to within thirty-five meters of the friendly positions. Within minutes, the entire perimeter was attacked by wave after wave of VC firing recoilless rifle, RPG2 rocket launchers, automatic weapons, and other small arms.

As the attack continued, the three artillery batteries began counter-firing in an effort to neutralize the VC mortar concentration, which continued to rake the entire fire support base. During the initial assault, Company B reported that its first platoon positions (southeastern perimeter) had been penetrated and that the reaction force from 2nd Battalion, 77th Field Artillery was required to reinforce this section.

0701 hours. This reaction force began moving toward the first platoon's positions. In the meantime, the remainder of the perimeter kept the attacking enemy at bay with a continuous barrage of small arms and machine gun fire. Supporting fire from two 105mm howitzer batteries and a battery of 155mm howitzers (SP) was called in at a range of less than one hundred meters from the outer perimeter.

0711 hours. The Company B Commander reported that his first platoon had been overrun by a human wave attack and that the platoon was surrounded. Air strikes were called in to the outer edge of the perimeter and along the eastern wood line.

0714 hours. A FAC (Forward Air Controller) arrived on the scene in a Cessna O-1E Birddog. The Cessna was shot down by heavy machine gun fire while flying low over the perimeter after directing only one air strike. Both the pilot and observer were killed.

0752 hours. Company B's Commander requested that 2nd Battalion, 77th Field Artillery fire beehive rounds into the southeastern and southern sectors of the perimeter. A twenty-man reaction force from Company A was sent to reinforce Company B's northeastern perimeter, which had been penetrated by another human wave attack.

0755 hours. Two more Cessna O-1E's showed up after being scrambled from Ben Hoa. F-100's and F-4 Phantom's were arriving by the squadron. Bombs were bursting at the edge of the perimeter. An AC-47 "Dragonship" showed up with Gatling guns blazing into the enemy, who were caught in the open.

0840 hours. The northeastern, eastern, and southeastern portions of the perimeter had fallen back to a preplanned secondary defensive line around the guns of the artillery batteries. During this time, the VC penetrated within hand grenade range of the Battalion Command Post (CP) and within five meters of the Battalion Aid Station.

To counter this new threat, a continuous and devastating hail of small arms and automatic weapons fire was directed at the frenzied VC attackers, while the remaining 105mm howitzers of the artillery batteries began firing beehive rounds "direct fire" into the attacking VC masses. Bombs were dropped within fifty meters of American positions. Supporting 105mm and 155mm artillery batteries threw up a constant wall of high explosives.

When the 2nd Battalion, 77th Field Artillery ran out of beehive rounds, high explosive (HE) rounds at charge one were fired into the charging VC at point blank range.

0900 hours. The situation, though tense because of ammunition shortages, was still under control. The northern, western, and southern portions of the perimeter were intact and under moderate pressure from VC who had worked their way up to within fifteen meters of friendly positions.

By now there were eighty-five fighter planes on the scene. The aircraft played a major role in breaking the attack.

Although pushed in, the northeastern, southeastern, and eastern portions of the perimeter were still intact. The defenders had contained and broken the neverending human wave attacks that had been thrown against them.

0901 hours. A relief column led by the 2nd Battalion, 12th Infantry Regiment broke through from the south and linked up with the besieged defenders. Joining force, 2nd Battalion, 12th Infantry supported Company B's counterattack from west to east to reestablish the original perimeter.

0912 hours. A mechanized infantry and armor column from 2nd Battalion, 22nd Infantry Regiment and 2nd Battalion, 34th Armor Regiment broke through from the southwest and began sweeping forward along the tree line toward the northeast.

0928 hours. The original perimeter had been reestablished and mopping up operations had begun.

1045 hours. Medical evacuation of friendly casualties and ammunition resupply had been accomplished. The battle area had been secured.

Artillery and air strikes continued to pound the route of withdrawal of the broken and routed VC attackers. For four hours, four hundred men of this battalion held off a determined attack by twenty-five hundred hard core guerrillas consisting of six battalions controlled by the 272nd NVA Regiment. A total of 647 Viet Cong were killed in action, including 200 by body count, and ten were taken captive. On the U.S. side, 31 were killed in action, and 187 were wounded.

In summary, Lieutenant General Jonathan M. Seaman, in his commendation to this brigade stated, "I want to extend my congratulations to you and your magnificent troops for their major victory at FSB Gold on the 21st day of March. Fighting against a numerically superior and well equipped foe, elements of the 3rd Brigade, 4th Infantry Division, with supporting elements, inflicted a devastating defeat on major elements of the 272nd Main Force Regiment. This is the most decisive defeat the Viet Cong have suffered in the III Corps Tactical Zone in my eighteen months in Vietnam."

James D. Holder, Del Rio, TX
Company A, 3rd Battalion, 22nd Infantry Regiment

Admiration for the Artillery

I was at the battle referred to as Soui Tre on March 21, 1967. Our reference, as I recall, was the battle of LZ Gold. I was a squad leader of some fine men, but then that is another story for another day. I remember this battle for many reasons, but one was a newfound admiration for the men of the artillery. I had always felt that they were not as good as infantry troops. But during the battle of Soui Tre, when we were informed that the enemy had penetrated our perimeter in three places, I watched the rear of our two-man position.

As I stared out there looking for the enemy, I noticed that amid the 82mm and rifle fire the artillery soldiers from 2nd Battalion, 77th Field Artillery were standing in the open without cover, continuing to load and fire the 105mm howitzers with beehive rounds and HE into the tree line. I saw many of these fine soldiers hit the ground one at a time and then it hit me like a rock—these men were falling from wounds. I came away that day with a newfound pride in the artillery folks, which I have maintained to this day. We had cover, they did not, yet they stayed on duty continuing to fire their weapons until they were silenced or ran out of ammo. My hat is off to the men of the artillery.

Gary Krek, Phoenix, AZ
Recon, 2nd Battalion, 22nd Infantry Regiment

Chasing the NVA

Gary Krek was also a participant in the Battle of Soui Tre and while answering an email inquiry from a man from 2nd Battalion, 12th Infantry Regiment who was in the battle, Gary wrote this.

Port, we may have passed each other or spoke a word or two at Soui Tre. After the perimeter was secured (loose use of words), I was with the group of three APCs who went on the rescue mission of the downed pilots from the Birddog that had been shot down earlier that morning. We ran into the retreating 272nd NVA Regiment and started our own little conflict. The word was sent out for a rescue party to come to our rescue. This didn't amount to much and as soon as my crippled APC was put back into working order, we were on our way again. When we arrived back at FSB Gold with the remains of the two pilots, the VTR had already dug up the two burial sites, and the enemy were being brought over to their final resting place. We stayed at Gold until after the award ceremony and moved out the next morning.

Gary also sent another interesting story attached to an E-mail note.

During the month of March 1967, we had been chasing the 272nd NVA Regiment around continuously. One morning we were sent to a large clearing where they were supposed to be. They must have heard us coming and split in a hurry. There were mines just lying on the ground for us—guess they didn't have time to bury them. We pulled into the zone in attack formation and then stopped. We had to wait for the 2nd Battalion,

34th Armor to catch up to us. As we were sitting there, I saw a metallic flash in front of our position maybe a hundred and fifty yards away (I was the driver side M-60 gunner at the time). I saw this NVA/VC stoop down and point a rocket right at us. I swung the M-60 at him but the TC's turret was in the way, and I couldn't get a shot. I started yelling at the TC that we were targeted and he had better open up with the .50 caliber.

He keeps saying, "Where?" and I am trying to get him to fire the damn gun. About then, there is a loud explosion and the next thing I know I'm covered with dirt (the little guy missed us). Within a second, the whole area is ablaze with machine gun fire and the tanks firing from behind me (wonderful thing that the 2nd Battalion, 34th Armor liked to do often. Same thing happened at Soui Tre). In the meantime, I still see him and still can't get a shot off. I watch him run off into the tree line, probably laughing his ass off. After that, I always kept my M-79 by my side.

James Frost, Saginaw, MI
Company C, 2nd Battalion, 22nd Infantry Regiment

My First Mission

While serving in Vietnam in 1967, our unit was away from Dau Tieng base camp for about two weeks. We had moved through the Tay Ninh province area near the Cambodian border. The four-day New Year Tet truce had ended. It was February 10, 1967, and I was nineteen years old when assigned to this unit of men who had trained together at Fort Lewis, WA. This would be my first mission.

Our company had set up a large open perimeter and was conducting platoon size search sweeps in the dense jungle. On this operation our unit was to stop Viet Cong buildup. Earlier in the week, headquarters had spotted a regiment sized VC unit near our grid location. It was about mid-afternoon when one of our platoons ran into an ambush while sweeping the jungle. Our platoon was called for backup. When we arrived at the ambush site, we immediately gave necessary firepower with our .50 caliber machine guns mounted on personnel carriers.

The platoon that was under attack was nearly out of ammo. Our RTO called in an artillery strike on the ambush site. With the intense pressure from our .50s, plus the artillery falling on the VC, we were able to retreat to the company perimeter. There were many lives lost that day and the days that followed. Our .50 gunner was killed in action, and I was wounded by shrapnel. That was my first of many firefights. I developed a lot of respect for the men of Company C, 2nd Battalion, 22nd Infantry Regiment (Mech) that day. They were a well trained bunch of soldiers.

Bob Babcock, Marietta, GA
Company B, 1st Battalion, 22nd Infantry Regiment

The Individual Soldier in Company B, 1st Battalion, 22nd Infantry Regiment, 1966-1967

This applies to all infantrymen—

He has many names and knows who he is. He might have been a rifleman, a grenadier, a machine gunner, a radio operator, part of a machine gun crew, a fire team leader, or a squad leader. His daily mission was like all infantrymen who came before or after him: "to close with and kill or capture the enemy through firepower and maneuver."

He was well trained, well motivated, and always did an excellent job. He knew he would not be rotated out of his front line infantry job. He knew that he had twelve months to work in the field seeking out the elusive enemy, hoping he would not be killed or wounded. He had two opportunities to leave the field— R&R and end-of-tour. Any other time he left, it was because of sickness, injury, or wounds.

He spent his year living the most primitive of existence. He always wore his steel helmet, web gear, and carried his weapon. He also carried a rucksack, weighing well over sixty pounds, in which he carried his essentials: ammo for his basic weapon, claymore mines, hand grenades, C-rations, bed roll, entrenching tool, machete, sandbags, writing paper, basic toilet articles, dry socks, and any other personal item he was willing to trudge through the jungle with. Most men eliminated all but the barest essentials: air mattresses and a change of clothes were among the first things to go. Cigarettes, writing paper, and the latest letter from home were the most cherished personal items. Sometimes, he was weighed down even further with extra machine gun ammunition or a mortar round.

Shaving and taking a bath in a stream or bomb crater were luxuries that happened maybe once a week. Leeches, mosquitoes, and bugs were as commonplace as the smell of sweat and body odor that permeated each man.

He seldom knew where he was and hardly ever looked at a map, compass, or talked on a radio. He depended on the leaders above him to tell him what to do. It was his job to do what he was told and to do it to the best of his ability.

All too frequently he was called on to sit with another man or two in an all night listening post outside the company perimeter. The nights seemed to last forever as he lay motionless, listening for the slightest sound of an approaching enemy. Another day, he would be called on to walk point and lead the company through the dense jungle. Constantly, the fear of running into the enemy was in the front of his mind. Caution and alertness became second nature to him. He learned to observe and react to his surroundings more than ever before in his life. All his senses were honed to a fine edge.

He learned what trusting your buddy was all about. He also forged friendships that he would never forget. White men, black men, Hispanics, and Orientals became closer to and depended more on a man of a different race than he had ever dreamed possible. These men were too busy to use drugs and to dislike someone who was different. Constantly in the field and returning to base camp only every three or four months, he did his job, day in and day out, as all infantrymen before and after him have done.

Henry Lenhart, Camarillo, CA
Company B, 4th Aviation Battalion

Martha Raye

This story concerns one of the greatest, most unselfish, and giving persons I have ever had the chance to meet. Her name is Martha Raye. As you probably know, she was an entertainer and movie star during World War II. But, my story is about her undying devotion to the men and women who served in Vietnam.

Martha Raye was not like most celebrities who visited the troops in Nam. She would go anywhere to visit and entertain troops. She would go out in the boonies to visit ten or fifteen troops with no regard for her own safety. She spent more time in Nam than any other entertainer. In fact, the U.S. Army made her a fullfledged Green Beret Lieutenant Colonel for her service in Vietnam.

I first met Martha on a rainy night at the 4th Infantry Division's main headquarters near Pleiku in 1967. I was a member of Company B, 4th

Aviation Battalion when I first saw her getting off one of our choppers. She had the biggest smile I'd ever seen. Just looking at her brightened the night. She and a fellow entertainer put on an impromptu show for all attending in the GP Medium Tent. The tent was filled to capacity as she sang songs, told jokes, and signed everyone's MPCs (Military Pay Scripts.) She had us laughing so hard that tears came to our eyes. When I got a chance to speak to her, I told her she looked like my mother-in-law.

Martha Raye said, "Poor lady!"

Martha was on her way to do a show at a Green Beret camp about fifteen clicks from base camp. It was our assignment to fly her out to the camp. We landed on the outskirts of the Green Beret camp just as the rain started to let up.

Martha gave us that large smile and said, "Thanks." We told her, "We will pick you up in the morning."

Little did we know what was to come. After returning to base camp, we settled in for the night (some sleeping and some on perimeter guard duty.) About midnight, it really started raining (as only monsoons can.) What we thought was thunder, was the Green Beret Camp being hit. With the heavy rain and bad visibility, we couldn't get our ship in the air. We could only watch and pray that Martha would make it through the night. The next morning brought a beautiful sunrise, and we were soon in the air. At first the Green Beret camp looked deserted. We could see that the NVA had breached the perimeter of the camp. Our hearts sank thinking Martha had been killed with the rest of the troops in that small outpost. The sound of our choppers brought folks running out of cover. All were waving, and in the middle was Martha, with one of the wounded. We found out later she had been a nurse in World War II and helped with the wounded in that war; she helped with the wounded the night of the assault in Nam as well. She would not fly out until she was assured that the injured were on their way out first.

That was the last time I saw her until 1982. The Green Berets were giving her a special tribute on Treasure Island in San Francisco. I just had to go and see her. I told the story to my wife, and she wrote a poem about Martha Raye, which I presented to her at the tribute. She read it and wept. Martha gave me her address and we exchanged Christmas cards until her death.

The poem says it all—not only for me, I hope, but also for anyone who was so lucky to have had the experience of meeting her in Vietnam. She was the greatest. I still have the MPC she signed in my safe deposit box. It is a true treasure to me. It reminds me of someone who made me laugh during the worst days of my life. Thank you, Martha.

Bob Babcock, Marietta, GA
Company B, 1st Battalion, 22nd Infantry Regiment

April Fool's Day 1967

On June 1, 1998, a helicopter pilot from the 4th Aviation Company left a notice on the 4th Infantry Division Association web page asking about a battle in February, 1967. A series of email notes ensued to answer that question and he offered this follow-up story.

April 1, 1967. I flew flare duty the night before. I was in bed when the call came in to take an S-2 to a Montagnard village. We picked him up, flew to, and landed near an infantry company. We began to lift off when I heard the popping sound. Funny— automatic weapons fire sounds just like popcorn at the movies. I was flying at the time as the fire raked the aircraft on the right side from front to tail. I felt it shudder, and then my left foot came up to my chest. Blood splattered across the instrument console.

The top of my boot had exploded when the armor piercing round came through. I knew I was hit so I gave control of the aircraft to the other pilot.

I could see metal tearing and smoke filling the cockpit, but it didn't last. Every light on the caution panel came on. We had no hydraulic pressure at all and the controls were frozen. We had leveled off about fifty to one hundred feet above the jungle and were traveling about 120 knots. We flew about a minute when the engine came apart. I made a Mayday call on the only radio that seemed to be still working. The aircraft began to settle towards the ground. As the aircraft settled, it began to yaw to the left. I now had a front row seat to watch the jungle passing by. We broke over an open area and the aircraft nestled in with us traveling about ninety miles an hour. The skids impacted the ground, the aircraft rolled straight forward, and I could see the dirt coming straight toward my windshield. Everyone got out but me. The gunner had been hit eight times with shrapnel and AK rounds; still, he came back into the aircraft and helped me get out. About twenty minutes later, a ship that had heard my distress call came into the area and picked us up.

Bob Babcock, the recipient of this note, was shocked. He looked into his collection of unpublished stories and found the following.

Every soldier wants to be paid on payday, whether he has a place to spend it or not. April 1, 1967, was no exception—it was the first day of the month, so payday it was. The company had been operating for the past several days in an area northwest of Pleiku, a relative picnic compared to the jungles we had been working in since November 3, 1966. The terrain was fairly open; it was sprinkled with a series of Montagnard villages, and the only enemy presence were a few bands of Viet Cong.

It was a welcome relief to be out of the jungle, off the "Ho Chi Minh trail," and fighting small VC groups instead of NVA regulars. Since it was payday, the company had not even sent patrols out. They were taking the opportunity to lay back, take it easy, and enjoy a well-deserved break.

The sun was shining brightly, and the countryside was beautiful as a helicopter approached the landing zone beside the company defensive perimeter. The Montagnard villages dotting the area had always intrigued me. I was riding in the helicopter, enjoying the view and the cool breeze blowing through the open doors as the pilot radioed Captain Ator.

"Oscar 6, this is Black Jack 53; mark your position, over."

Harry Troutman, Captain Ator's radio operator responded back in his familiar North Carolina drawl, "Black Jack, this is Oscar 6 Echo; our position is marked, over."

"This is Black Jack 53, I see purple smoke, over." "This is 6 Echo... Roger purple... Bring it on in. Out."

As the helicopter started its flare to hover onto the LZ, I grabbed my M-16 and my brown briefcase full of MPC (military payment certificates) and prepared for a quick exit from the chopper. Pilots don't like to stay on the ground in a potentially unsecured area. I jumped to the ground, and the pilot accelerated and headed back up into the sky as I casually walked toward the company.

The sound of gunfire punctuated the calm as bullets raked across the departing helicopter. The chopper lurched forward as the pilot lost control. The copilot reacted quickly, regained control, and nursed the crippled machine to a hard landing not too far from the LZ. At the sound of gunfire, I quickly sprinted to the safety of the company perimeter. (It would have been interesting to have a stopwatch on me to see how fast I ran).

Bravo Company reacted quickly to the gunfire. Before the rotors on the chopper had stopped spinning, a squad of men had formed a skirmish line and were moving across the landing zone to find the VC who had fired the shots. Another squad quickly grabbed their steel helmets and rifles and headed in the direction where the helicopter had gone down.

The following note went back over the net.

You're not going to believe it—I was the guy you left off in that Montagnard village when you were shot down that day. I was not the S-2 but the Executive Officer of Company B, 1st Battalion, 22nd Infantry Regiment, going out to pay the troops. (A copy of the above story was attached.)

Don Rawlinson, Dothan, AL—Company A, 4th Aviation, wrote back.

I am sitting here in near shock. I showed what you sent to my wife and she could only shake her head. I still can hardly believe that you're the guy that jumped off with a brown briefcase.

A month later, on July 5, 1998, the two vets got together in Dothan, Alabama. They swapped stories while their families sat and listened. If you haven't figured it out by now, it was yours truly, Bob Babcock, Marietta, GA—Company B, 1st Battalion, 22nd Infantry Regiment, the author of this book, who was the lieutenant on the chopper.

David Hegberg, Dekalb, IL
Company B, 1st Battalion, 22nd Infantry Regiment

What Did I Get Myself Into?

In 1967 I received my orders to go to Vietnam. I reported to Oakland Army Terminal on schedule. After a day or so standing in formation listening to names being read off, I figured out the name the sergeant was trying to say was actually mine. He needed a few lessons in pronunciation. I went forward, and our group was put into a big warehouse where we spent the next day in a building with no windows and no way to escape. We boarded a bus and were taken to Travis Air Force Base where we boarded a C-141 cargo plane. We were in fatigues, and it was being called a combat mission. The plane had been fitted with seats across the width of the plane with only two windows near the back. The first day we landed at Midway Island in the Pacific Ocean. The Navy personnel were very nice to us and one gave me some writing paper so I could write home. The next day, we went to Clark Air Force Base in the Philippines. The cabins we stayed at reminded me of a Boy Scout camp, with screens on the windows and bunk beds. You could buy San Miguel beer from a machine.

The next day we went on to Pleiku Air Base. A bus took us through Pleiku and out to the 4th Infantry Division Base Camp, Camp Enari. The first few days were spent at the 4th Infantry Division Replacement Company, where we watched films on what to do and not to do in the country. On our last night there we were taken out of the base camp perimeter to practice an ambush patrol. It was almost nighttime when we set up. No lights were to be used, and silence was a must. The next morning, after not much sleep and changing watches, I was astounded to see we had actually camped in a horseshoe configuration. None of us knew our group had actually camped right across from each other. If we had started shooting, we would have been shooting at one another. Green troops are edgy anyway, and it's a wonder something hadn't happened. We marched back into camp and then were sent to the HQs of our new units.

I was assigned to the second platoon, Company B, 1st Battalion, 22nd Infantry Regiment. The first sergeant seemed to be always upset. The day I was to take a chopper to the field, I missed it. That didn't help his disposition any. I helped to build a building for the rest of that day, but made sure I was on the next day's chopper out to the firebase. As we circled the outpost, I could read the words, "REGULARS BY GOD" written out in sandbags before the chopper landed in the LZ (Landing Zone). My company of men were manning the perimeter of this outpost also known as "Regular Hill." It was very hot and muggy.

The next morning another company of men came in and then it was our turn to leave. I had my rucksack filled with C-rations and personal items, my M-16 rifle with three hundred rounds of ammo, and my medical bag strapped over the top. A machete, a blanket, and a poncho were rolled up under the rucksack. We moved out into the forest, with rolling foothills, and trees standing tall, like at attention. Our company walked most of the day, and that night we stopped in one area of higher ground, no one saying anything, silently eating our C-rations. As darkness fell, I lay down on my blanket trembling, because soon the 105mm howitzers started firing from the firebase. I could hear the rounds whistling through the air and exploding in the distance. What in the world did I get myself into? My only thought was, "Will I ever get to go back home again?" I hugged the earth hoping we hadn't got a short round and that the enemy wasn't driven back toward us.

Morning came. We hadn't had much sleep, but we moved out. During the day I would follow the guy in front of me from a distance of about forty yards, depending on the density of the terrain. Because of the heat, your mind would wander and you would think of all sorts of things. You had to keep an eye on the guy in front of you because if you lost him, the guys behind would be just as lost as yourself. Elephant grass and bamboo thickets were the worst, because it was so tall and dense. We worked our way back to the LZ after several days, and hurried into a bunker.

"We just got hit a short while ago," a guy said.

I hadn't heard anything as we had walked toward the camp. We were now leaving that area of operations. Our company stayed on the perimeter watching other companies of men come in and leave by choppers until it was our turn. The choppers came and I jumped on board. Some of the very last to leave said the NVA were overrunning Regular Hill with the words "REGULARS BY GOD" still there.

We were taken to a more open and flat area for our new AO. It was a beautiful spot, and our company dug in. Some of the guys dug foxholes while others cut down trees to make an overhead bunker. Sandbags were filled with dirt from the foxhole. The corners would be about three sandbags high with a log going over it the width of the hole. Logs would then be placed over the length of the bunker and then sandbags were placed over the top. There would be just enough room to slip under the log and into the bunker in case of an attack.

Before we could put the overhead timber on for bunkers, the enemy found us. Someone from the tree line started shooting into our perimeter. The foxhole I wanted to get into was taken, so I lay behind some sandbags behind the foxhole. When the shooting stopped and I got up, I noticed the sandbags had been shot up; they had been shooting at me. A little guy from Hawaii was coming back from the water point with a few other men and was credited with killing an enemy soldier in an open field. I went out with my platoon to check on the area where the dead enemy soldier lay. I felt hate for this guy since he seemed to be the reason I was there. We were told by radio to take his clothes back to camp with us. No one would touch him, so we returned to our camp empty handed.

The next day was payday for us, and our executive officer flew out by chopper. His name was First Lieutenant Bob Babcock. The chopper touched down, and he got off. Then as the chopper started back up there was enemy fire. I jumped into a burn pit and had to put out the burning rubbish as the rounds came in. The guys fired back as Babcock came racing in. It was like a moving picture happening in front of me as I tried putting out the flames from the burning rubbish. I had been told that medics weren't supposed to get dirty filling sandbags, but when I didn't have any place to go, I soon realized I had to look out for number one. After that, I made a foxhole so deep I could hardly get myself out of it.

E. Q. "Skip" Fahel, Sarasota, FL
Company B, 2nd Battalion, 22nd Infantry Regiment

Breaking In

I was lucky for the first month I was with B Company. My platoon did not see any direct action. We had a variety of missions and covered a lot of ground in the Brigade area of operation. The quiet time gave me a good opportunity to get to know the men and the men to get to know me. It provided me the time needed to get accustomed to life in the field and to gain self-confidence in my leadership and decision making ability. It also gave me a chance to work on my map reading.

It was an advantage being assigned to a mechanized unit because you did not have to carry everything on your back. When we dismounted and walked, all we had to carry was our ammo, water, and a few rations for the day. We were able to carry an increased load of ammo, which added to our ability to continue an engagement with the enemy.

The platoon could carry an extra M-60 machine gun. This made movement easier, and once we did get into contact, we appreciated the greater mobility because of less weight. Another noteworthy item about a mechanized unit was the firepower available. If you got into contact, and the tracks were with you, it was great to see the jungle and anything else being torn apart by the .50 caliber machine gun. Also, the three 81mm mortars were available to provide quick, high explosive fire support that was so often needed.

However, if you carried everything with you, there was no need to go back to the base camp. We used the base camp only to get to the other side of our area of operation. We would pass through base camp entering one gate and exiting the other. We would only stop long enough to get fuel and supplies; then continue our movement. We did not stop and spend the night at Camp Rainier until July 1967, and that night was cut short.

Even with the lighter load, the first few weeks were difficult on me. When we were dismounted I had my steel pot, flak jacket, water, M-16, .45 Caliber pistol, compass, maps, and one or two cans of C-rations. Not much of a load. What made it hard was the heat and humidity. Within fifteen minutes of starting the movement on foot, I was dripping wet from sweat and exhausted. Nothing could prepare you for the introduction to the climate. During that first month, I lost twenty pounds. Over time I got used to the climate, and my body strengthened.

The movement through the bamboo was the hardest and took the most out of a person. Cutting a trail through thick jungle was not too bad if there was a high ceiling of trees to keep you in the shade. In the jungle, you had to contend with all the insects, especially the red ants. The worst thing that could happen was to have a nest of red ants drop from the trees on to you. At night there were the mosquitoes—thank God for insect repellent. Walking the rice paddies was easy, but you did have the sun beating down on you. We had the advantage of operating on relatively level terrain with many clear areas. We did not have to climb up and down hills or mountains.

We could return to the tracks at night, have a hot meal, cold drinks (including beer), ice, and other comforts that were not available to the other infantry units. Being mechanized, we could get supplies and mail every day. Everything was carried in our tracks. We had radios, chairs, tables, clothes, soft drinks, beer, blankets, pillows, paper and pens, and reading materials. I remember getting into the track one day after resupply, and all the ammo was under the cases of beer and soft drinks. The tracks also provided excellent protection from small arms fire and bad weather— and gave us a dry place to sleep. At night I had a cot set up in the track to sleep on. Later, I slept on the bench of the APC. But I always slept with my boots on.

During these first thirty days, the platoon conducted sweep operations; both mounted and dismounted, provided road security, and went on night ambush patrols. We ran the road between Dau Tieng and Tay Ninh and around the Black Virgin Mountain. The company went deep into War Zone C and operated around the Prek Klok firebase. The company came under ineffective mortar fire and some sniper fire, but no heavy contact; however, several times, other companies in the battalion were in heavy contact. It was a calm time that was soon to be shattered.

Ambush—May 18, 1967

At 0700 hours the first platoon moved out of the battalion laager position to the contact area of May 17. Their mission was to locate and recover the remains of the

U.S. troops killed in action that was left in the contact area. At 0800 hours, all elements of the battalion with the exception of Company B moved out to FSB Fang. Company B would remain in the laager until the first platoon returned and the remains medivaced, then follow the path of the battalion to FSB Fang. At 1030 hours, Company B moved out to join the battalion. The order of march was the first platoon, Command Group with the one M-113s of the second platoon, weapons platoon, and the third platoon.

With all troops mounted, the company made its way northwest. When the first platoon reached Highway 13, the distance between the first platoon and the last element of the battalion was approximately five thousand meters. As the last M-113 of the third platoon headed west on TLT 13, the enemy ambushed the company.

The enemy fired RPG-2s at the lead and rear M-113s of the third platoon. The three rounds that were fired all landed short. As the RPGs hit, the enemy opened up with small arms fire directed at all four M-113s of the third platoon. All of the enemy fire was coming from the north side of the highway. The platoon reacted to the first RPG hitting the ground by dismounting from the M-113s; the track commanders moved the .50 caliber machine guns to the north and opened fire. The troops dismounted to the south side of the highway, and started returning fire to the north. The platoon leader stayed in the track on the radio, communicating with the company commander, informing him of the ambush, the action that the platoon had taken, and that the platoon did not have any casualties at the time.

The battalion commander, who was flying over the battalion, was notified of the contact and took charge of the artillery fire and air support. As the Battalion Artillery Officer called in the fire support, the battalion commander directed the air support that was being provided by gunships flying cover for the Battalion. The first artillery fire support was on the way within three minutes of the first contact, and two minutes later the gunships were ready to make their first gun run.

During these first minutes, the third platoon directed a high volume of fire to the north, causing the fire from the enemy to decrease. After the first artillery rounds hit, the enemy fire stopped. The artillery fired a total of twenty-four rounds when a hold was placed on them so that the gunships could make their run. The Battalion Commander directed that the two gunships make their runs keeping the fire to the north side of the highway. Both gunships made one run; their machine gun fire was to the north of the highway, but the rockets hit both to the north and south of the highway. The third platoon was lucky that it did not have anyone hit by the rocket fire.

The platoon leader called the company commander telling him that the rockets were hitting to the south of the highway and requested that the gunships not make another run. The battalion commander confirmed that the gunships would be called back and directed that the artillery fire mission be resumed to the north side of the highway. The artillery fired another twenty-four rounds to the north of the highway, and the platoon leader requested a cease-fire.

The platoon was not receiving fire, and the platoon leader requested instructions from the company commander whether the platoon should hold in place or move to the north side of the highway to establish contact with the enemy. The company commander directed the platoon to move to the north side of the highway, but to just provide security for the platoon. The platoon was instructed not to move more than twenty meters north of the highway. The platoon leader directed that the first and third squads move across the highway to provide security. The two squads moved into position, and there still was no enemy fire.

As the third platoon waited for additional instructions, one RPG was fired at the lead M-113 of the first platoon. The RPG hit the .50 caliber machine gun, killing the gunner. There was no other enemy fire. The first platoon opened fire to the north, and artillery was called in to the north of the highway. After a fifteenminute wait, a medivac unit was called in to evacuate the killed in action of the platoon.

After the medivac left, the company moved out to join up with the battalion at FSB Fang. The firebase was mortared later that night but suffered no casualties.

Bob Gamboa, Palmdale, CA.
Company B, 3rd Battalion, 8th Infantry Regiment

Operation Francis Marion—May 26, 1967

Reports from S-2 indicated the NVA 32nd and 66th Regiments were somewhere in the Chu Pong mountains, a vertically challenging AO near the Ia Drang River Valley. My company that day was dug in waiting for Charlie Company to link up on our hill for the night. My squad was sent out to check out Charlie Company's flank. We were out about two hundred meters when we heard AKs open up. Charlie Company was ambushed and my buddy, Captain Powers, was the first to die. We first met in Tuy Hoa when he read my name tag, "Gamboa." He claimed his best friend at West Point was a Gamboa. I told him that there was no relation.

Every time he saw me back in the rear he told me he wanted me to be his RTO, and I would always say "No," because, I said, my Company B was the best in the battalion, and he would smile about my bragging.

The NVA were all up in trees mauling Charlie Company. My squad was about one hundred fifty meters from the firefight. We closed to maybe one hundred twenty-five meters. We could hear screams and obscenities of both our troops and the enemy. My CO, Lieutenant Marinovich, ordered my squad over the radio, all six of us, to close in and help C Company. Meanwhile, as we got closer down the draw, our artillery and the NVA mortars stopped us. We radioed back, explained the situation, and were ordered to pull back.

The yelling, crying, and the explosions continued from the battle. Those sounds have been in my nightmares throughout the years. As we pulled back, I was filled with mixed emotions. We could not help C Company. We were glad to get out of a very serious situation. We started back to my company's night defensive position and started receiving sniper fire. We made it back to our hill, and my platoon was left as security as the rest of the company went back to the rescue of C Company.

Our company commander was wounded as the enemy started dropping mortars. As they neared the C Company perimeter, fighting was brutal and intense. When our companies linked up, they counterattacked. When my company was fighting downhill, all the NVA dead had on Red Berets, signifying that they were part of an elite unit of the 32nd regiment. Finally, we saw our company coming back up the hill. My squad went down to the battlefield, mostly quiet now except for our artillery and the occasional snipers left behind to mask their withdrawal. Rucksacks littered the battlefield as we sorrowfully carried the bodies of ten grunts plus sixty-nine wounded to our LZ. We stacked their bodies onto the choppers, set up our perimeters, and dug in for the night. Enemy losses were ninety-six killed in action and two captured. They were part of the 32nd and 66th NVA regiments.

Jim Stapleton, Atlanta, GA
Companies A and C, 1st Battalion, 22nd Infantry Regiment

Malaria Pills

In the central highlands we had to take two types of malaria pills—a daily small white one (dapsone) and a weekly large orange one (primaquin)—and roll our sleeves down each night. The chain of command was responsible for watching their soldiers take their pills and reporting compliance. Some of us were so concerned with contracting malaria that we took two white pills a day and two orange ones each week. Thirty-three years later, I have no known side effects, and I love tonic drinks.

Unfortunately, we had some soldiers who had such a fear of being deployed in the jungles that they purposely avoided taking their pills so that they would contract malaria and be evacuated to the malaria unit at Cam Rahn Bay. As the company XO, I had several trips to the medical treatment facility to pay soldiers from our unit who were undergoing treatment for malaria. Many of them were disappointed that they were not evacuated out of the country, and the pain and discomfort of malaria was much worse than they ever expected. Also, the after-effects of malaria potentially lasts a lifetime.

Despite regularly taking all pills and required precautions, many of our best soldiers still contracted malaria and suffered along with those who used malaria as a way out of the jungle.

Jim Stapleton, Atlanta, GA
Companies A and C, 1st Battalion, 22nd Infantry Regiment

Premonitions

In Company A, two soldiers who were killed in action had definite premonitions of their deaths in Vietnam. Lieutenant Dick Collins, the first officer killed in the division, feared that he would not return alive. At dockside, just prior to boarding the USNS Nelson M. Walker for our voyage to Vietnam, Dick asked his wife, Linda, to take from her wallet a love poem he had started as a West Point Cadet and never finished. He told her he wanted to take it and finish it on the ship because he felt he would not return alive to finish it. His father was killed in action in World War II.

Our company commander's RTO, Private First Class Fitzgibbon, was killed because of mortar fragments in his inner thigh. He fought death all night, but when the medivac chopper called in saying they were having difficulty finding our LZ, he gave up. When preparing to ship his personal effects home, I found a handwritten note in the side pocket of his duffel bag, "Save this bag to ship my body back home."

Jim Stapleton, Atlanta, GA
Companies A and C, 1st Battalion, 22nd Infantry Regiment

Combat Strength Forward

As the battalion went into action in the central highlands, it was a division imperative that our foxhole strength be maximized. The Company Executive Officers had the mission to get the base camp strength to as close to zero as possible. Lieutenant Russ Zink, XO of Company B, had the best results. He and his driver were the only ones not forward. The rest of us XOs were aware of his results, as was the battalion commander. We were counseled daily. The other imperative from division was to "clean up the base camp" and get tents lined up.

Of course, the only manpower we had was our "stay-behind" people. While most of us had sufficient soldiers to comply, Lieutenant Zink did not. One day the Assistant Division Commander came to the Company B site and told Lieutenant Zink that he would return in one week and wanted to see all six of his tents that were to the left of the fire barrel moved over to the right of the barrel. Knowing that he could not and would not ask soldiers to come back to the rear, he carefully planned a solution. One week turned into two, and finally the ADC did return to find all six tents to the right of the fire barrel and commended Lieutenant Zink for a much better looking area. Russ and his driver were able to move the barrel to the left of the last tent by themselves and maintain their record with the fewest soldiers in the rear. In due course, all the tents made it to the concrete and partial wood pads constructed by the engineers and Company B continued to have their soldiers forward where they belonged.

Jesse Davis, Albany, OR
4th S & T Battalion

Living With Green Plastic Bags

Like the many who will read this story, I was a kid of the 1950s and 1960s. I got my driver's license in June of 1962, graduated high school in May of 1964, and, after a brief stint working at a truck stop in central Ohio, I got a "real" job at a factory in April 1965. I got engaged in October 1965 and was ready to "live the life"—you know, just like Ozzie and Harriet. Little did I realize all that would change in a very short time after October 1965.

On December 9, 1965, I was inducted into the U.S. Army, sent first to Fort Knox, KY, held there in a reception center until December 20, then put on an airplane (not a jet, but a four engine gas powered job) and sent to Fort Lewis, Washington. Basic training was taken with the 2nd Battalion, 22nd (Mech) Infantry Battalion (with 252 guys). As luck would have it, I was one of only seven guys who scored high enough on their entrance test to get out of that battalion before AIT. I was sent to the 4th S&T (Supply & Transport) Battalion to be a mechanic on trucks. I was elated to learn that I was not going to Vietnam in an infantry battalion.

My time in the S&T battalion was boring. We did all the stuff that I assumed all S&T personnel did: wash trucks, go to classes, go on maneuvers (play army), and then wash more trucks. After learning we had too many mechanics, I received orders to go to a meeting of the "Bath Unit" for the Brigade going first to Vietnam, the 2nd Brigade. I went to the meeting but was not thrilled with the thought of telling my grandkids (thirty years in the future) that I spent a war in a Bath Unit. Now don't get me wrong; there is nothing wrong with being a Bath Unit member, as we all had jobs to do. Some guys were infantry, some were truck drivers, some medics...but for me, I just didn't want to be a Bath Unit guy.

Lieutenant Whitson was the leader of this Bath Unit. I asked him one day, if he had anything other than a Bath Unit.

He said, "Yes" and added that he was also to be the leader of a Graves Registration Unit, and that he did not have anyone selected for those jobs.

I told him, "I am your man."

Training started shortly thereafter. We learned "by the book" the procedures that were used during World War II. We learned nothing that would set the stage for what reality would be like in Vietnam.

Our first body came to us during the time that the base camp (later Camp Enari) was in its infancy. While the troops were still sleeping in pup tents, someone had come off perimeter guard, taken a clip out of his 45-caliber pistol, forgotten the round in the chamber, pointed it at his tent mate, and pulled the trigger. His buddy was dead, instantly, of a gunshot wound to the head. We had no place to process this guy, so the medics lent us one of their jeep ambulances, and an officer from the 704th Maintenance Battalion rode shotgun in the jeep, while we took the remains to Camp Holloway.

If you remember—and how could anyone forget?— the monsoons had all the roads within the base camp looking as if they were mud fields, and at the time we had to make this trip to Holloway we could not get through the mud. The officer from the 704th flagged down a huge Tank Retriever in their battalion, directed the guys in it to hook up to our jeep, and we were dragged through the mud, looking into the back of a radiator that measured four to five feet across and had heat coming from it that would cook a steak. We went to the main road, unhooked, and headed for Pleiku.

When we got our second body in, we had the guys from the 1st Support and Supply Battalion from Qui Nhon in the camp helping us learn what would be expected of us. It was the body of an infantryman who had straightened the pin out on a grenade, but it was still attached to his web belt. He had snagged the straightened pin on a bush or vine, it was extracted from the grenade and exploded while still on the belt. This man, much like the first guy, was not cosmetically injured. After that, things got worse.

Two sergeants from the 2nd Battalion, 8th Infantry had a claymore mine explode "point blank" on them. The bodies of these guys I will remember to my dying day. I have always asked myself, "What did these two guys do in their lifetimes to die in such a terrible way?" Yes, it was instant death, but these guys were the first I handled who would not have an "open casket" funeral. They were badly mangled. We transported these two guys in two APCs. The first had a squad of infantrymen in it, which was led by (ironically) Lieutenant Mark Enari, who the base camp would later be named after. I was in the second APC with the two bodies.

After that, guys drowned in JP-4 Jet Fuel when their "Goer" overturned on them. A guy who was modest about relieving himself left his area during a night patrol and was shot by his own guys while returning to the area. Another guy drowned while on patrol by walking into a large sump hole that he thought was shallow. One guy was shot directly between the eyes (one shot), while we were sixty-five miles south of the base camp. We processed the body of a North Korean soldier who had been helping the VC at that same place. The body of a captain was the last one I handled before coming home in July 1967. He had been riding in a jeep on one of the mercy missions out to one of the Montagnard villages and was hit in the chest by a 40mm rocket on his way out from the base camp.

I know many of you lived in the field during the time of which I speak. I lived in a GP Medium tent. I know you saw things that would make you remember them the rest of your life. So did I. I know you thought many of us rear area men were doing nothing while you were humping the hills. I lived a life where the tent flap could open at any time of any day with a litter filled with one of your buddies. I know that I did everything I could do to make sure you and your buddy's family knew he had been treated with the highest of respect. That's how it was living with green plastic body bags.

Bob Gamboa, Palmdale, CA.
Company B, 3rd Battalion, 8th Infantry Regiment

Too "Short" for This

Another day in the jungles. Our patrol was out maybe six hundred meters when we spotted a squad-sized NVA patrol. We were spotting signs all over. There were red markings on trees, rocks, and fresh trails. You could actually smell them, and to this day, I sometimes think I can still smell that scent. We radioed back and were told to follow them while trying to avoid contact.

The NVA crossed a small stream, went up a hill, and we started to follow. We were scared sh-tless, most of us were really "short." We crossed the stream and started up the hill when we were called on the radio to return back, "ASAP."

We were all relieved and returned to our company perimeter to dig in for the night. According to intelligence, we were supposed to get hit real big that night. Nothing happened and next morning our company went back to the previous day's spotting of the enemy. We got up the hill and again we could smell those bastards on top of the hill. We found a regiment-sized camp, over two hundred bunkers, a hospital, latrines, some equipment, ammo, etc.

The NVA had just pulled out, back to Cambodia, and my squad had almost gone up the hill the previous day. One squad against maybe a whole regiment. We were scared, really scared, and too "short" for this. Battalion engineers were choppered in to blow up the bunkers.

Lewis Easterly, Montgomery, AL
Company C, 1st Battalion, 12th Infantry Regiment

Unusual Incident

Once when I was spending the night at the FSB south of Ban Blech, an unusual incident happened. The FSB was located on very flat ground, but several very large, deserted termite mounds were scattered inside the perimeter. These termite mounds were about eight or nine feet tall and fifteen or twenty feet in diameter. Close to the helicopter pad, the company commander of the rifle company guarding the FSB had placed a .50 caliber machine gun on top of one of these mounds. It was about thirty or forty feet to the left of where I was sleeping. Around 0100 hours, there was a horrible shriek from the direction of the termite mound, immediately followed by a burst of fire from an M-16. Everybody was awake.

Everybody was scared. The word finally came down, "Go back to sleep. It was just a snake." About an hour later the same thing happened again. This time everyone was more disgusted than scared. The next morning we found a boa constrictor about sixteen to twenty feet long and about as thick as my thigh, stretched out next to the machine gun position.

This was during the dry season, and in the central highlands it would get quite chilly at night. The machine gun team had built a bunker for the gun and then built their hooch just behind the bunker. One man was on duty, and the other two were sleeping in the hooch. One of the men felt something moving, and when he reached over to push his hooch mate away, he felt the snake slithering between them trying to keep warm. He screamed and then shot the snake. I would probably have died from fright.

Al Fuller, Wilmington, DE
Company B, 2nd Battalion, 22nd Infantry Regiment

Short-Time Ambush Patrols

The time frame was July and August of 1967, somewhere in War Zone C around the Black Virgin Mountain, also known as Nui Ba Din. We were getting short, and I mean real short, so short that our "short-time" calendars were approaching the real critical areas. The company would take a laager position around the base of the mountain and send squad-sized ambush patrols out each night. Usually, one squad from each platoon would go about seven hundred to one thousand meters out to pre-designated coordinates that battalion, or higher commands, had determined were likely avenues of enemy approach or movement.

My usual squad of eleven men was down to about seven due to casualties we had taken. I didn't feel good about the situation, being short and undermanned. I was talking this over with another squad leader, Dennis McCourt, from Arnold, Maryland, who I believe was with the second platoon and who was in the same boat as I was—short, and short of men. It didn't take long before we came up with an ingenious idea. I would take my seven men out of our perimeter in the direction I was supposed to go and he would do the same for his patrol. Then we would meet at a location that both of us had agreed to, link up squads, and call our situation reports back to the perimeter. Mac McCourt, our RTOs, and I would be sort of in a command group and I would call and say, "Bravo Six, Bravo Six. This is Bravo One, over."

Then from the other end you would hear, "Bravo One, this is Bravo Six, go ahead, over."

And I'd reply, "Bravo Six, situation negative, out."

Mac would then make the same report, and we'd repeat this every hour. It went on like this all night until about dawn when we'd split up and approach the perimeter from the directions we were supposed to be set up in. Although this is not "approved" military tactics, in this way we overcame the shortfall of men in our unit, at the same time giving all the men a little more sense of security.

Raymond Warner, Mena, AR
Company C, 1st Battalion, 22nd Infantry Regiment

Central Highlands of Vietnam—October 3, 1967

Our company was tasked with setting up a very temporary firebase with two missions: to provide artillery fire support for a sister battalion operating to our southeast and to serve as bait to NVA units operating in the area. This second mission was significant in that we were out of range of any artillery support except for the famously inaccurate "Long Toms." We were at the fringe of their range. The firebase consisted of our infantry company and a mixed battery of two 105mm howitzers, three 155mm howitzers, one 40mm duster on tracks, and one Quad 50 mounted on a truck bed.

We were in place for about a week before being hit. We had time to dig great fighting bunkers and clear good fields of fire. This duty was a welcome relief from humping our rucks in the mountains. Our CO, Captain Lee Kleese, was an exacting professional. He expected everyone to give his best every time, all the time. Observation Posts were deployed by day and listening posts (LPs) at night.

Not long after supper on October 3, 1967, the first report from a listening post came in with an excited, fear-filled voice telling of the enemy all around and very close. They were directed to escape and evade back into the defensive perimeter. The word was quickly passed, and we were on one hundred percent alert. The two listening posts reported seeing mortar aiming stakes being placed, and they counted two mortars. Within moments an RPG impacted on the command bunker, and mortar rounds began to fall on our position. Then the ground attack started. It was a fantastic light show of incoming and outgoing tracers.

Captain Kleese got the "twin 40" crew up and firing and then got the Quad 50 into action. The twin 40s ran out of ammunition, and the Quad 50 crew fired until all four guns overheated and malfunctioned. The artillery tubes lowered and commenced direct fire, effectively covering about half of our perimeter.

There were many seen and unseen acts of courage that night, such as the helicopter flight of two "Black Jack" choppers escorted by two gunships, one of which was shot down on its first pass. A "slick" (helicopter) landed in the middle of the fight and evacuated two of our wounded.

Captain Kleese, who guided the chopper in, asked the slick pilot, "What in the hell are you doing out here?"

His reply was classic for that time and place: "Heard you were in trouble and scrambled some volunteers to bring in ammo and take out wounded."

It was only after Spooky began to hose the area down around us that all incoming fire ceased. I remember the smell of blood, death, feces, gunpowder, and fear. Our company casualties were two badly wounded. There was one dead from the artillery unit. There were eight to ten less seriously wounded that we evacuated at first light. This fight proved the folly of a light infantry frontal assault on a fixed defensive position.

The next morning we began to pull the dead NVA out of the jungle. A large hole was scraped out by a self-propelled gun with a blade attached, and the dead were laid to rest. The air began to fill with command choppers as the division commander and all the staff "horse holders" descended on our position. He directed us to saddle up and begin the chase. We never caught them but found numerous fresh graves next to the main trail we followed. We were directed to dig up the graves of those brave men to satisfy a body count requirement, the thought of which still sickens me after all these years.

However, I was proud to be an American that night. The artillery crews, the helicopter crews, the gun crews, and most of all, my compatriots in my infantry company gave a full measure of devotion to duty. America should have been proud of her sons that night. Specialist Fifth Class Raymond W. Warner, the company senior medic, was awarded a Bronze Star for valor and Purple Heart for his actions that night. Captain Kleese was awarded a well-deserved Silver Star. I located him after thirty-plus years, and we now stay in close touch.

Tom White, Gloversville, NY
Company D, 1st Battalion, 8th Infantry Regiment

A Man I'd Like to Meet

I was assigned to Company D, 1st Battalion, 8th Infantry Regiment as a rifleman on October 1, 1967. The company had just come into a forward firebase to pull perimeter guard and daily patrols. This was the method the 4th Division used to rotate their units operating in the jungle, to give them some rest and lighter duty. A platoon sergeant was sent back to the base camp in Pleiku to pick us up. He was very impressive to us and gave us many tips on how to rig our rucksacks and otherwise handle our equipment. One piece of advice he gave us was to take off our rifle slings, as they would only get in our way. Having grown up in the Adirondack

Mountains of northern New York, where I often carried a pack, I knew the advantages of being able to slip your thumbs under the pack straps and give some occasional relief from the weight of the load you were carrying. Without a sling to drape the rifle over my shoulder, I wouldn't be able to do that. Therefore, I chose to leave my sling on.

When we reached the firebase, we were briefed by the company commander and the first sergeant on the operating methods of the unit. We were told that we would be working from the firebase for a couple of days while us new guys got familiar with the area. But shortly before dark, we were told that a large enemy unit had been spotted, and we would be moving out at daybreak. Knowing that I hadn't yet fired my rifle, I requested permission to sight it in.

Initially the first sergeant said, "No, just put it on automatic and pull the trigger," but then he relented and said, "OK."

Well, to my surprise, my rifle didn't work; it had a broken firing pin. The pin was replaced, and I got to sight the rifle in.

The next morning we were in the air on my first combat assault. As we approached the landing zone, the crew chief of the helicopter hollered that it was a "hot" LZ (landing zone). The LZ was small, and the helicopters weren't landing, but just hovering a few feet above the ground for a few seconds while we exited. I was the last one off the left side, and as I was going out the chopper started lifting up. My ass cleared the deck, but my pack didn't. I was tossed towards the front of the chopper. My rifle flew off my right shoulder, and the sling went over the runner of the raising chopper. There I was, lying on the ground while my rifle was leaving with the chopper!

I'm sure the look on my face was one of astonishment, but I'll never forget the look on that door gunner's face. It could only be interpreted as, "You stupid FNG." The door gunner then unbuckled himself and got out onto the runner to get my rifle, which he threw at me. Now there's a man I'd like to meet.

With rifle in hand, I ran to catch up with my squad members and "hit" the ground in between two of them, only about one foot in front of them, when up popped a cobra snake about three feet in front of me. That snake scared me so bad that I jumped up and ran way around the right flank. Wow, one week in country and only fifty-one to go. And, oh yeah, that snake has come back to haunt me many a night since we met thirty-three years ago.

Bob Smyers, Fort Lauderdale, FL
2nd Brigade Long Range Reconnaissance Patrol

Men Called Lurps

This is a true story. I observed the men making up the Long Range Reconnaissance Patrol Platoon. Men I speak of here are of the same makeup of all human beings, and that is of flesh, with its strengths and weaknesses. Fear is natural, but these men, though they had fear, were able to overcome it. They were men you would consider as either being plain crazy, or men who had guts and nerves of steel. "Plain crazy" was the comment most often heard from those on the outside looking in. Outside of being a long-range patrol member, the only ones who may have an insight to the courage and tenacity of these men called "Lurps" would, in my opinion, be the chopper pilots and the door gunners. ("Lurps" is the word describing Long Range Reconnaissance Patrol members. The acronym "LRRP" sounds like "Lurp" when you pronounce it.) Lurps and the chopper crews had something in common; they both lived on "the edge." Chopper crews risked their lives on each insertion and extraction.

I remember Warrant Officer Pepper risking not only his life but also his career when he had to pull my team and me out of a hot firefight. He had no gunships to back him, but he came in for us. Had he not have taken the risk, I fear my whole team would have been lost, as we were outnumbered and being surrounded. Regardless of your view, I can only say, being one of them (Lurps), that they were brave and daring above all else they may have been. Everyone was there by choice, as the army did not, to my knowledge, assign anyone against his will to a unit such as the Lurps, due to the dangers they would face—dangers beyond what the average infantryman would face.

Regular infantrymen were assigned to squads, which in turn was a part of a platoon, which was a part of a company, which was a part of a battalion, which was a part of a brigade, which in turn was a part of a division, and so on up the line. The Long Range Reconnaissance Patrol Platoon was assigned to the Headquarters Company for administrative purposes, but it was a unit unto itself. They worked directly for the brigade commander who might dispatch teams to a battalion to investigate areas of interest to them. Though referred to as the Long Range Reconnaissance Patrol Platoon, they never operated as a platoon, but as several small units, called teams.

Whereas the regular infantrymen traveled in numbers, Lurps did not. In fact, teams at the time of my service in Vietnam were mostly made up of four men. During my tour I did witness a one-man insertion. I, in fact, inserted him. His name was John "Vic" Powers. He was trained as a sniper at the Recondo School in Nha Trang. I do not know by whom or how the mission was approved, but he rappelled into the jungle to overlook a large valley. His task was to observe and fire on long-range targets. It was only a two-day mission that proved unfruitful, but it took guts.

I saw two-man teams inserted twice—small in numbers, but very successful on both missions. Twice I saw two, three-man teams inserted. Both had a team leader but one was controlling both, as the situation dictated. One went without incident, but one was successful in engaging an enemy of superior force, which chose to run rather than fight, due to the effective positioning of the two Lurp teams and the element of surprise. Later, after my tour, and as operating procedures changed due to more experience, teams varied in size in order to be more effective.

Lurps worked deep in enemy-held territory—often so deep that radio relay stations had to be set up on mountaintops in order for teams to have contact with the closest friendly unit. Many times, Forward Air Controllers or planes called Headhunters (those who looked for troop movement, supply lines, etc.) were sent up to relay for teams deep in enemy territory. This even failed at times, allowing for some intense moments of uncertainty for the men on the ground. The uncertainty was because the radio was the Lurps' lifeline; it's too bad we did not have cell phones then. When deep in enemy territory, Lurps could not rely on a leg unit (walking infantry) to get to them when they were "in the soup" so to speak, or contact with the enemy. Even the mechanized infantry took too long as the jungles were often dense and had natural barriers. No, Lurps relied heavily on high-angle fire weapons (artillery) or gunships for survival.

Lurp teams traveled relatively light and rarely traveled on trails or went crashing through the jungle. They moved with great stealth, trying always not to disturb the foliage or the landscape, so as to maintain secrecy. Their objective was to get in and detect the enemy without the enemy knowing they were there. Then they were able, according to their mission, to bring havoc on the enemy with ambushes, gunships, artillery, fighter planes, and, at times, with bombs.

Normally, if a Lurp team was doing its job, it was Charlie or the North Vietnamese Army that was caught off guard. Lurps had to stay alert all the time due to their small numbers, keeping all directions covered at the same time. Each man watched his sector, his weapon on rock and roll. When contact was made, it was normally to the advantage of the Lurps, as they stayed on ready. Charlie and the NVA thought they were all alone if they could not hear American troops or see a lot of air activity. Rifle companies were easily detected as they made a lot of noise when moving on search and destroy missions. The size of the company alone was enough to give them away in many cases. The enemy counted on this and often used it to their advantage.

But with the Lurps playing their game, sneaking and peeking, it became hazardous for the enemy. They got lax if the area seemed to be void of activity and would develop a sense of false security. This was to the Lurps' advantage, allowing them to often catch the VC or NVA with their weapons slung or cradled on their shoulder like a hunter coming in after a hunt. This was sweet when you were set in ambush, ready to spring on the enemy using the element of total surprise.

If the ambush was properly executed, the VC or NVA never had a chance to endanger you with return fire, as they were killed, badly wounded, or, if extremely lucky, they ran like hell. The enemy hated the Lurps with a passion and even put bounties on the men in the tiger uniform and the short black weapon (CAR-15). We learned this during interviews with captured soldiers. After the war, enemy officers said they feared the Lurp teams more than any other force, as they always showed up where they were not expected. Lurp units are credited with bringing havoc on much superior forces that prompted the high prices ($1,000 to $2,500) being placed on their heads.

It was not unusual for Lurp teams to get so close to the enemy without their knowing it that they could reach out and touch the ankles of the passing soldiers. I have personally been that close. Teams found themselves at times completely surrounded, but yet without detection. These situations called for guts and a lot of discipline in order to keep your cool while waiting for the opportunity to present itself. Talk about an adrenaline rush! Man, there is no high like it! I guess that is part of the reason men became Lurps. It was an adventure like those men have sought from the very beginning, and still that spirit lives to this day. It is hard to describe; you almost have to live it to know what it was really like. Of course, you had to be ready to die any minute and many did just that, taking the risk to be able to live on the edge. Belonging to a unit such as this, you would either live to boast or die and be boasted about.

To look at some of the men I am talking about, you might think, "No way is he a Lurp." Then there were those you would expect to be Lurps. Looks really do not define the man on the inside. As the old saying goes, do not judge a book by its cover—likewise with the men of the Lurps. All volunteers, they were a variety of men from many different backgrounds as well as military skills. Men that made up the Lurps were recruited from line units. I know we had infantrymen, artillerymen, tankers, and probably a cook, mechanic, and most likely a clerk. I know one who gave up a gravy job driving a jeep for the brass at base camp to be one of us. Regardless, we all wanted it and knew we had to be extra alert as we would be depending on each other to survive. Men in units of this type develop a love and a bond between them that stays with them to the grave. The closeness between men in these units is as close, if not closer, than with a family member. It is probably closer, as you each depend on the other for your next breath—especially if in contact for a sustained period.

This frequently happened when contact was made deep in enemy territory during monsoon (rainy) season, or at night. I have personally been in these situations a few times, and you really rely on the other guys holding together and giving all they have to survive. It is not like a rock fight where you may go home with a few bumps; these were bullets, and one could send you home in a body bag.

Lurps were for God, Family, and Country in most cases, and believed in a fair shake for all. They were generous men and had compassion even though they put on a hardcore appearance. They shared and they cared for one another—often times proving this by getting wounded or killed for one of their own. A couple of good examples were Dan Harmon, who, after saving the life of one team member in an ambush, lost his own while trying to save his team leader. The team leader was rescued but died two weeks later due to his wounds. Both were on their last mission and would have gone home once the mission was complete.

Likewise, Charlie Britt was killed on his second tour while performing a rescue mission for a downed helicopter crew five days before he was scheduled to return home. He gave his life for those that had saved many Lurp teams from an early demise. These are the kind of men that made up the Lurps. These are the men I served with, and I will always remember them for all the days of my life. Many are physically gone from the realm in which we live, but as I live and breathe, I will always hold them in my heart and speak of them when I get a chance. I do not want America ever to forget these men, or any man or woman who has served this great nation, and gave all for the freedom we enjoy.

War still runs rampant throughout the globe, but as long as there are men like the men of the Lurps, liberty still has a chance.

Today, I am in contact with a few I served with. I cherish every one of them and will continue to look for others all my days. Lurps, as well as all veterans who fought in the Vietnam War, have melted back into society, but a new day is dawning and many are looking for their buddies of long ago, to be reunited and to share what we can of what we did. War still runs rampant throughout the globe, but as long as there are men like the men of the Lurps, who are willing to pay the ultimate price, liberty still has a chance.

This is a true story as I remember it and is meant to provide an insight from the perspective of a Lurp team leader and platoon sergeant with the 2nd Brigade, 4th Infantry Division, 1967-68. I dedicate it to all who have served this great nation and especially those who gave all.

Dick Arnold, Indianapolis, IN
Company A, 1st Battalion, 35th Infantry Regiment

My Mother, the Patriot

I guess all wars are hard on moms and dads but at least in my family, Mom seemed to carry more of the burden regarding her first-born being in harm's way. Based on a conversation I had with my dad not long before his death, I now realize he was very concerned too, but being from the old school, chose not to show it. True to form, with Mom being the dominant figure in the marriage, she also assumed the lead role in energetically doing all she could to support the war effort in general, and my well being, specifically. It was well known in my Vietnam platoon that I received far and away the most packages from home. Mom had discovered that home baked goodies held up remarkably well in transit when packed in popcorn, and she averaged sending one package a week.

Some of the packages included things like toothpaste, candles, vitamins, the hometown paper, and pre-sweetened Kool-Aid. (The Kool-Aid went into the canteens to make some of the yucky water we drank more palatable and also worked well with fresh coconut milk. We honestly tried for a while to learn how to shinny up the coconut trees but usually resorted to bribing the kids to do it for us or blasting clusters down with our M-16s.) In addition to her herculean mailing efforts, she could not resist dabbling in the business of being the watchdog for truth in all local media pronouncements concerning the war.

Martinsville, Indiana, in 1967, was a sleepy town of about ten thousand souls, but it did proudly sport a fledging radio station. Now one can fill only so much air time with news of the Traffic Court and garage sales notices, so in the summer of '67, the station covered the local National Guard unit who was playing soldier at Camp Atterbury. They did a live interview with a sergeant who reflected that the training was going well, but that recent heavy rains had created some worrisome mud. "A mistake to cover this non-news?" you might ask. Rather, a whole series of mistakes.

Mom had been listening and immediately called the station with three more or less concise observations: first, what made them think that anyone cared about these "play soldiers;" second, why didn't they interview some folks that had "real" soldiers to worry about; and third, how would that sergeant like to sleep and fight in that mud all the time?

Then there was the situation with the unfortunate Mr. Danny East. Danny was a couple of years ahead of me in school, joined the Air Force, and was stationed at Danang. The local paper was doing one of the traditional "our boys at the front" pieces and featured a letter from Nam that Danny had sent to his Mom. He mentioned some obviously embellished harrowing escapades involving guarding the airfield perimeter and capped his letter by saying that overall his tour wasn't bad, but that the PX did not have his size underwear.

Mom no sooner finished the article than she was pounding away on her old Underwood typewriter, working up an incendiary letter to the editor. Dripping sarcasm, she led off by berating the editor for wasting valuable paper space on inconsequential matters and then turned her formidable wrath on Danny. Did he realize that while he was safe and sound in Danang that her son's unit was heavily engaged barely thirty miles away. And further, he should quit whining about wrong size underwear as her son could not even wear any because they literally rotted off in the heat and humidity. So, take that and choke it down, Mr. East!

Yes, brother Dave, who was still living at home, allowed as how Mom was sure embarrassing to be around at times.

However, her finest hour would come during the circumstances of me being wounded. On October 9, 1967, I caught a piece of shrapnel in my shoulder. It was relatively minor, though it did become infected and I ended up spending about three weeks in the hospital. It wasn't that bad—I was able to listen to the World Series, binge on cold apple juice, and met entertainer Martha Raye who informed me that her husband was also from Indiana. (Martha was a trooper. She made countless trips to Vietnam, including every Christmas for several years, and told reporters that while she had a family at home, nothing was more important than these kids. She was also a registered nurse and was known to have pitched in and helped out at times. She went too far when she volunteered to go to a forward aid station that later came under mortar fire. General Westmoreland then sent down a directive that under no circumstances was she to go near a place like that again.)

I wrote letters describing what had happened both to Mom and to a girl I was seeing before I left—the basic stuff to the girl and a lot more detail in Mom's letter. My parents lived in the country, outside of town, and at that time in small towns like Martinsville, the country folks usually received their mail one day late. That is exactly what happened with these two letters, which normally would not have been a problem except that this wasn't a normal day. The two women (my mom and my girlfriend), occasionally talked by phone, comparing notes and all, and they unfortunately chose the day when the girlfriend had received her letter but Mom hadn't yet.

So, after a few minutes of small talk Docy, my girlfriend, asked, "So how do you think Dick is?"

At that, of course, the well-tuned antenna that all mothers possess started sensing danger. "What do you mean, how is he?"

"Didn't you get his letter?" Docy replied.

From there things went decidedly downhill. Mom had her read the letter to her about ten times; repeatedly asking if was in my own handwriting. Finally, Docy was ordered to bring the letter to Mom, ASAP, so its authenticity could be verified.

While waiting for the courier to arrive, Mom decided to conduct some reconnaissance on her own. At that time our congressman was William

Bray, who resided in Martinsville. A legitimate World War II hero, he had been congressman forever, and, while once a very capable man, he was now in his dotage. (More likely, what we would call Alzheimers now.) He was given to wearing bow ties, smiling endlessly, and staring vaguely into space when asked anything of substance.

Anyhow, Mom reached the Great Man himself, who was of course of no help, but he did offer her the number of one of his aides who handled these matters. The aide in turn directed her to the Army's Causality Department in Washington, D.C. Mom's emotions by this time were out of control and she was alternating between shouting on the phone and crying.

Her main message to the poor sergeant at the Causality Department was, "By God, they had managed to locate me when they wanted to draft me so they should be able to find out exactly how I was now."

He attempted to reassure her that it was SOP that if a soldier was wounded to the extent where his survival was in question, the army automatically sent a telegram to the family. But that barely registered with Mom. Brother Dave, then working 2400 to 0800 hours and trying to get some rest, woke up, heard Mom hollering and thought Dad had been in a wreck on his way home. Sister Wendy, who besides the family dog Duke, was apparently the only one to even marginally display any calmness, later noted it would have been comical if had not been so serious.

Dad and Docy arrived simultaneously and Dad, surveying the wreckage of his once peaceful home and in the best tradition of fathers everywhere— attempted to interject a little levity. He studied my letter intensely and opined, "The kid writes well, doesn't he, Phyllis?"

Of course all this got him is one of those wifely, withering, "Bill, how can you at a time like this?" looks. By now, Mom was holding the letter up to the late afternoon sunshine, confirmed it was my handwriting, noted the absence of any bloodstains, and finally decided I was probably OK.

My letter to Mom arrived the next day, and with two pieces of confirming data, she now felt much better. However, still angry with the aforementioned Mr. East, she turned my letter over to the local paper as evidence of what "real" soldiering was about. They promptly printed it, accompanied by my army photo under a huge headline, "Local GI Escapes Communist Massacre." (It wasn't that bad, but it was bad enough. I am going to write about that day as the capstone to these stories.)

At any rate, Mom sure loved me, meant well, and I guess that is what really counts.

Bob Walkowiak, Canton, MI
Company B, 3rd Battalion, 8th Infantry Regiment

Jungle Living—Things to Know

Here was my basic system for food:

Open all the meal boxes you have. Remove and save the plastic pouches with the salt, pepper, sugar, creamer, instant coffee, cigarettes, matches, and toilet paper. Pick out all the fruit cans of peaches, pears, and fruit cocktail. Keep the sliced ham, pork, and beef. If you get beans and franks, keep those, too. The cheese and crackers cans are good for snacks. You need to carry some hot cocoa packets. They're a nice change from coffee when you add cream and sugar. So pull them out of the B3 cans, and throw the cookies away, that way it's lighter to carry. Keep a couple of backup spoons so you can replace the one in your pocket if it gets too black. Make a new stove if you need one. Take a short can, remove the top, and with the P38 can opener put holes in the side of the can on both the top and bottom. Replace your P38 can opener regularly or carry a spare. Never carry the "ham and eggs, chopped" or "ham and lima beans," or the bread. All were inedible.

When LRRP rations were available, I would grab them. The spaghetti and beef stroganoff were very good, as were the indigenous rations. They may have looked bad, but if you followed the directions, they were OK. I liked them. We could never get heat tabs, so we used C4. We would pinch off a small amount of the explosive and roll it into a ball. We'd put a little tit on the ball, set the ball of C4 on the ground, and light the tit. Next, we quickly placed our "stove can" over the ball of flame and started cooking. Once the fire started burning, it could not be put out. I always carried two sticks of C4, one for blowing an LZ, and one for cooking.

Your second best friend is a green towel. Get one. Take care of it. Draped around your neck, it keeps the sun off and the bugs out. You can easily wipe the sweat or rain from your eyes. If anybody gets hit, jamming it in the wound will stop most bleeding. At night in the wet season, it will wick the water away from the roof joint of your poncho hooch. During slow days, it's a pillow, a card table, or a sunscreen. Some nights, the bugs are so bad you can't sleep unless it's over your face. Finally, if you're ever lucky enough to get a real shower, use it the right way.

Dick Arnold, Indianapolis, IN
Company A, 1st Battalion, 35th Infantry Regiment

How Many Scared GIs Will Fit Behind One Large Rock?

After our fight on November 9, 1967, we hung around a few days to search the now deserted NVA base camp and hospital. We found a great deal of rice and some armaments, but the most impressive find was uncovering an underground field hospital—complete with operating rooms, fairly sophisticated surgical equipment, and lights rigged to run off a gasoline powered generator. Once again, it may have been a "guerrilla" war with the Viet Cong, but the NVA were more a truly modern army than they are generally given credit for. No wonder they fought so fiercely for three days to hang on to the place.

We blew up the armaments, hospital, and any other tunnels or bunkers we found, while bagging the rice and shipping it back to be distributed among the needy peasants. Most of the rice may have made it to the peasants, but it seemed a mighty strange coincidence to us that for days after a major rice haul, that was all the mess halls in the rear served. Rice and beans, rice and fish, rice and pork, just plain rice—rice ad nauseam!

Late on the afternoon of the thirteenth, all the work was done and we were standing around in small groups waiting for the choppers to come get us. It was our company's turn to go to the rear for a few days to lick our wounds, get some badly needed rest, and welcome some new replacements. We were smoking, joking, and playing like kids will do, telling big stories about how much beer we were going to drink, and generally acting like teenagers hanging out at the local pool hall rather than the soldiers we were, or at least trying our hardest to be. "Big Man" Kevin Hobson, another machine gunner, was holding court and for the umpteenth time replaying his latest heroics from the Ninth for a large group of admirers. He told a different version every time.

This time he did admit to being just slightly scared but repeated one of his favorite sayings, "You got to bring some to get some!"

Then, quickly, word was passed that there had been a change of plans. In the military, "change of plans" is synonymous with bad news. You could bet your autographed picture of General Westmoreland that whatever your status was currently, it was shortly going to be infinitesimally worse. It turned out that an American unit one valley over had been pinned down all day in rice paddies outside of a hamlet, and they were in imminent danger of being overrun.

Since we were the nearest unit, we got the call. It was decided to chopper our three rifle platoons directly into the hamlet in a lighting strike at dusk—two of the platoons would act as a diversionary and supporting force while my platoon would attempt to reach the trapped outfit. (An infantry company had three rifle platoons and a weapons platoon. The weapons platoon had the heavy 81mm mortars and generally did not hump with us, but set up on a nearby hill to support us with the mortars, and to be the reserve force.)

During my year in Vietnam, we made perhaps a dozen of these combat assaults. They were for a variety of reasons: rescue missions like this one, efforts to complete a cordon against a trapped enemy unit ("find the bastards and pile on"); missions to get into places where "hard" intelligence had pinpointed enemy activity, and others. They ran the gamut from innocuous to very hairy, but as was our wont, as simple grunts who would have to jump from these choppers, we only wanted to know one simple thing—was the LZ likely to be "hot" or "cold?" That is, would we be getting shot at or not? This LZ had all the earmarks of being a very hot one.

As soon as we boarded the birds, I could tell by looking at the door gunners that this was very serious indeed. Usually they would talk with us, but this time they were nervously checking and rechecking their machine guns, and you could tell they were listening intently to communications on their headsets. It turned out that a 1st Air Cavalry Division recon "Blue" team had been lured into landing their chopper by an NVA standing out in a rice paddy and making motions that he wanted to surrender. An NVA antiaircraft battalion was dug in the village. They promptly shot down the recon chopper and blasted away at everything sent to attack them or rescue the stranded men. It was about a ten-minute flight, and the pilots were flying at treetop level so as not to give the assault away until the last possible moment. It is very exhilarating going 125 mph with your combat boots literally brushing the tops of the trees. You pray the pilots have steady hands.

A few minutes out, the choppers split up to land each platoon in a different location. The three choppers carrying our platoon actually followed a river bed for a while to use as much cover as they could, but eventually they had to pop up from the trees, and from about five hundred yards out, we came at a dead run for our LZ. My eyes quickly spotted the six marooned Americans, and I noticed their destroyed chopper and several more that had been shot down in various places.

But what I noticed the most were those damn, green tracers coming at us. The NVA had a heavy 12.7mm (51 caliber) machine gun that they fired at choppers with, and every fifth round was a tracer. Our tracers were red; theirs were green. Therefore, when you saw a green tracer, there was no doubt who, or what, it was intended for. The door gunners were spewing out the rounds trying to protect us, but our only real hope was to get on the ground as quickly as possible. Since the choppers are the most vulnerable when disembarking troops, landing was absolutely out of the question. They barely slowed down to a decent air speed when the door gunners let it be known, politely, but firmly, that it was time to get our butts out. Over the roar of their machine guns they shouted, "Good luck!" and out we went. We jumped from about eleven feet up. The paddy was muddy and offered a reasonable cushion. Miraculously, we all made it down unscathed, as did the choppers that had delivered us.

With my pack and machine gun, I sank down in the mud to my knees, but that wasn't the worst part. I had neglected to fasten the strap on my helmet, and the jarring landing caused it to come down with a resounding whack right on the bridge of my nose. (I'm glad Sergeant Noels wasn't there to see me.) By the time I had extracted myself from the mud and my eyes quit watering, everyone else was already moving and seeking cover, with small arms fire cracking overhead. I hurried to do likewise. (As any patriot, would say, "real" grunts can explain the difference between rounds that are merely whining overhead and those that are cracking. Rounds that are passing safely overhead have a whine to them. Those that are uncomfortably close give off more of a cracking sound. Folks, these were cracking.)

Due to the intense ground fire, our choppers had actually let us out one paddy away from our original destination. Therefore, we could not simply rush up to the stranded guys; we would have to work our way there. In a far corner of the paddy, I spotted a large, black, lava rock. Thinking that this would be a marvelous place to catch my breath, maybe lay down a little supporting fire, and generally see if there was a plan to this madness, I scampered on all fours to it. Upon reaching it, I found that great minds think alike, or at least scared great minds do. Roughly half the platoon was behind the rock. A classic case of, "Spread out, men. One round will get you all!"

I scampered on all fours to a large, black, lava rock. Upon reaching it, I found that great minds think alike, or at least scared great minds do. Roughly half the platoon was behind the rock.

Platoon Sergeant Johnson was threatening us with the tortures of the Inquisition if we did not spread out. But I noticed that "ol' Sarge John" was not exactly leading by example. He didn't seem in much of a hurry to move out himself. Whereas we were usually game and tried to be brave, we were not foolhardy, and we certainly were not stupid. I mean, those rounds were beating a crescendo against that rock, occasionally even throwing off sparks. Even the intrepid Big Man had apparently decided that, just this once, his vendetta against the NVA could be put on hold for a few minutes and that, perhaps, discretion truly was the better part of valor.

The real problem was that the fire wasn't coming from the side of the hamlet where the recon guys were, but from a tree line to our right, and it was very difficult to get a fix on it. Fortunately, the first platoon had landed near the tree line, and we started hearing a brief, but intense firefight.

Though we suffered eight wounded (they all survived) in ten minutes, the tree line was cleared, and the surviving NVA were sent scurrying back into the village. With our flank now secured, we started moving carefully toward the recon group. We finally were able to reach them. The platoon spread out along the dike, and we started pouring fire back into the village wherein a form of a draw was arrived at. The NVA had damaged many choppers (which after all was what they were really interested in), and we had rescued our fellow Americans. They were sure happy to see us. They had long ago run out of water and food. We gave them what we could spare and settled in for a long, miserable night in the mud.

As it always seemed to do at the worst possible moments, it rained all night. Not a driving rain, just a steady, soaking one that the gods bring down to remind soldiers who is really in charge. In addition to the rain, it was a very eerie night. Still afraid that the NVA might work up a ground assault, artillery was fired all night long into the village and to within a few yards of us. It was so close that occasionally an odd piece of shrapnel would land, sizzling, into the water near us. Also, the NVA had put an RPG round into a downed chopper near us. It burned all night long, and every once in awhile rounds on board would "cook off," scaring the devil out of us.

When dawn came we cautiously poked up our heads, did a little "recon by fire," and when no one shot back, decided it was safe to move around. We stretched our cramped, wet limbs and used our heat tabs and little stoves made from empty C-ration cans to get some coffee and hot chocolate going. As we did nearly every day in the field, someone called out a cheery, "Good Morning Vietnam!" emulating the daily lead for Armed Forces Radio Network in Saigon. (An interesting tidbit. Before Adrian Kronenaur, the D.J. that Robin Williams played in Good Morning Vietnam, Vanna White's television buddy, Pat Sajac, was the D.J. in Saigon.) I was busy calculating how much taxpayer money was lying around in destroyed choppers. It was easy. One million one, one million two...

War can be very strange. A fluke or an anomaly can kill you just as quickly as a bullet or a grenade. Sometimes when you think you are safe, you are not. There is always danger lurking around the edges. Our battalion commander, Lieutenant Colonel Kimmel, came flying overhead in his command chopper at several thousand feet along with his staff of two majors and a captain. When one of his four companies would get in a fight, he would be there at first light to appraise the situation, occasionally landing and making small talk with us. (Though he was certainly a "no nonsense, old army" man, he was very supportive, constantly inquiring as to whether we had everything we needed and trying his best to explain what we were trying to accomplish.)

Some men thought they heard one heavy machine gun burst; others said that no, it was a simple mechanical failure. Whatever, we all heard a loud "ping," and looked up to see the rear rotor blade fly off Kimmel's chopper. The rear rotor is what gives choppers their lateral stability; it is nearly impossible to land safely without it. It looked for a few seconds that the pilot might get it down but it was not to be. The tail swung completely around, and the chopper came spiraling down, exploding on impact. We were shocked—it had happened in a twinkling. We rushed over there, but everyone was dead, still belted in their seats. One of the door gunners had apparently tried to jump when he gauged they were near the ground; we found him a hundred or so feet away in a clump of trees. He had been killed when a tree limb hit his head.

Winners and losers. No reporters or bold headlines—just another day in the war.

An interesting postscript: Several years ago I was reading a Vietnam book titled Brennan's War, by Matthew Brennan. In one chapter, he was describing how they had been pinned down all day in a rice paddy with many choppers shot down, etc. He mentioned some grunts coming to their rescue and their colonel's chopper crashing the next day. At that point I knew he had to be writing about us. I got his address from the publisher, and we exchanged a couple of letters. It turned out he originally was from Washington, Indiana, joined the army as an enlisted man, served three Vietnam tours, and received a battlefield commission as an officer.

He recalled "the rush to the big rock" and said that, in fact, an NVA sniper had shot at them all day from behind that rock. When we rushed for it, the NVA went splashing back into the tree line, but as he diplomatically put it, "you guys probably could not hear him since you were splashing so hard yourself."

Amen to that. Matt said the whole day was "very intense," and that the NVA shot down a total of twenty choppers that day.

Bruce Wesley, Easton, PA
Battery A, 5th Battalion, 16th Field Artillery Regiment

Dak To—November 1967

This was probably the most fear-filled time in my life, when three NVA infantry regiments and one NVA artillery regiment jumped into the northern area of Dak To from the sanctuary of Laos. Their objective was basically to take this area by surprise and, I believe to this day that this was the start of the Tet Offensive. We were at a firebase located around Kontum in November 1967.

We had received orders to pack up and head north, destination unknown to a lot of us. We had no idea where we were headed. Later on we found out, when we pulled into a large area surrounded by huge mountains. Our battery moved to the far end of an airstrip and began digging in. We started to get a bad feeling, seeing the 173rd Airborne Brigade coming in on choppers and starting to dig in also. My battery was Battery A, 5th Battalion, 16th Field Artillery, 155mm self propelled (SP) howitzers. I was a member of the fire direction center (FDC) crew that worked up the data for the guns to fire. Things were quiet and calm, but not for long. We received radio messages from the 173rd Airborne unit, which had just made contact with the NVA on Hill 875. It seemed that all hell had broken loose around that mountain area.

I will always remember the young radio operator screaming into the radio for first round, shell HE (high explosive), on his position. Our fire direction officer (FDO), First Lieutenant Apple, had to tell him that we needed coordinates and needed to adjust with smoke rounds first. This was an artilleryman's nightmare. You wanted to do so much very quickly, but you didn't want to hurt your own guys. The NVA were all around them, and we couldn't shoot at that time. Later on in the battle, Battery A had plenty of chances to pour it on.

The 4th Infantry Division was working at another hill, 1338. They had captured a general and many NVA supplies. Our battery was never in one place very long. We constantly moved from one fire support base to another. I can't count the number of holes we dug and sandbags we filled.

My worst time came after eight months with the 4th Infantry Division. After Dak To, I was transferred to the 1st Cavalry Division at An Khe. I had to leave all my buddies behind. This was my last assignment in Vietnam, finishing my tour in August of 1968.

Dak To—Hill 724

The following is an attempt to quantify and record my memory of events that occurred over thirty-three years ago. Accuracy may be debated, but this is my truth as I saw it.

Start of the operation

Alpha and Delta Companies were inserted on November 4, 1967, and both had been in contact with the NVA almost from the very beginning. By November 8 or 9, the situation was deteriorating. Captain Taylor, Company A CO, was killed in action, and casualties were mounting. "Saber," our battalion commander, made the decision to commit his reserves some time during the afternoon of November 8, or 9. (The exact date is unconfirmed.)

Bravo and Charlie Companies were located at the firebase we had built on Hill 1001. At this location, the battalion had a battery of five 105mm howitzers, a section of 4.2-inch mortars, and a section of 81mm mortars. Captain Falcone had been spending most of his time in the Battalion CP with Saber and the staff officers monitoring the situation on the radios. In addition, the group developed plans for the next phase of the battle.

The platoon leaders were called to the Company CP just after noon for a briefing on the following day's movement. At that time, the orders were to prepare for a combat assault (CA) the next morning. For this operation, an 81mm mortar squad was attached to Bravo Company. Our mission was to join and reinforce Alpha and Delta Companies in order to continue the original operation. "Six" (the CO) instructed the platoon leaders to draw four days of C-rations and some LAW rockets. Each man was to carry as much water and extra ammo as possible. In addition, ammo for the 81mm was divided up between the platoons. The platoon order for the CA was established. As was his custom, "Six," his two RTOs, and the three-man artillery forward observer team went in on the last chopper of the first lift. Field First Sergeant Dickerson, his RTO, and I were to supervise the loading at the firebase, and come in on the last chopper.

Night Before the Combat Assault

Only those who went through a similar event can imagine the experience and understand the mental confusion we were encountering. Each of us went from the emotional highs of, "We're going to kick ass and take names," to the stomach tightening fear of the unknown. We all handled it individually in our own way. For me, the mechanics of packing kept my mind on business. Did I pack!

Faced with the choice of what was going to keep me alive longer, a can of peaches or two more magazines of 5.56mm, I opted for starvation. Therefore, after picking over the case of Cs, only a few cans of the really "good stuff" made the cut. Munitions were a different story. I was a walking ammo dump. We were lucky enough to get some footlockers full of empty magazines, so I added two more bandoliers to the four I already carried. Then, just for good measure, I added five more bandoliers of loose ammo. Here is the total list as I recall it:

Over fourteen hundred rounds of 5.56mm ammo; ten hand grenades; two smoke grenades; two trip flares; two pop flares; one claymore; one belt of M-60 ammo; two sticks of C4; four canteens; one bladder bag for water; C-rations; two ponchos; poncho liner; air mattress; machete; one radio battery.

Sleep came late, the sun rose early.

Dawn

It was cold at first light. I didn't know if that was causing the shakes or not, but a jungle sweater helped. The ache in the pit of my stomach was stopped with "C-rats." Since carrying them was out of the question, I pigged out, and ate all I could. The sky was cloudless and a deep clear blue. The day was going to be very hot.

Combat Assault

We "saddled up," moved into the Firebase LZ area and waited for the choppers. How long the company waited is unknown. Being last, it seemed like two days. There was rifle fire on the LZ and mortar fire. We had to select another LZ, but some birds were getting through and un-loading our men. Somewhere a chopper went down. More waiting. The last lift was just before dark. We came into a small LZ that was surrounded by higher ground. The light was fading fast, so all that could be seen were just patches of blasted bamboo. Just after the sun set, the radio watch for the night was established. After finding a soft spot next to the CP bunker, I curled up in a poncho liner and slept. The night was uneventful.

November 11, 1967

With the dawn one could see clearly the high ground on three sides of the night location. We were the fish in the proverbial barrel. The commander held a short meeting on the orders for the march. Bravo Company would hold the night location until Hill 724 was secured by Alpha and Delta Companies. Then our company would proceed to the hill and join up with the other two. This would be a short move, no more than five hundred meters, but the troops would be out of the fish barrel and on much higher ground.

A and D Companies moved out shortly after 0800 hours and cautiously worked their way to Hill 724. The route from our night location to the hill was a simple one: move along a small saddle to the hill and, after making a left turn, climb the high ground. With the hill secured by 1030 hours, we began to move out of the night location to join up with them. Again, Sergeant Dickerson, his RTO, and I were assigned as "tail end Charlie." We watched as the first three platoons slipped into the bush and disappeared from view. As our group and the last platoon began to move, the pop of mortars could be heard. With no place to go but up, we started to run.

We never heard the shells land—too busy running. Running is not the right word, because you really can't run with over one hundred pounds on your back. Your back was bent over so far that your hands almost touched the ground. A fast walk was more like it. Nevertheless, it was a 100-yard dash to me. By the time we gained the saddle and made the left turn at the bomb craters, most of the company was out of sight. Our group of maybe fifteen or twenty guys was the last to reach the hill. As we rounded the last crater, we encountered a mass of downed trees. The OPs that were posted directed us through the tangle. I didn't know it at the time, but we were to be the last people to see them alive.

As the last of the log tangle was navigated, we joined the company. The scene was a typical one with rucksacks dropped everywhere, men taking a breather, and the first to arrive were just moving out to clear the fire zone. The only answer to the usual question, "Where is the company CP?" was pointing fingers and saying, "Over that way, I think."

The first person we saw was Collins. Jim Bury was a short distance away with Taylor and "Alpha Charlie." "Six" was nowhere in sight. As my rucksack hit the ground, I grabbed a canteen, and slumped down.

"Where is 'Six'? someone asked.

"Up talking with the other COs," came the reply. "This the CP?" another asked.

"Don't know. 'Six' just told us to wait here."

As Collins sat down next to me, he asked, "Where should we put the hole?" "I don't know," I said. "Wait for 'Six.' He'll tell us where."

No one can teach you the sounds that different weapons make by just talking about the different noises. The learning comes from experience and is burned into you by necessity. The hollow pop of an outgoing mortar, the "krump" of a landing shell, the "whoosh-bang" of a RPG, all have meaning. With enough dumb luck, you learn. The talent, once acquired, is never lost. To this day, the difference between the light, sharp pop of an M-16 and the louder, deeper bark of an AK has never faded from memory.

Just as I finished speaking, the popping of M-16s started, slow at first. Maybe two guys on semi-auto, firing deliberately. The next moment, a roar of AKs kicked in on full auto. A second later, our other M-16s and M-60s opened up. We didn't know it then, but in that one instant, all the OPs were lost. The initial "mad minute" stretched into two, then three. The deafening noise lasted for hours. Jim Bury yelled at Collins and me to get down. We jumped behind a small log as the roar grew even louder. Both of us just lay there and laughed uncontrollably. A case of nerves can do that to you. After about five minutes, we settled down and went to work. The CP was in good hands, so I told Collins I was going to see what I could do in one of the platoons on the line. I crawled low toward the heavy firing, not realizing I'd never see Collins again.

A person's perspective changes when he's crawling on his belly under fire. Feet become yards, a single minute is ten, and out of sight is the other side of the world. That's the way it was as I crawled into the firefight about thirty feet away from the CP. "Doc," the company's head medic, was struggling with someone on the ground. I realized as I moved to help that the guy had been hit and was just thrashing about. As we got him under control, the hole in his head was apparent. The soldier couldn't open his eyes, and the unintelligible sounds coming from him were like drunken animal grunts. Doc worked feverishly to get an IV started. I found a machete to hang up the bottle, but each outburst from the soldier was shorter than the one before. He was sinking fast. Seeing him weaken, the truth was evident. I grabbed Doc's attention and verbalized my thoughts.

"He's not going to make it. There are wounded all over this hill that need help.

You must leave to work on them." "No!"

Doc didn't want to hear about it, but the truth won out, and he moved on.

I was alone with a man who was bravely fighting his last battle, and I couldn't just leave. I put an arm around him, and spoke into his ear. He was told that there was nothing we could do to stop him from dying. I'm sure he heard and understood, because a violent animal sound exploded from him and he fought on. As I apologized for our inability to save him, the fight for his life ended. I've always believed he understood the situation, and didn't feel alone. Hopefully, some day I'll know if he forgave us for failing.

During this time, I happened to roll over on my back in order to try to get a better look around. The sky was a beautiful deep bright blue, but it looked funny. The visual effect was like having stars or streaks in your eyes. Then I realized that what I was seeing were bullets and shrapnel flying overhead. Anyone who stood up or even got too high was sure to be hit, if not killed, by the fusillade of lead and steel passing over us.

The only thing that resembled any kind of cover was a small four-inch log which already had two guys squeezed behind it. As I made it three, we started to get overrun. What was left of the platoon in front by the log tangle, pulled back up the hill to our position. On the right, one man raised up to fire as he withdrew and was promptly shot dead. A sergeant dropped down next to me on my right and began to fire.

On the left a fellow with a pump shotgun retreated up the hill. He stood tall as he walked backwards, firing every few steps. No panic, just grudgingly giving up ground in that hail of bullets. He slapped more shells into the pump shotgun, and as he raised the weapon to fire, a bullet went through his jaw. Just then Chicom grenades sailed over the log tangle, and shrapnel began to plow into us. As I watched the grenades explode in front of the position, I said to no one in particular, "Where should we pull back to?"

At that, the sergeant drew his hunting knife and plunged it into the dirt in front of us.

"We stay here! Don't move from this spot!"

That's how that little log became home for the next five hours.

Sarge grabbed a LAW (Light Antitank Weapon). Seeing this, I cleared the backblast area of troops and wounded. Sarge went up on one knee and fired. That sure slowed them down. The NVA weren't as eager to come through the downed trees any more.

The jungle in front of our position was alive with flashes. I had no idea what they were until Sarge told me. I really felt stupid. I started to fire my M-16, but it jammed.

Out came the magazine. Lock the bolt open, shake out the shell on top of the jam, and put the cleaning rod down the barrel to knock out the empty. Hand load one shell, and shoot. Knock out the empty with the cleaning rod. That's how it went.

After repeated jams, the M-16 I had was pitched, and I found a rifle that would work correctly. With the entire tangle of downed trees alive with muzzle flashes, the new rifle ate up the magazines on full automatic. The guy next to me had an M-60 machine gun and plenty of ammo belts, but he wasn't firing. While changing a magazine, I politely inquired about his lack of participation.

"It's broke," he said.

"What do you mean it's broke?"

"Well, once you start firing. You can't shut it off. The trigger housing falls out of the gun."

I told him that was OK as long as he kept it pointed down hill, "So get going."

He loaded up and promptly ripped off a 200-round burst into the logjam of trees in front of us. At that rate, I knew we could be out of M-60 ammo in just a few minutes. Something had to be done to fix the gun, and quickly. The pins holding the trigger housing in place were missing, so I put two grenades into the downed trees, and kept the cotter keys to replace the pins. The gun worked fine.

At the log, two guys on my left were trying to start a foxhole. There were no shovels or entrenching tools available. They were using a machete, a stick, a plastic spoon, and their hands. Progress was slow, but at least the dirt was piling up on the other side of that little log.

About this time, Doc came back after checking for wounded. He told me that the command post had been hit by a rocket and everybody there was killed. Things were very bad and getting worse. Wounded were piling up everywhere. Supplies were sure to run low, and he wanted me to hold some of his morphine for him. I had to promise to keep it safe, and only give it to him when he asked for it—no one else—no matter what. He looked on as I placed the small flat box in my top fatigue pocket and buttoned the flap. If I was killed or seriously wounded, he would know where to look for the morphine. Doc moved on, and I went to pitching more grenades.

Doc looked on as I placed the small flat box in my top fatigue pocket and buttoned the flap. If I was killed or seriously wounded, he would know where to look for the morphine.

By now, I had given up on the M-16, because ammo was getting low, and without my glasses, seeing the NVA was a problem. The fact was, I could do more damage with an M-79 and hand grenades. This was partic-ularly true against targets in the logjam (by the tall trees) just in front of my position. I could just make the throw to the other side of the tangle. Plus, the grenade launcher was accurate enough to hit the small trees just behind the large ones where the NVA were hiding. The only thing that stands out during this period was picking out the sound of a single rifle shot on a regular basis. The direction and general location was all I could make out. A count between shots indicated a regular five-count beat, just like an old style bolt-action type rifle. I started the count with the shot: one, two, three, four, shoot. On one and two, I rose up with the M-79 grenade launcher. On three, I lined up the target, and on four, I steadied and fired.

The rifle never fired again. Much later, a guy told me he saw me shoot an NVA with my M-79. This must have been the situation. After that, I put hand grenades and M-79 rounds everywhere people could use as fighting positions in or around the trees and the logjam.

What I did not know at the time was that two of our guys were hiding in there. All of a sudden they flushed like rabbits and ran up the hill. Johnnie Dollar had been hit with some light shrapnel, but the lieutenant was creased by a bullet to the head. It had knocked him out and he had just come to. The guys that were with him thought that because of all the blood he was dead, so they left him when they had pulled back. Once the medics got a hold of him, they slapped a chest bandage on top of his head like a granny cap and tied the strings under his chin. He sure looked funny crawling around after that. Every time he moved, he would land on the trailing strings, making his head bob up and down like a chicken picking corn. After the fight, I learned how he was hit. An NVA soldier was standing up, popping out from behind a tree and shooting at us on a regular rhythm. The lieutenant saw him and tried to line up on him the next time he popped out. What he didn't know was that another NVA at the base of the tree was covering the decoy. He shot the lieutenant in the head. The bullet went in the front of the helmet and out the back, but it only grazed the very top of his head. It knocked him cold, and he bled a lot. Maybe the decoy was the NVA hit by the M-79.

About three or four NVA machine guns and some riflemen were still firing at us from the downed trees. A man was sent back to find out if we could get artillery support to blast them out of the location. When he returned, the word was that the firebase could only give us some 4.2 mortar fire. After adjusting the fire, all we could get them to do was put four rounds about seventy-five meters out. The effect was minimal, but must have shaken up Charlie.

Next the artillery forward observer got some jets on call. This really lit the area up. Even though the 750-pound bombs went in about five hundred meters away, the pilots put the napalm and CBUs (Cluster Bomb Units) directly on both sides of the perimeter of the hill behind my location. (The hill was an ellipse, and I was on one end). We managed to talk the pilots into strafing the woodpile with their 20mm cannons. I popped smoke for our position and marked the woodpile with red. The very first pass was on target. You could see the shells exploding in the pile. Charlie didn't like that at all, because on the next pass they opened up on the jets with machine gun and rifle fire. I ordered our group to lay down covering fire on the remaining passes to make Charlie as unhappy as possible. We didn't lose any planes, so I hope it helped them. As the dust cleared, I could tell that the volume of fire was cut by about one third.

The scratching in the dirt to my left was actually starting to look like a hole.

What teamwork! One man was digging and the other was shooting.

By this time my hand grenades and M-79 shells were running out. Most of the platoon's ammo was packed in the rucksacks that were lying on the ground between us and the NVA near the log pile. That meant hunting some up was the only choice because I wasn't going out there. Moving towards the right, I got some shells from the guys in the small bomb crater and dropped them back at my fighting position.

I moved back toward the CP area checking rucksacks as I went. Most were already empty, but I managed to pick up enough various types of ammo to last for a little while longer. This meant that all the spare ammo in the area was used up. Still being short of M-79 rounds, the search was expanded past the crater on the right, to a bunker further on. Sliding down the bare hillside to a well dug fighting hole, the greeting was, "Sniper! Go back!"

Already committed and past the halfway point, I continued, finally stopping next to the hole. They grabbed me and pulled me into the hole. The guys didn't think too highly of giving up their M-79 ammo, or my chances of getting back. They were sure the sniper would get me, but I got the shells.

When I finally got back with the ammo, the process to pick off the two remaining machine guns continued. Since the 4.2-inch mortar could not be adjusted close enough, I tried a request for 81mm mortars, but was turned down. The hill was out of range for the small tubes.

While wondering where our 81mm mortar was, I peeked over the small log and saw the tube and base plate about twenty-five feet in front of us. This was not good, because it meant that someone had to go out and carry it back.

Crawling to the CP, I asked if they had a problem with my putting together an operation to get our mortar back. They didn't object. I pulled about five guys together and told them my plan. Someone had to go out and get the tube while we provided covering fire to keep the NVA's heads down. (Great plan, eh!) Who wanted to volunteer?

Hosack said he'd do it. A flak jacket materialized and he put it on. The shooters were set up on either side of him to sweep the area. The signal to start was when I fired the launcher and the M-79 grenade blew up.

With the crack of the explosion, we opened up. Hosack stood up and moved out down the hill. We were all firing madly to cover him. As I reloaded the M-79, he reached the mortar. We kept up our fire. He then dragged the tube and bipod back up the hill to our location. We had done it, and he was safe. Before I could call off the fire, Hosack dashed back down the hill. I'd forgotten about the base plate, but he hadn't. Again, he made it safely back. Hosack was braver than any person there. I know that I didn't have the guts to go after that mortar.

On the left, the hole was almost eleven inches deep, and might cover a single person. A second bedroom was being added as quickly as possible. The best part was that the dirt had piled up higher than the log and was adding more protection. We were in "fat city."

From that moment the remaining events took on a life of their own. At least two machine guns had to be taken out, and our pickup team of players moved rapidly to achieve the goal. Part of the mortar team was still available, so they were ordered to move the gun to the crater and set the tube up. A few men were directed to pick up as many of the 81mm mortar rounds as they could find and deliver the ammo to the crater. The machine guns were marked as targets. We used the standing trees as aiming points because from the bottom of the crater, that was all the gunners could see.

The guy who took charge of the crew didn't feel we could get the shell as close as was needed, but we had to try. I'd spot for the adjustments. We had all of ten rounds, so there was no time to play around with big adjustments. The crew lined their sight up on the indicated tree, cut the charge to minimum, and elevated for close-in fire. In order to see the shells land, I had to move from inside the crater back across eleven feet of open ground to my original position. Then after the shell landed, reverse the trip back to the crater and deliver the adjustment. The first round was a little long, maybe sixty-five or seventy-five meters. I went back to the crater.

"You're on line, but drop twenty-five meters," I said. "No way. Can't do it," someone replied.

"All right, drop what you can," I said.

He made an adjustment, and I went back to the observation point, calling for the shot. After the hollow pop as it left the tube, the shell could be seen going almost straight up into the blue, cloudless sky. Seconds later, it landed on target with a cracking whoomp. One machine gun was down. ...back to the crater, line up on the next tree, move to observe by the log.

I called for the shot. The hollow pop, as it left the tube, was followed by five to eight similar pops from just in front of us. INCOMING! On the left, the hole was just large enough for two, and if they really pushed toward the bottom, only a few inches of them were exposed. I didn't jump in, more like on top of them.

"Hey! This is our foxhole get out!" someone shouted. "Shut up! I'm overhead cover," I said.

With that, we reached an agreement just before the shells landed. All the explosions seemed distant. They must have hit the CP areas in the middle of the perimeter. Nuts. I missed our mortar shell landing. I moved to the crater to call for another shot. As I topped the lip and went down the inside, the first thing I saw was a leg. Just a leg, no pants. It was black, maybe a boot, and the leg stopped at the hip. I tried to look around to assess the situation but saw nothing. My brain and eyes didn't work. I could hear nothing, just silence. None of my senses would function. It was like being in a fog, no sight or sound. Somehow, I knew they were not wounded but dead. I had to get out, and did, but I don't know how. I went back to the log and told them to get some men into the crater.

That section of the line was wide open. I never went back. The NVA crew on that 60mm mortar was really good. All the rounds landed in the crater. We were fortunate that the counter battery fire was not followed up by an assault. If they had attacked as a follow-up or part of a plan, none of us could have gotten off the hill.

The remaining machine gun, with a few riflemen, continued to grind away at us. I kept trying to get them with grenades but was never successful. The shadows lengthened, and the sun began to set as the remaining

NVA slipped away. When dusk began to move into dark, we began to think about standing up to move around. Just then we got directions to go out and collect the "rucks" plus anything else useful. We were running short on ammo, and the hope was that some of it might be still left in the rucks. Water was also low. One group covered as the other moved down the hill to get the rucks. Part of the guys down the hill stood watch as the others carried the packs back up the hill. Everyone waited for the NVA to open up on us. The tension was unbelievable. No talking.

Those covering or watching strained their eyes in the dim light for movement. Their ears listened for the approaching sounds of the enemy. I stole a quick glance around and saw the men instinctively being drawn to different cover points. Each was waiting for the mad minute to begin. Nothing.

The soft sounds of equipment being moved or men quietly walking up the hill were the only breaks in that silence. The job was done, and we all moved back to our positions. Then, the rucks were rifled looking for water, ammo, and grenades. Going through a buddy's ruck was like invading his private space. The entire time a vision of an angry confrontation filled my mind.

"Hey, that's mine. What do you think you're doing?"

It never came. There were too few of us left, and that made it all the worse.

Then word was passed to start cutting an LZ. The area directly between my location and the crater was the most cleared, so that became the LZ. While the choppers were flying to our location, we chopped down the last few small trees. Upon arrival, the ships couldn't really land; they just hovered with one skid on the side of the hill. Resupply was hastily thrown out, and the wounded were quickly loaded. Between birds, all of us worked to expand the LZ or fortify our positions. There was one large tree blocking part of the LZ and making it difficult to get in and out quickly. I went to work on it with a machete, as the flares from the 4.2-inch mortars lit up the whole scene. Part way through the chopper operation, the tree fell with a crash. After that, the pilots had an easier time of it getting in and out of the LZ. The resupply and evacuation moved more quickly.

I can't remember all the guys we helped onto the choppers. The only one I recall was "Mo." His arm was in a sling and his head was bandaged. I never saw him again, but I heard he was OK and later became a door gunner.

The guys from the log and I moved down the hill about fifteen or twenty yards and dug a fighting hole. We were just outside of grenade range from the logjam, but our grenades could reach the tangle, because we were going down hill. We packed in our rifles, an M-60, and my M-79. Each time a chopper came in we helped to unload it because we were so close to the LZ. Also, we were able to get all the ammo we thought we needed for the night attack that was expected. We ended up with a case of 5.56mm for each rifle, three cases for the M-60, one case for the M-79, and one case of hand grenades, plus some pop flares.

With the wounded evacuated and the foxholes completed, the four of us settled in for the night. An LP was sent out to spend the night just this side of the logjam. They were only twenty-five yards in front of us. About an hour or two after they went out, the NVA hit them with grenades. The team pulled back to our lines, because two guys in the group had been wounded, and their position was compromised. Each of us took a turn at guard, but no one could sleep. We just waited for the attack. Artillery was firing H&I (harassing and interdictory) fires with their entire battery into suspected enemy positions. Some B-52s dropped their load, but it was a few clicks away.

First light began, and all of us were standing to, ready for the next wave. It never came. The 66th NVA regiment must have had enough or else they just got tired of beating on us. I don't really know for sure. The only sure facts were that Bravo Company had 165 men who went up the hill that day. The fight started about 1300 hours and over the next six hours, 68 men were wounded badly enough to require hospitalization. Luckily, 78 of us managed to struggle off the hill with only minor cuts, scrapes, and shrapnel wounds. The medics quickly patched us up for another day. The real tragedy was nineteen of us who would never come down from that hill.

With the dawn we crawled out of our holes. Dazed, shell shocked, without sleep, the "Thousand-Yard Stare" was in every eye. Slowly, a few men moved. Here and there, the silence that blanketed the area was broken. Disjointed voices could be heard asking where people were. The replies varied.

"He was on OP. Nobody got back."

"Saw him on a chopper. ...didn't look good." "I don't know."

Off on the right came, "Here's a gook; look how close they got." "My God, there are bodies everywhere."

"One's alive over here!"

Like moths to a flame, we moved to the sound of the voice, asking, "Where?" "Here. Should I shoot him?"

"No. Where?" "Over here." "Over by the LZ."

A group formed at the edge of the LZ, near two guys who were pulling an NVA from under a downed tree. Part of the top had landed on him when the tree went down. It looked like he had crawled up to throw some grenades at us, but I realized he was after a chopper or me because the downed tree was the one I cut the night before. The POW was in bad shape. The tree had caused some serious damage, so we carried him to the CP on top of the hill. Later I saw Saber sitting at the main CP next to Captain Falcone's body just staring at the POW lying on a stretcher. The guy was in the sun, and all attention was being denied him until our people were taken care of by the medics. Not even water was allowed. After we got off the hill, I heard that the POW died.

At that time we didn't know who was running the company because the company commander, the field first sergeant, a platoon leader, and a platoon sergeant were dead. Another platoon leader was wounded. Even with all that, we got the word to have a patrol sweep the area in front of our position. Several of us moved out from the left and started to ease down the hill across the edge of the napalmed area.

We began to run into the dead bodies of the enemy about fifty feet from the edge of our perimeter. Next, the patrol swept around the logjam to secure the area. The objective was to look for our guys who were on OP duty. They were found, but they were beyond our help. The dead NVA were lying everywhere in and around the logjam, about twenty-five or thirty of them. I got as far out as the NVA 60mm mortar position. The location wasn't hard to identify because of the empty shell containers, cut charges, and even a shell they had left behind. Knowing how the NVA dragged off their dead, they must have lost a lot of men because they were unable to pick up all of them.

Most of their weapons, however, were gone. I found one body at the base of the large tree where a machine gun was positioned. I didn't check him out because he was curled up in the fetal position and may have been rigged with a booby trap. The logjam was a very good fighting position. The logs were two feet or better in diameter and piled two or more high. The three trees that withstood the bomb blasts that had created the original craters were four to five feet in diameter. Standing there by that body, I was protected from the chest down, and felt safe. I moved back to the hill and made our report.

An airborne unit, likely the 173rd Airborne Brigade, got orders to replace my company because we were no longer an effective fighting force. As the replacements were dropped off, we departed. The first group to land jumped off the chopper and could not believe what they saw. NVA and U.S. bodies were lying everywhere, right where they fell on the LZ. I felt ashamed because it had never dawned on me to start picking them up. Our group just sat staring into the fog that still covered all of us. Our bodies were partly working, but each mind was frozen in time.

Out of the fog, a voice ordered me, "Get in a chopper." I did.

After landing at the Dak To chopper pad, we just stood around, not knowing what to do. Finally, the few of us who had gotten out started to move toward the battalion area, walking across the airstrip. Just then, two slicks arrived and started to hover about five feet off the deck. Each had a landing net filled with cargo. The pilots dropped the nets on the pad by the aid station. Our dead spilled out. They were starting their journey home.

Jim Stapleton, Atlanta, GA
Companies A and C, 1st Battalion, 22nd Infantry Regiment

Dak To Debriefing—MG W. Ray Peers— CG 4th Infantry Division

In December 1967, Major General Ray Peers was the Commanding General of the 4th Infantry Division, Lieutenant Colonel William J. "Bill" Livsey was the G-3, and Major Mike Malone was the Deputy G-3. Captain Bruce Shipley was the aide to Peers. Bruce was one of the most highly decorated officers in the division and in the war. Livsey went to command a battalion and Shipley went with him to command his second rifle company. I was the G-3 operations night duty officer and then replaced Shipley as the aide to MG Peers.

The Battle of Dak To had just been completed, and MG Peers and LTC Livsey were called to Saigon to present the battle from start to finish to the USARV (United States Army, Vietnam) staff and to the HQ-DA (Headquarters—Department of Army) historical unit. It was interesting to me how the battle was reduced to Red (Enemy) and Blue (Friendly) arrows and star clusters to indicate contact points. As the briefing was prepared and presented, arrows and clusters were adjusted to fit the presentation board in the room. The briefing was edited to fit the time allocated by time and film. Having studied military art, I now had some insight as to how and why the arrows and contact clusters came to be so convenient to the presentation.

January—December 1968

Highlights of 1968 include the major battles surrounding the Tet offensive early in the year and continuation of Operation McArthur. Tactics changed from company-wide operations and larger size search and destroy missions to patrols conducted by small units with large units poised to react when contact was made. After the Tet offensive, public opinion at home turned against American involvement in Vietnam. Pacification operations continued throughout the year. Major General Charles P. Stone commanded the division. Three 4th Infantry Division soldiers earned the Medal of Honor in 1968, and 736 were killed in hostile and non-hostile actions.

Michael Richards, Adelphi, MD
Company C, 1st Battalion, 8th Infantry Regiment

A Noel Visit

On January 1, 1968, Charlie Company, 1st Battalion, 8th Infantry Regiment, was at the farthermost position on a ridgeline at the junction of Laos and Cambodia overlooking the Ben Het Special Forces base. This was before the next six weeks of the 1968 Tet Offensive.

As the farthermost position, we were informed of a special visitor coming to our position for a Christmas and New Year Celebration. It was not until the last minute that we were informed that this was not a senior officer, but a USO person and a "female" to entertain the troops. Being so far out in the boonies, it was a delight to us that we had a lady coming to see us. We were all giddy with excitement.

The first order of business was to insure all pants buttons were buttoned to the full ladder (no zippers were used in Vietnam), and shirts were to be worn by everyone. Needless to say, when a blue-eyed blonde in a mini-skirt stepped off the Huey and entertained us for over one hour, every jaw dropped in awe that this lady would come to the front line. We were all amazed that someone would go so far as to put herself in harms way to entertain the troops.

I believe the name she used was Chris Noel and that she was a radio disc jockey from Los Angeles. She didn't know that by her coming to the most remote foxhole in Asia how much she inspired the troops. Her special effort will never be forgotten.

The next six weeks were a different event, but I can assure you, all buttons were buttoned for that event. It is a pleasant memory.

For some reason, I received no stories about the 4th Infantry Division's involvement in the 1968 Tet offensive. The division was heavily engaged at Camp Enari, in Pleiku, in Kontum, and in other locations in the central highlands. Just so our reader doesn't look in vain for Tet 1968 stories, there aren't any. And the reason is, none of our veterans submitted them. Now we will continue with what happened after Tet 1968. —Bob Babcock

----

Bob Walkowiak, Canton, MI
Company B, 3rd Battalion, 8th Infantry Regiment

The Dog Bone—February 1968

The wind and noise swept through the helicopter cabin as always, loud enough so that talking was only possible if you yelled to the guy next to you. This one was going to be a piece of cake. Just chopper in and pull security for a bit while the firebase was torn down, and everything that had been accumulated over three months was either destroyed or flown out. No problem, I thought. Looking out the door, you could see the dry season was in full swing. The jungle was a dirty green, and shell and bomb craters pockmarked the landscape everywhere. The chopper passed over large burned-out areas where napalm had been dropped. Where was it? I thought that if I kept looking close, I might recognize something, but I didn't. The entire area looked new to me, even though I knew it was down there somewhere. We hadn't been back in this area for almost three months, and everything seemed changed. I was still looking for Hill 724, when the "Dog Bone" came into view.

One look from the air was enough to name this firebase, and it had stuck. In the middle of the jungle was a giant reddish brown outline of a dog bone. The knobs on each end were not large enough to stand alone as a base of operations, but by connecting them together across the saddle, the twin knobs formed a giant firebase. In its prime, at the height of the battle for Dak To, the base commanded the whole backside of the Dak To ridgeline. With a battery of 105mm howitzers at one end and 155mm howitzers on the other, the massive firepower could be directed throughout the valley; however, that was then, and this was now. Our job was to tear it down and move on.

The 155mm howitzer battery was already gone, and the choppers were dropping us on the empty half of the base. Stepping off the chopper, all of us must have thought that this was going to be just like R&R. The bunkers were built large and comfortable, and we just had to move in. The command post was set up in a central bunker large enough so that the whole group of us could sleep under cover together. They even gave us hot chow in the evening.

The next day or two the company rested, pulled a couple of patrols, guarded the perimeter, and generally worked on our tan. Then the work started. Chinooks started to arrive to pull out the 105mm howitzer battery. They would fly into the other knob and hover just long enough for the cargo nets to be hooked up and then took off with their loads. I was a good hundred and fifty yards away, but the noise still drowned out every sound. As one of the choppers left and our hearing returned to normal, two mortar rounds landed. I was just standing there and watched the shells blow up by the 105mm howitzer battery. "INCOMING!"

We all hit the bunkers and waited. Nothing. We eased out of our holes, listening for the telltale pop of NVA mortars that generally signaled such an attack was coming, but the hill was back to normal. The Chinooks returned for their next loads, and the entire process was repeated. Only this time, the rounds landed just short of the wire, and we were a little slower getting in our holes. After about the fourth time, we didn't even take cover, because the NVA on that mortar were the worst shots in the world. They had put a good twenty rounds into us and only got one inside the perimeter. They were terrible.

The next day the extraction continued and so did the mortar attacks. We, on the other knob, just sat back and watched the show. In would come a Chinook, hook up a load, fly out, and the shells would land after the chopper had left. Every time was the same, and most of the rounds exploded outside the wire—really strange. That night I couldn't get it out of my mind. They could not be that stupid to continually miss the chopper pad without making a correction, and why was the bird gone before the rounds landed? When the lift started the next morning, I sat on top of our bunker and just watched the show while trying to figure out what was going on. Then it came to me. The NVA were not trying to hit the chopper on the pad. Because the choppers took off in the same direction, and flew the same pattern, they were waiting for the bird to fly over and hit it on the upsweep of the mortar's arc. That's why they didn't care where the shells landed. I quickly talked to our CO, and we relayed the information to the pilots. Now when they left the base, they would go left or right, but not straight. The shells stopped. I really felt good that the observation may have saved a crew.

Later that afternoon most of the heavy stuff was off the hill. The next day we would leave for the Dak To airstrip. That night, we divided the beer and soda our supply sergeant had sent in on the last chopper with the hot chow and kicked back. Warm beer, hot chow, and a solid bunker roof over your head—this was heaven for us grunts. It didn't matter that the last shower was ten weeks ago or that some of the fatigues were rotting off the guys. All that was going to get fixed at Dak To the next day. It was going to be the first day of March, but I'd swear it was like Christmas Eve.

In the morning, the last few lifts of equipment were completed, and the slicks were sent in to pull us out. The landing zone was on the top of our knob, and the platoons knocked down the bunkers as they pulled out. Our procedure was always the same. The command post personnel went in first and out last, so I knew there was plenty of time before we got to leave. Only four birds were in the extraction, and the flight to Dak To was longer than usual, so things were starting to drag. About half of the company had left when I dropped my rucksack on the roof of our bunker and climbed up on top. I was just standing there looking over the hill and watching the guys move to the pad to get on the choppers.

Suddenly, everything went black, and a stabbing pain went through my chest just as if a nail was being driven through me. I could actually feel it traveling in my body. The next instant, I'm floating and spinning ever so slowly, and the little voice in my mind calmly said, "Oh, I'm shot."

Then the sound of a very small, distant explosion entered my mind... A mortar? When the motion stopped, I was just in darkness, feeling nothing.

The voice continued. It went right through and blew up. This is not good.

You're dead.

Slowly, the black was replaced by red. Consciousness was returning, and I felt warm. It was the sun. The warm sun was shining through my eyelids. I don't think I'm dead. No pain.... Don't move, that could make it worse, and this could be very bad. Wiggle your toes. OK, they move. Now try your fingers. OK, they move, too.

My eyes fluttered open for just a second. No blood was spurting.

What the hell happened? Like it or not, you have to take a look, and check it out. As my eyes opened, I had to squint in the blazing sunlight. Everything seemed to be working, but there was a dull pain in my chest, and no blood.

Damn, a mortar round is pretty big, what's going on?

As I looked down the front of my fatigues, I was amazed not to see a fist-sized gaping bloody wound. Well, something had happened! Raising my fatigue shirt, I looked at my chest. There, an inch above the right nipple was a small hole about the size of a thumbnail. Shrapnel? My eyes closed again, and my body just soaked up the warmth of the sun.

Close by a voice said, "I think he's dead, but I'll check him anyway."

As hands rolled me on to my back, I opened my eyes.

"I'm OK. It's only in the chest," I said.

Close by a voice said, "I think he's dead, but I'll check him anyway."

As hands rolled me on to my back, I opened my eyes. "I'm OK. It's only in the chest," I said.

The medic took a look and agreed. I got up, and walked the twenty feet back to the bunker to get my rucksack. The mortar round had landed almost at my feet. That was why they thought I was dead. The side of the bunker, and the ruck took most of the shrapnel. The blast threw me.

The medic had returned to the LZ area, and was working on one of our guys who had been hit in the back and leg. As I walked up, dragging my ruck, the medics were slapping bandages on him as he sat there on the ground.

A new one took a quick look and said, "You're OK. Sit down," and returned to patching up the other guy.

My head was spinning. I sat down, and watched them working, as another load of us went out. ...POP, POP, POP...INCOMING!

Everyone dived for the bunkers, leaving the two of us sitting there. I got up, started to run, and realized the other guy couldn't get up because of his shoulder and leg wounds. Returning, I grabbed him and pulled him to his feet. I threw his arm over my shoulder and just ran. He hobbled, and I carried. The shells landed just as we stopped next to a large bunker wall. Just then, I realized we were outside of our perimeter, wounded, alone, and didn't have a weapon between us. So, I started to drag him back to get on a chopper.

"Are you OK?" I asked him.

"Yeah, but my shoulder is broken, and you got my bad arm," he said.

Switching sides, we hobbled back to the LZ. The choppers were back to pick us up. It was the last lift, and we made the last bird.

As we lifted off, I sat in the door, feeling really pissed that I hadn't been able to fight back. We swept low over the wire and started to climb. In frustration I began to pitch my grenades out. The first must have hit the ground, but as we climbed, they made airbursts. The gunners and pilots went crazy. They thought the biggest anti-aircraft gun in Vietnam was going to put one up our butts. By the time they figured out what I was doing and tried to stop me, my grenades were gone. However small it was, I had done something to fight back, and I felt better. After landing at the Dak To chopper pad, I hopped a truck to the aid station. Our medics didn't want to just clean me up and put on a bandage, like I asked. When I got to the aid station, the place wasn't too busy. They were poking and prodding the other guy from my company, so I just stood around and waited. Finally, a medic or doc comes up and asks me what I'm doing.

"Just waiting around to get this hole in my chest bandaged so I can get back to the company," I said.

That set them off but good. They had little to do, so I was now the "pokey" of choice. Two of them listened to my chest, poked some, and announced, "We need X-rays."

"Look, slap a bandage on it, I've got to get back to the company," I said.

Three x-rays and some more good pokes later, I got the bandage. As I started to leave, they handed me the x-rays, slapped a tag on my fatigues, and put me in a chopper with a couple of stretcher cases. Destination was the 71st Evacuation Hospital near Pleiku.

When the chopper landed, I hopped out, tucked the tag inside my fatigues, and stood off to the side. My plan was to just walk off, but I didn't know where I was. The doors to the hospital opened, and people were streaming out. They scooped up the litters and carried the guys inside as the bird took off.

I'm stuck, alone, on the pad with no place to go except in.

I walked to the door, and looked through. Inside was an operating room that looked like a large garage, and everyone was busy with the two stretcher cases. It was late and I was tired, hungry, and still mad at the world. So the ruck got dropped against the wall, and I squatted on my helmet with my rifle against my shoulder as I searched for a can of peaches. I knew the drill. They'd get to me soon enough.

A "round eye" nurse walked over. She got hit with my best icy, stay away, don't mess with me glare, and walked right through it.

"What are you doing here?" she asked. "Peaches, I'm hungry," I said.

She saw the string on my fatigue shirt, and pulled out the tag. Turning on her heel, she said, "Come with me."

I hadn't smelled anything that good in my life, so I kept my mouth shut and followed her to a table where I sat down. The stench was rolling off me in waves. It was so bad in this confined area that even I could smell it, but she never even wrinkled her nose. She just went to work removing the bandage, and prepped me for the Doc.

Soon he came over, flushed out the hole with some solution in a turkey baster, cut around the edges of the hole, and put on a clean bandage. After announcing that I'd be OK, he left. I picked up the ruck, put on the helmet, grabbed the rifle and was almost out the open door when she stopped me. Looking outside, I could tell the sun was setting. I had to hurry since we couldn't travel after dark. She was standing behind me talking softly.

"Why don't you stay here tonight?" She offered. "Can't! Got to get back," I said.

"We can get you a hot shower and clean clothes." "That sounds good."

"Come on with me, and we will get you fixed up." "All right."

"Now put your equipment in this room, and we'll save it for you."

I dropped the ruck and helmet, but held onto the rifle and two bandoliers. "You need to leave the rifle here," she said.

"Like hell! It stays with me!" I argued loudly.

She talked softly. Fatigue and confusion were spreading over me, and I was hurting more and more. In the end, the little kid with a gun gave in, took a shower, and went to sleep. The next morning, I couldn't even get out of bed because the pain was so bad. Then I got the good news.

"You don't eat unless you walk the two hundred feet to the mess hall."

I missed eating that morning because the mess hall was closed by the time I got there. It took over a week to start walking without a shuffle.

Jesse A. Romo Jr., Lockhart, TX
Company D, 3rd Battalion, 12th Infantry Regiment

Headline Story from "Ivy Leaves" Newspaper

Polei Kleng, Vietnam: "Enemy forces paid a stiff price as twenty-four of their soldiers died while attempting to defend a hill against the 1st Brigade's Delta Company, 3rd Battalion, 12th Infantry Regiment."

The story behind the headline: As we were moving up, we were getting hit, and, I mean we were getting hit hard. We dug in that night with our hands and our steel pots. They had us for now. Morning came and lead started to fly again. There was a giant tree lying in front of me.

It's now or never, I thought.

I landed on top of a body. I couldn't tell whose—ours or theirs, but the body exploded and it smelled bad. I gagged night.

I lunged over it as we were still taking heavy fire. I landed on top of a body. I couldn't tell whose—ours or theirs, but the body exploded and it smelled bad. I gagged. Jeff and Cato grabbed me and we all went back over the fallen tree. As we went over again, we were taking heavy fire, due partly to them seeing the M-60 that Cato was carrying. He was good because he kept their heads down for us, but we weren't moving too far again. We dug in for another We were suffering from hunger and too little water to drink, but we were still alive. The nights were just as bad as the days. We could hear the NVA; they were still there. Was I scared? You bet I was, but that went away when I thought, It's him or me. I am not dying here, no way. It seemed like a whole year instead of eight days.

Yes, we took the hill, but a lot of good men died. We checked the hill out to see what we could find. The enemy was dug in all around this hill. They were not on the top of it but around it with tunnels. Two hills were joined together with a "finger" connecting them. Bunkers were everywhere. There had been more than a company of NVA located there. No one ever said otherwise, and we stayed on that hill for a while. The NVA kept coming back for more for the next three days. Not heavy, but just enough to let you know that they were still there. So were we.

I was glad to move out, finally. The war didn't stop there. It still went on with me in it, along with my friends. These are the guys I will never forget. We were close.

Dennis Whitt, Fairfield, CA
Company B, 1st Battalion, 22nd Infantry Regiment

Regulars, by God

Dennis sent the following article, clipped from a copy of "Ivy Leaves" in Vietnam in 1968.

Camp Enari: From hundreds of battles in the past, the 1st Battalion, 22nd Infantry Regiment has emerged victoriously as the "Regulars, by God." After more than a century of fighting our nation's battles, the battalion, which has been involved in some of Vietnam's fiercest combat, now has adopted a new distinctive trademark.

The wearing of the black scarf as a neckerchief was initiated by a soldier who recognized the desirability of clearly distinguishing the fighting troops of this traditional infantry battalion.

The color black is significant as it affords the soldiers a subdued color tone not easily identified in the wooded regions and jungles of the central highlands.

It is also a constant reminder of the dark, uncertain future and destiny that all soldiers must face in the defense of our nation's principles.

And foremost, it is in mournful memory and recognition of the gallant, courageous comrades, "Regulars, by God," who so valiantly fought and made the supreme sacrifice.

John Pastrick, Fort Dodge, IA
Company A, 1st Battalion, 22nd Infantry Regiment

Chu Mohr Mountain—April 1968

After several days under constant small arms, rocket, and mortar fire atop Chu Mohr Mountain in the central highlands of Vietnam in April 1968, our final morning came. I only remember it was quiet and from daylight until about 1100 hours no enemy fire had come in (unusual). The company commander decided to use two platoons—ours, which was second platoon, and another from the other side of the perimeter and go out in a line and slowly sweep to see what we could find. We never really got to see the enemy, only the dead ones. I think they had left the mountain.

We moved out in single file until we had gone out about thirty-five or forty yards. That's when two guys in front of me noticed a small bunker with an NVA helmet lying outside it along with a knife. Inside the bunker was a spider hole dug underneath our location from on top of the mountain. A man by the name of Bob Brown asked if he could put a few rounds into the spider hole. After alerting the other platoons what was happening so they wouldn't fire, Bob fired off about five or six rounds, and there was no response.

We slowly moved another ten or fifteen yards. I can remember standing on top of some thick vines and armed only with my ammo belt with a few magazines and my M-16 rifle. The sniper fire started again, and I dropped belly first into the vines and got tangled in them with my ammo pouches. Pulling and tugging, twisting and turning, I watched everyone else head back up towards the top of the mountain, except for the man carrying the M-60 machine gun and the man with him by the last name of Schumaker. The M-60 man was hit but was able to move back with Schumaker's help. This was happening fast (I was concentrating on how to get out of the thick vines).

I finally said to myself while the sniper fire still popped around me, "Take the damn ammo belt off, stupid."

I did. I left it behind and ran like hell to join the others.

The word was to grab what we could of importance and start moving off the mountain to the artillery firebase, about five clicks away. I can remember walking back all through the daylight hours and when it got dark, they sent up illumination rounds to help us see. When we got to the top of the mountain, I remember being so tired I went over to a bunker inside the perimeter and collapsed on top of the sandbags. The next morning, before we were air lifted to Dak To for hot chow and showers, we all gathered together to listen to a chaplain give a sermon and pray for the ones who had given their lives.

Even though I didn't know many men in my company, since I was still a new guy, I remembered the faces of the wounded I helped carry down the mountain and the names of Michael York and a man by the last name of Hall. To this day, I still see the wounds and ask myself how some of them lived. They were messed up. For the first time I felt that I actually got to see how much punishment the human body can take.

Back at Dak To we started to come to terms with what we had just been through. Not too many months before this, I was cruising the hamburger stands in Indianapolis with my high school friends, going to high school basketball games, and dating a sweet and attractive girl I'd planned to marry. But all that could never compare to the feeling I got when I was not considered a FNG any more. Short timers and old timers started trusting me, and I started taking on other duties and feeling good about myself.

Fred Gould, Ridgewood, NJ
Company A, 2nd Battalion, 8th Infantry Regiment

Have You Ever Seen a Pink Elephant?

An easy way to determine when someone has experienced too much trauma and emotional stress is when they start hallucinating and seeing things that do not exist. With this in mind, I'd like to relate the story of when I saw a pink elephant in the middle of the central highlands jungle west of Pleiku, Vietnam.

We were on a routine patrol on what seemed to be one of the hottest days I spent in Vietnam. It was nearing the end of the monsoon season, so we were not only wet and dirty, but we were almost exhausted due to the heat and humidity. We had been walking patrol since approximately 0700 hours with a brief stop at about 1000 hours for rest and a half-hour stop for lunch at noon. It was now approaching 1500 hours, and I had the unfortunate duty of being the point man, the first person in the line of march.

I was about twenty yards in front of the column as I made my way around a bend in the trail that led into a large clearing. As I cleared the jungle vegetation and took my first step into the clearing, I saw movement at the opposite end of the clearing. I immediately motioned to the patrol to halt and wait until I could determine what the movement was. Then, to my total amazement, a pink elephant came out from behind some vegetation and started to walk across the open area.

I stopped, rubbed my eyes, and even shook my head, but the pink elephant was still there. At this point I was starting to question my own sanity and wondering if I had been in Vietnam too long. Having observed something that couldn't exist, I walked back to the rest of the platoon and announced I had just seen a pink elephant.

After some immediate laughter, and comments like "Gould has finally lost it," the lieutenant and sergeant walked up the trail to see for themselves. Guess what? They saw it also. In a way, this brought great relief to me because I wasn't the only person to witness something that couldn't exist. Then, as quickly as it appeared, it walked back into the vegetation and disappeared. Later, we discovered what had caused our unbelievable sighting and were reassured that we were not imagining the entire incident.

The soil in the central highlands area of South Vietnam is red clay. Therefore, during the monsoon season, the rain creates mud puddles (red mud) used by the local animals to cool themselves once the rain stops and the heat and humidity set in. They slosh around in these puddles and get covered by red mud. Once they leave the puddle, the heat dries them off, and the red mud turns into pink dirt. They remain some color between red and pink until it starts raining again, and the falling rains washes them off.

Donald. P. Brathwaite, Laurelton, NY
Company C, 3rd Battalion, 8th Infantry Regiment

Tiger Pulls Switch on Lyrics: Holds That Man!

Firebase BlackHawk, Vietnam. Specialist 4th Class Donn P. Brathwaite's experience is sure to be the basis for a great conversation stopper in years to come: "Did I ever tell you about the time this tiger grabbed me..."

Originally from the Bronx, New York, I was a member of a short-range patrolfrom Charlie Company, 3rd Battalion, 8th Infantry Regiment working in "VC Valley."

The patrol had selected a night position and was just settling down when we heard movement in the bushes nearby. Half an hour passed, but nothing more was heard or seen.

Then suddenly I heard a rustling in the brush again, very close to me. As I raised my head and peered out into the darkness, I found myself looking into the luminous green eyes of a jungle tiger.

Before I had time to react, the animal had me by my neck and head and was dragging an 180-pound soldier off into the jungle. Unable to yell for help because the tiger's jaws held my mouth closed but still holding my weapon in my hand, I was dragged about fifteen yards before managing to work my weapon into position and fire two shots point blank into the animal. The tiger let out a roar, dropped his prey, and ran off into the night.

After the patrol reported the incident, the area was saturated with 81mm mortars. That morning, blood trails were followed, but no tiger was found. I was covered with the animal's blood and had teeth marks in my neck and face but was able to walk back to the perimeter, thankful that the tiger didn't just want a quick snack.

Bert Nicholson, Wheaton, IL
4th Military Intelligence Detachment

Water Buffalo

When the 4th Infantry Division established the Dragon Mountain Base Camp (later Camp Enari), the practice was to keep an infantry company at the camp for security. This practice was discontinued for reasons unknown to me, and during my tour in Vietnam from June 1968 until June 1969, base camp personnel helped with security that was provided by the artillery, armor, police, and air units that were stationed in the Camp. 590

During one of the patrols of the TAOR (Tactical Area of Responsibility), personnel from the 4th Military Intelligence Detachment and the 4th Engineers were trucked outside of the perimeter and took up a sweeping position for the day's mission. We went out in five-ton dump trucks provided by the 4th Engineers. These were pretty good vehicles for transport because of the great defense against the mines that produced many of the division's casualties.

During the sweep I got into some tall elephant grass. I was looking up at my general objective, Dragon Mountain, so I would not get lost, and pretty soon I was in the grass. It was then that I heard a loud rumble followed by a passing water buffalo. The animal was as big as a Buick, and he passed within inches of me. If he had been a foot or two over, he would have run me down, and I would have been a casualty. There were many ways to get in trouble in Vietnam, and this was one of them.

Fred Gould, Ridgewood, NJ
Company A, 2nd Battalion, 8th Infantry Regiment

Saga of a Listening Post

After a very long day of patrolling on a search and destroy mission near the Cambodian border, our company set up camp for the night. As usual, we set up the company perimeter, dug three-man foxholes, and prepared for what we all hoped would be an uneventful and quiet night. Unfortunately, we had encountered enemy activity late in the afternoon, so we all knew Charlie most likely had our night position already plotted and under observation. Knowing this, we all knew the calm of the night could turn out to be another life or death struggle.

Each evening as the company set up its night position, three Listening Posts (LPs) were positioned in a triangle approximately seventy-five to one hundred yards outside the company perimeter. On this particular night, I was selected to lead one of the three-man LPs. I was very concerned, because one of the two men selected to go out with me had only been in country for five days (we called them "Greenies"). Knowing that Charlie was probably going to probe our position during the night and that it was going to be pitch black because there was no moon out, I asked for a replacement. That request was met with contempt and a stern word from the company commander who said the "boy" had to learn how to be a soldier and carry his weight in the company. Just after darkness set in, the three of us slipped out of the company perimeter and headed for what would become an unforgettable night on LP.

The usual operation of an LP was to set up at approximately 2100 hours and pull one and a half hour watches until 0600 hours the following morning. I assigned the first watch to the "greenie" and because this was his first LP, I decided to stay up with him to give him the emotional support a new guy needed.

That shift was totally uneventful and at 2230 hours he went to sleep and I pulled the watch until midnight. At midnight, the third man took over and had an uneventful watch until 0130 hours. The greenie started his second hour-and-a-half watch.

At approximately 0145 hours, he woke me up and said he heard movement to the front of the LP. I figured it was his nerves, so I remained up with him for about fifteen minutes. Hearing nothing, I went back to sleep. A half hour later, he woke me up again with the same observation. Once again, I remained up with him for another fifteen minutes, but still heard nothing. I then tried to calm his nerves and I went back to sleep. At 0245 hours he woke me again and, needless to say, I was pissed. I was losing my entire night's sleep due to someone I didn't want on LP in the first place.

This time I knew his nerves weren't the problem because I heard movement about thirty yards directly in front of us. I immediately woke up the third guy, and we all listened for additional movement. After two more incidents of movement, I contacted the company command post, and informed them we had confirmed movement that appeared to be someone crawling toward our position. At that point I instructed the other two guys to head into the company perimeter, adding that I would remain behind to continue to observe the situation. As odd as it might seem, my main concern at that point was that the other two men would make it safely back inside the company perimeter.

Now I was totally on my own with the enemy approaching my position. After about a half hour, the movement had come to within about ten yards of the LP. At that point, I radioed into the command post to inform them that all hell was going to break loose out here and that I would be making a dash for the perimeter. I called in specifically to make them aware that a single person would be running for the perimeter and that the troops on the perimeter were not to fire at me as I was coming in. Unfortunately, that had happened several times before and we shot our own guys by mistake.

After gathering my thoughts and nerves, I got ready for what might be my last moments on this earth. I put my M-16 on "rock-n-roll," took aim at the approaching enemy and popped off the entire magazine. At that point, I immediately got to my feet and ran for the perimeter as fast as my legs would carry me. For the remainder of the night, we had no additional contact, but we remained on alert and ready for anything Charlie could throw at us.

In the morning we made a sweep of the area to find traces of the contact and determine if we had to be on alert for the possibility of additional action to come. After about a half hour into the sweep, the guys in my platoon started to "bust my chops" because no one found any bodies, blood trails, or any trace of the enemy I shot. By this time, I was starting to get very annoyed because I knew it wasn't my imagination and that I hit what I shot at.

Then one of the guys yelled out that he found the body. This immediately relieved my feeling of self-doubt as we all hurried over to where the body was found. There, lying on the ground, with about ten bullet holes in it, was a wild dog about the size of a German shepherd. Needless to say, the guys had a great time telling dog jokes for the next couple of weeks.

The next time I went out on LP, the guys back on the company perimeter started to bark like dogs, and one even meowed. I didn't mind the joking around because from that day on, everyone who went on an LP with me knew I would watch out for their safety and that I hit what I aimed at.

Rick Adams, Spartanburg, SC
HQ Troop, 1st Squadron, 10th Cavalry Regiment

The Longest Night

Our mission was to recon Hill 1151, which was located thirty kilometers due east of Camp Enari at map reference BR104325. The four man LRRP team's name was Four-Bravo. The team leader was Gary Price, I was the radio operator, and the names of the other members escape me.

The preparation for the mission and the insertion techniques were familiar to us, a procedure that we repeated on a regular schedule. Two "Shamrock" UH-1 Huey slicks and two Cobra gunships from Delta Troop brought us from base camp. The Cobras stayed high above, ready to respond with covering fire; one Huey carried the team, and the second Huey served as the decoy ship and for our retrieval if we were downed during insertion. Earlier in the day, we had done a flyover, and the landing zone had been picked. We also selected some artillery impact areas so we could adjust fire from the predetermined points. The insertion was made at 1530 hours.

Once on the ground, we established radio communication and moved out southward toward the point at Kong Tieck. Insertions always give an adrenaline high. I sat in the doorway of the UH-1 with one foot out on the skid while the choppers shaped the landscape, using a false LZ tactic in case we were being watched or heard. I was nineteen and sensed a tremendous rush of power as I leaped off the chopper and headed for a tree line.

It was June 23, 1968; I had been in the country eighty days. This was my sixth mission, but the first with this team. Each team member knew his job and did it well. The point man had the immediate front and usually walked with his weapon set on full automatic. The second man in formation watched the right side, the trees, and handled the compass. The third man was responsible for the left side. He kept track of the distance traveled and handled the map. This usually was the team leader's position. The last man covered the rear.

The team carried two PRC-25 radios. Procedures were to change direction every fifty meters and never walk on a path. We found a good night position and spent the first night with negative sit reps. Sit reps are situation reports that are given every hour on the half hour. At night we did not talk or smoke. Often, sitreps were given by simply breaking squelch with the radio handset. Our night location was perfect. We were in some large timber that had fallen. It was good cover, and we had a good view of the lower valley.

The next morning, we ate, did our business, and buried all the trash. We continued on our way up the side of Hill 1151. It began to rain, sometimes very hard. We stopped, and the four of us sat in a circle with our backs together, pulled a poncho over us, and peered outward. At about 1030 hours, the pounding of my heart erased the sounds of the rain tapping on the poncho.

We heard voices, many voices, about twenty-five meters to our northeast. I called it in. In the heavy rain, the NVA were able to walk up on our position undetected. We collected ourselves and quickly moved southward.

We now heard more voices and movement to our left and back down the mountain from where we came. At one point, a squad of NVA walked so close that their legs were clearly visible as we lay silently in the prone position. We were in a world of hurt, as they say. They certainly did not know we were there— they were hollering back and forth. The rain continued off and on through the afternoon, which affected our movement. We continued to hide, and slowly the hours passed until darkness approached. I had been giving our sit-reps by breaking squelch. We had to get out of there so the artillery could fire. We received instructions from base to move southwest down the mountain's steep side until we reached the blue line, which meant the river of Dak Trouille.

This also meant we would have to crawl through some NVA. The team leader, Gary Price, said he would crawl ahead and clear the way, hold up the illuminated compass face, and we would crawl to him. So that's what we did, through the darkness, ten meters at a time. We crawled through the NVA positions and down the steep side of Hill 1151. We crawled all night, and, at first light finally reached the blue line. I reported to base on the radio that we had reached the river. Within two minutes, anyone on that mountain began paying a heavy price. Every piece of artillery that could reach that position opened fire. We had done our job, and after a twoor three-day stand down, we prepared to pull another mission.

Rick Adams, Spartanburg, SC – HQ Troop, 1st Squadron, 10th Cavalry Regiment

Delta Tango

Delta Tango meant "defensive target" to a mortar man—likely places of high enemy activity such as trails at river crossings, locations where enemy weapons or food caches had been found. Targets were selected during the troops' daily search and clear operations. Then at random times during the night we would drop in a few surprise rounds of high-explosive (HE) shells from our "four-deuce" mortar vehicles, the M-106 Armored Personnel Carriers. This form of harassment fire was very effective, we learned during the following day's sweep through these areas.

On October 21, 1968, we were operating in an area about fifteen kilometers south of Camp Enari, and just east of Highway 14 along the Ia Ring River. Bravo Troop was positioned in typical night formation, which consisted of three fully mechanized mobile platoons. From each platoon, the M-106 mortar APCs were positioned inside an outer perimeter of tanks and tracks. I was on the first platoon mortar track, B-19—call sign, "Best Hand Four-Deuce." Ron Miska was "Scarlet Four-Deuce" on track B-29 of the second platoon, and Cass Lewis was the gunner on B-39 of third platoon—three mortar squads always ready to answer a call for a fire mission.

This night, we would fire our Delta Tangos from my track, B-19. We had several targets selected and began firing around 2200 hours. Unknown to us, A squad of Viet Cong demolition men (sappers) had set up outside our defensive perimeter. Their mission was to watch for the muzzle flash when our mortar fired. They would then know where to fire their B-40 rocket. Miska and I were in the track firing the gun, while the other squad members set charges and prepared additional mortar rounds. We had completed one set of targets, and as Ron and I stepped out the back of the track and turned to the right, a B-40 rocket came in, striking the upper rear door and showering the crew with hot shrapnel. Ed "Mongoose" Brosch and Roy were hit.

The vehicles on the outer perimeter immediately opened fire, and the sky was lit with flares and tracers. We checked on Ed and Roy and called for a medic. The other squad members—Willie Holland, Bill Zink, Cass Lewis, Ron Miska, and I—started firing mortar illumination around the perimeter. We had a "hang fire" on an illumination round, which required us to disengage and lift a very hot mortar barrel and dump out the jammed round. We did it in record time and continued to fire illumination rounds.

The perimeter became silent after about ten minutes. A dustoff was inbound to get Ed and Roy, so we had to stop firing the mortar illumination. The VC had chosen only to strike quickly and run this night. The effectiveness of Delta Tango's was never questioned from that day forward.

Bob Noce, Troy, MI
HQ, 1st Squadron, 10th Cavalry Regiment

Seven Short Stories

West of the Oasis (West of Camp Enari), Pleiku Province, July 1968 After my first days with the squadron, the S3, Major Tony Ardizzione, hesitantly observed to me that he, in the CP, had difficulty understanding my radio transmissions from the command helicopter. I didn't know how to fix that. By chance, he went up with me one day shortly thereafter. Normally we didn't fly in the same chopper so we wouldn't both be put out of action if it went down. He told me with some elation that he now knew the cause of the problem. I had to take the cigar out of my mouth when speaking with the lip mike.

Ban Me Thout East Airfield, Darlac Province, Summer 1968

Ready to leave the 1st Brigade CP Fire Support Base one afternoon after coordination with the S3, my chopper crew chief told me of a pair of 22nd Infantry soldiers nearby whose battalion resupply ship had been diverted. They were sadly stuck there with a case of quarts of ice cream, fast threatening to flow away in the heat of the tropical dry season afternoon. Could we take it? Yes! We detoured to C Troop, I think it was, and gave it to them, with the chopper's aluminum floor now laced with rivulets of melted ice cream.

On one of my few visits to the Division Tactical Operations Center (TOC) at Camp Enari, Command Sergeant Major Frank Mouri managed to scrounge up a couple cases of beefsteaks. My Command and Control chopper (tail #535) was chronically underpowered, and it had a homemade radio console weighing hundreds of pounds, and it was the dry season, which meant high DA (density altitude) and very thin air. We took off down the Pierced Steel Planking (PSP) runway bounced like a stone skipped on water. Unfortunately, the division's 4th Aviation Battalion Safety Officer observed the incident. I took the blame.

Western Pleiku Province, South Vietnam, Summer 1968

While Command Sergeant Major Frank Mouri and I were visiting one of the ground cavalry troops, I sent the C&C chopper back for fuel. This was a risky decision, as it left me stranded for about forty-five minutes, and I'd be stuck if the balloon went up somewhere else in the AO. After I'd conferred with the troop officers and Frank had seen NCOs and troopers, I was waiting sitting on a log at the edge of a cleared LZ for the chopper, with a young trooper with M16 to protect me. I idly blurted out that I sure could use a good Mexican meal. He agreed, and I observed that the best Mexican restaurant I'd ever eaten in was in Barstow, California. He was from there, knew the restaurant, and was delighted. I really cheered up a lonesome young soldier that day. Made me feel good too.

Darlac Province, South Vietnam, Autumn 1968

I was flying in my command chopper during a quiet period just snooping around, when I spotted a large tropical lily-like flower in a field surrounded by woods. I had the chopper land, I picked the flower, and we returned to the squadron CP without incident. Entering the S2-S3 track tarp area with lily in hand, I told the S3, Major Tony Ardizzione, that I needed a vase.

He bellowed out to my S3 air, Bill Hamilton, "Get the colonel a vase!"

Now, neither the table of organization and equipment (TO&E) nor the prescribed load list (PLL) had a vase listed. But Bill, being a quick thinker, came up with a 90mm round's expended cartridge (shell) case. It was the best we could do, and the huge lily certainly added a lovely touch to the grimy command post.

Asking me where I'd found it, Tony was aghast seeing the map location and said, "Don't ever do that again."

The squadron was west of Ban Me Thout for a big threatened NVA campaign. We were about one hundred clicks south of Camp Enari up at Pleiku, and we depended primarily on overland resupply down Highway N14, since much of our stuff was heavy loads. Additionally, much resupply for the 1st Brigade came down that road. We normally provided a Cav platoon plus a chopper to fly over the convoy for security. From time to time a vehicle would have to drop out for maintenance failures; if it wasn't near enough to either end of the trip to be towed back or onward, we'd leave it at the Special Forces Camp at Buon Blech east of the infamous Chu Pong mountain. Well, our crews were glad to have a safe haven, and the green bereted snake eaters were just delighted to have an armored vehicle or two snuggled up to their isolated command post. I was grateful, and we developed quite a rapport. Discovering that their higher HQ had them continuously on B rations (all canned food) when they weren't out on patrol, and they got no coffee, I told Command Sergeant Major Frank Mouri, my sidekick, to get hold of an "SP" pack, a 2 by 2 by 2 carton for each one hundred men for three days containing candy, cigarettes, coffee and so on. He squealed that they were just about impossible to get under the table. He got one anyway, and I put it aboard the Huey when I took my turn at convoy escort over flight. Because the next chopper was late coming, we were short on fuel and couldn't land at the special forces camp. So, the Crew Chief, Corporal Nutter, kicked it out over the pimple hill that was their CP. As luck would have it, two NCOs were in the tiny mess at midmorning coffee break when the SP pack hit the tin roof with a huge bang. They thought it was incoming bullets. Because they were so grateful and liked the squadron so much, they left that huge downward bulge in the corrugated iron roof as a fond and humorous memento or reminder. Many laughs!

Ban Me Thout, Darlac Province, South Vietnam, Autumn 1968

The squadron CP was located some ten clicks (kilometers) west of Ban Me Thout city, and 1st Brigade HQ was at the large Ban Me Thout East airfield ten clicks east of the city. The Brigade TOC (CP) continually had difficulty with voice radio transmission. One day while sitting in our S3 track idly monitoring the brigade command radio net, I heard the brigade CO, Colonel McChrystal, repeatedly trying to contact his TOC from his chopper. Finally I broke in on the net and offered our services to relay for him.

He said with a good deal of exasperation apparent in his voice, "Thanks, but I have them in sight now and will land and deliver my message face to face, together with choice comments," or something to that effect.

Tony Ardizzione, Bill Hamilton and I all chortled. Our squadron Commo officer, Captain Whitman, had told me that the reason for brigade's difficulty was that they sat on top of a large iron ore deposit. We never told them.

Kontum Province, South Vietnam, December 1968

Now under 3rd Brigade control, we were tasked one day to recon and clear as necessary the dirt road from Kontum City about fifty kilometers northeast to the special forces camp at Plateau Gi, midway on the road to Qui Nhon on the coast. The road had been built by U.S. civilian contractors in the early 1960s, and no friendlies had been up the road for a couple of years at least. A Cav platoon from B Troop, I think, got the mission. The lead M48A1 tank was commanded by an "instant NCO," a buck sergeant promoted at the end of his AIT and sent straight to Vietnam. Those kids had lots of spunk but were awfully short on experience. At the first five or so Bailey bridges (portable bridges used to cross small streams and rivers) over shallow streams, the young sergeant dismounted, checked abutments and bridge stringers, making back of the envelope rough calculations to conclude crossing was safe and he was right. At the next bridge, he tired of this time consuming procedure. His CP probably was on his neck on the horn, so he just eyeballed it from his cupola and proceeded on.

Unfortunately, this bridge was a longer span high above the streambed, and it didn't survive the M48. When I arrived in my chopper, the beast of a bridge was on its side with the rear sprocket a foot from the near abutment and its muzzlebrake a yard from the far one. It was a mess underneath. Now we'd just received a very experienced Chief Warrant Office. We weren't supposed to have that senior a CWO in the squadron, but we'd lost our captain motor officer due to family emergency. I radioed back to the CP to send him up in another chopper with his bedroll and to send every other operable M88 recovery vehicle in the squadron up the road. When he arrived, I told him to get the tank out and not to come back until he did. I left him the platoon for security in the high plateau jungle. I didn't expect to see him for two or three days and just hoped that the NVA or VC didn't catch on. He arrived back at the base before dark the first night with all vehicles. Fortunately, no one was hurt in the road wreck, and the tank was in surprisingly good shape. Some egos were bruised, though. I asked him if he would be our squadron maintenance officer, as we had a dire need. Warrant officers cannot by law be required to assume command positions, although they may if it is voluntarily. He took the job and was a crackerjack.

Polei Krong, Kontum Province, South Vietnam, December 1968

One day an irate radio message came in from 2nd Brigade HQ over the command net that my tanks had collapsed a bridge. Now, we did do this on isolated occasions, but I knew we had no tracks in that area that day, or I didn't think so. The culprits turned out to be a platoon of M42 twin 40mm Dusters. They all look like tanks to walking infantry.

January—December 1969

Highlights of 1969 include the conclusion of Operation McArthur and conducting of Operations Wayne Grey and Putnam Tiger. Operations continued in the central highlands as the division provided a screen along the Cambodian border and the Army of the Republic of Vietnam (ARVN) moved into positions to protect the civilian population centers of the central highlands. Under the command of Major General Donn R. Pepke, he concentrated the bulk of his forces near the population centers and used them as rapid deployment elements within his extremely large area of operation. The only tank battle of the war was fought by tanks of 1st Battalion, 69th Armor outside the Special Forces camp at Ben Het where they destroyed two Soviet built tanks. The policy of "Vietnamization" had begun with U.S. Army units gradually turning over their missions and areas of operations to the ARVN. One 4th Infantry Division soldier earned the Medal of Honor in 1969, and 610 were killed in hostile and non-hostile actions.

Greg Rollinger, Rosemount, MN
Company A, 1st Battalion, 8th Infantry Regiment

Vietnam—Arrival and First Patrol

I arrived in Vietnam on December 9, 1968, after being drafted on July 8, 1968, and spending my first five months of military life in basic training at Fort Campbell and AIT at Fort Lewis. I had been given the option of selecting my MOS during basic by extending my active service by one year, but I was determined to put in my two years of active duty and get out. So I took my chances. Nobody had ever clued me in on the army decision-making process, or how I should conduct myself in order to get a non-combat MOS. So I did my best on all the aptitude testing and army skills training, thinking that things would take care of themselves. I was therefore somewhat surprised when, towards the end of the basic training cycle, my name was called during formation one morning to qualify with the M-16. I became an 11-Bravo infantryman, and my life would never be the same.

After AIT and a short leave, I found myself at the 90th Replacement Center in Ben Hoa, Vietnam. There were four of us—Billy Smallwood, Rick Bochenski, Marlon Troxel and myself—who had all gone through training together and went to Vietnam on the same flight. Marlon and I were the closest, and when we were given the opportunity to name a unit we would prefer an assignment to, we asked for the 4th Infantry Division. Billy went to the 1st Cavalry Division and Rick was assigned to the Big Red One. (1st Infantry Division).

These were not enlightened decisions. We based it mostly on the information we had been given that there were fewer booby traps to worry about in the 4th Infantry Division's AO. We had no idea what we were getting into as far as either the terrain we would soon be humping, or the fact that we would be facing NVA Regulars.

After receiving our assignment to the 4th Infantry Division, Marlon and I rode a bus back over to Tan Son Nhut Airbase, were flown up to Camp Holloway, outside of Pleiku, on a C-130 and were bused over to the 4th Replacement Center at Camp Enari. We had already been three or four days in country without a rifle or any other weapon. Finally, after a couple of days of in-country orientation at Camp Enari, I was assigned to Company A, 1st Battalion, 8th Infantry Regiment. I was given my field gear, an M-16, loaded onto a duece and a half, and headed out to Dak To, where A company was operating. I said good-bye to Marlon before I left, since he had been assigned to a different unit, Company B, 2nd Battalion, 35th Infantry Regiment. Little did I know that this would be the last time I would see or talk to him. I later received a form letter from the Department of the Army, along with a returned letter that I had sent to Marlon, informing me that they could not deliver my letter since he had been killed in action on March 16, 1969.

The convoy to Dak To was uneventful. I was surprised by my introduction to the war to this point. The only directions I was given upon boarding the truck were, if the convoy was ambushed, dismount the truck on the opposite side and return fire. There was nobody in charge of this group of six replacements sitting in the back of the truck. Driving through the cities of Pleiku and Kontum and into the countryside on Highway 14, I felt uneasy not knowing what1077 to expect. The nonchalance of everyone I encountered made it seem like there couldn't have been a war going on. They all acted like we were on a drive through the countryside back in the States.

Upon our arrival at Dak To, we were directed to a tent where we would report to the Company A First Sergeant. Within five minutes of getting there, we were on our way to the helicopter pad since Company A, 1st Battalion, 8th Infantry Regiment was currently being resupplied. I had never been on a real helicopter, since the army only used mockups for practicing loading and unloading during AIT. When we got to the pad, the Huey was already there idling and being loaded with mail and other supplies for the company. We grabbed our rucksacks and other gear, jumped on board, and away we went.

Alpha Company was operating off Hill 1049, which is located about fourteen clicks directly south of Dak To. Hill 1049 was at the southern end of a ridgeline that extended up to the northwest, towards the Cambodia border. To the south and east, grassy plains extended off into the distance. To the north and west was triple canopy jungle.

The top of the hill where the company had dug in was void of any greenery and was covered with several inches of dust. The chopper pad was located thirty feet or so down the east side of the hill on a grassy knoll. We were instructed to keep our heads down when we exited the helicopter, since if you didn't on the uphill side of the chopper, there was a good possibility that your head would encounter the Huey's rotor as you proceeded up the hill. In fact, the story was that a FNG had done exactly that a short time before and had been decapitated on his first day in the field. When the chopper set down, we cautiously unloaded and waited until it had taken off before we headed up the hill to the company CP.

Captain Hockett, the CO, greeted us at the top of the hill and called his platoon leaders together to divvy us up. Two of us were assigned to the third platoon. I was assigned to the second squad, and another replacement from New York (I think his last name was Roth,) was assigned to the third squad. We had a platoon sergeant, Staff Sergeant Grinstead, who led me over to where my squad was located.

As we walked down the hill towards the second squad bunker, Sergeant Woodall, the squad leader, greeted me with the words, "Looks like we got a new M-60 machine gunner."

Not knowing what to say, I didn't say anything. I soon found out that the load for me to carry up and down the hills and through the jungle of the central highlands had just become much heavier.

The squad was made up of guys from all over the U.S. There were four guys from Georgia and Alabama, including Woodall and Posey, the current M-60 gunner. I was happy to find another Minnesota native in the squad, Richard "Bugs" Moran. I immediately connected with him, and we became good friends. It was a great bunch of guys, and I immediately felt accepted and a part of the squad. They were all more than willing to tell me how to survive in the boonies, show me how to pack my ruck, teach me how to cook C-rations, and all the other practical things you don't learn in training. Woodall had me set up my sleeping gear in the hooch he shared with Posey, Flannery and Hughes. I settled in as best I could and started marking off the days until I would go home.

First Patrol

Shortly after my arrival in the squad, our turn came up to conduct a short-range patrol. Woodall got his briefing and passed down the word to the rest of the squad to prepare us. The patrol was to be a three-day ambush with the primary location about three clicks to the northwest of Hill 1049. This being my first hump, Woodall gave me a break and had me carry my M-16 instead of the M-60 so I could observe how patrols were run. Since we were going to be out for three days, we each procured nine meals of C-rations and discarded what we didn't want. After filling our canteens, checking our weapons, and packing our rucks, we saddled up and headed out through the wire.

The first thing I learned after we passed through the perimeter wire was that everyone ignored what we had been told in training as far as carrying weapons was concerned. The first sound you heard was the bolt slamming forward on all the M-16's, chambering a round. The second sound you heard was the M-16 selector switch clicking off safe, to either semi or full automatic. The rifle was held at the ready, with the trigger finger just outside the trigger guard. The guys who had been in country for a while knew that the seconds gained by being ready to rock and roll could mean the difference between life or death. Later in my tour there were times when officers made us stop and clear our weapons when they heard us chambering rounds. So we would, but then quietly ease the bolt forward by holding on to the charging handle.

The patrol headed down off Hill 1049 through tall elephant grass that was over our heads. We followed the prescribed route into the triple canopy jungle and eventually made it to our ambush site. We set up on a small knoll where we had good cover and could observe a trail going through the area. After getting into position on the perimeter, setting my claymore out and positioning my gear so that I was prepared to react, I waited nervously for the start of my first night in the boonies.

With the high canopy and the thick bamboo filtering the light, it got dark early. After the sun had set, it was pitch black. You could not see your hand in front of your face. The jungle was full of many strange sounds that I didn't have a clue what their origin was. The mosquitoes were so bad the only escape was to use your poncho liner like a cocoon to try to keep them off your exposed skin. The night was uneventful, but I'm sure I didn't sleep. I couldn't wait for the sun to come up to give me the security of daylight. It was obvious we were not the owners of the night.

The next day began clear and peaceful. The only sound was the occasional bird chatter, letting us know we were in their territory. Since we were staying in the same location, we took advantage of the time when we were not on guard to write letters home and get some rest. In the early afternoon, I was propped up against a tree writing a letter when we suddenly heard the sound of bamboo and brush breaking down over the hill behind where I was sitting. The noise got louder and louder. It sounded like an entire NVA company was coming through the jungle and didn't care how much noise they made. I grabbed my M-16 and lay on my stomach, sighting my rifle where I knew the enemy would soon be cresting the hill. The rest of the squad was doing the same. To say I was scared would be an understatement. This would be my first action, and we were just a squad of less than ten guys, going up against what sounded like a much larger force.

Then they were upon us. Over the hill came four orangutans running through the underbrush as if it wasn't even there. When they saw us, they stopped in their tracks and stared. I'm sure my M-16 was shaking, and they soon figured out we were more scared than they were. After a couple of minutes, they headed off in a different direction, tearing through the jungle as they did before.

I regained my composure and thought about what had just happened. Nothing in training had prepared me for this. I was being rudely introduced to the jungle and had just gotten my first lesson as to who was in control. I was learning that not only did we have to be on constant guard against the enemy, but also the real inhabitants of the jungle, the wildlife.

The rest of the patrol was uneventful. When we had completed our mission, we packed up our gear and headed back up to the top of hill 1049. I felt relieved once we had walked back through the wire and joined the rest of the company.

Thus was my introduction to Vietnam and to what lay ahead of me for the coming year. Before leaving, I would experience the terror of firefights, the exhaustion of company operations, and the harsh realities of trying to survive in the jungle. I would get so thirsty I would drink water out of scum-covered, stagnant pools; get so filthy dirty that my uniform would literally rot away before I got a clean one; and I would see more wildlife than I had ever seen in a zoo back home. Snakes, spiders, fire ants, mosquitoes, monkeys, elephants, leeches and tigers lived where we operated. The jungle was a harsh world for the infantryman. You had to live in it to know it and to survive it; you had to respect it. I was lucky. I survived.

Donald P. Brathwaite, Laurelton, NY
Company C, 3rd Battalion, 8th Infantry Regiment

Operation 'Clean Up' Sweeps Local Hamlets

News item from Camp Enari: Operation "Clean Up" is being conducted in the Pleiku and Kontum Province area with plans to rid the cities and towns of loose waste and garbage. The combined effort, between U.S. and Vietnamese Forces, will continue under the supervision of the 4th Infantry Division, who are providing transportation, material needed, personnel, and engineering support within their resources in the effort.

In all areas where American units have contributed to an unsightly or unsanitary condition, commanders are taking direct action with U.S. assets to rectify the situation.

The division is also initiating cleanup campaigns with the Montagnard villages and hamlets for which they have civic action responsibility.

A complete police of eleven major highways in the designated areas has been conducted to one hundred meters on each side of the road with periodic inspection being made by Ivy Division headquarters to monitor the progress of the campaign and to insure that the job is being completed.

Upon the completion of the initial cleanup, a schedule will be organized to maintain the area on a continuing basis.

So remember, Ivymen, the next time you have trash which you wish to get rid of, wait until you have a trash can. It is a lot easier to maintain clean and sanitary conditions if everyone does his share in the beginning.

Thomas O'Connor, East Amherst, NY
Battalion Surgeon, 1st Squadron, 10th Cavalry Regiment

Rats

Rats are a part of life in Vietnam. Whenever and wherever we set up, there were rats. Either they had a superb communication system, which is unlikely, or they were so ubiquitous it merely seemed as though they followed us about. It fell to me, the Medical Officer, to do something about this rodent plague. I don't remember anyone ever being bitten by one, but there always was this emotional outcry whenever one fell onto the face of a sleeping GI. Whenever we were in a camp, there was no trouble getting the mosquito nets strung since they also served to keep the rats off the sleeper. It ordinarily was a problem trying to convince the troops to use their nets, because malaria was viewed as a way out of the country, but telling them about bubonic plague and the rats carrying the bacteria was a strong persuader.

There was no real solution to the rat problem, but that did not dissuade us, particularly after we got out the rat traps. These were odd rat traps, made all of wire, and when sprung, very much like the Bouncing Betty mines, would get the tripper about the midsection. The bait was anything edible, since the rats showed no discrimination in their culinary tastes. Actually, peanut butter worked best since it easily stuck to the trap. The bait was a minor problem in contrast to setting the trap. The trap had to be bent over on itself and then the latch was fixed. The latch, of course, was a trigger, and long before we got any rats, we were able to smash any number of fingers and knuckles of GIs.

The great hunters fanned out through the camp, carefully placing the traps. I placed one along the edge of my cot and the tent wall just behind the sandbag. I had seen a gray rat running there while I was lying in my cot.

The following morning every trap had a rat. In fact, one of the traps had two rats. Our success was fleeting, unfortunately; the rats got smarter, and the rate of killing them fell off to just a few each day. Then again, I think that the population was depleted enough that there were fewer to be trapped. I'm confident though that they were all replaced with a new round of baby rats. For a laugh, I would report the daily results at the staff meeting each night until the CO found it no longer amusing. I think he was just jealous since our success was greater that his.

Thomas O'Connor, East Amherst, NY
Battalion Surgeon, 1st Squadron, 10th Cavalry Regiment

The Patrol

Even in the morning it steamed. The sun was barely up, and we were sweating beneath our helmets and flak jackets. We were to go on a foot patrol through the bush that paralleled Highway 19. The reason I was going was simply that I was bored and I wanted to do something, so I asked the CO if I could go, and he agreed. I wanted to play soldier. I had a grease gun that I had gotten from one of the tankers. It was heavy and I had two magazines. I also had a ton of medical equipment with me in a large pack that I had on my pack. I was not bright enough to minimize the weight by spreading it among some of the other people.

The beginning was easy. We walked on the flat through some very open country and then into the hills that rose at some ridiculous angle and then plunged at a more ridiculous angle until we entered a wood that was dense and impassable. I became entangled for a moment and since I was last in the column, the rest of the troops never noticed that I became separated. I could hear the noise they were making in the bush ahead of me, but I could see nothing. For one of the few times in my life, I felt a charge of fear. I knew that I was afraid of being captured more than anything else, but I also knew that I could easily get killed by my own troops if I startled them abruptly.

Suddenly the dense brush came to a clearing, and there they all were out in front of me. Oddly, there was one guy with the odd name for a soldier—"Slaughter" standing in the clearing. He was standing in the shaft of sunlight that made him stand out from the world in this ethereal glow, He stood there just for the instant. The next time I remember seeing him he was dead.

The patrol came down this short grade to a small river. We waded the river and then began to climb the other side. It was steep beyond all reason. I slid back to the bank of the river several times because of the steepness, the wetness of the ground and the weight of my pack. I finally managed, with some help, to pull myself up the hill by grabbing onto some branches. I reached the top breathless, nauseated, dizzy and wishing that I had been in better shape or that I might not make it further. A rest was called, and the lieutenants in command pored over the maps, and from the most casual observation I could see that they were lost. I went to talk with them and suggested that the South was directly ahead. Their compass was not working, but my ears were. I could hear the traffic in the distance on the highway. I knew it went north and south, so our orientation was complete.

Within moments the radios were active, and the lieutenant came to tell me that the helicopter was coming to get me. They wanted me to see a Vietnamese chief who was sick. The LOH (Light Observation Helicopter) came for me. I gave my pack to my unhappy medics who, I think, were beginning to appreciate that one must be sure not to be the recipients of heavy packs that could have been made lighter with some judicious advice. In the middle of the flight, the officer who saw me with the grease gun suggested that I might do myself a lot of harm if I was not careful with dangerous playthings. By the time we got to the area of the sick man, the pickup was called off. I never knew why. That night the CO asked if I had enjoyed the Boy Scout walk in the woods. He said that he knew that nothing was there simply by flying over it. I knew then the difference between the man who flies and the man who walks. It is from A Day in the Life of Ivan Denisovich by Solzhenitsyn. "A man who is cold cannot even talk to a man who is warm."

Thomas O'Connor, East Amherst, NY
Battalion Surgeon, 1st Squadron, 10th Cavalry Regiment

The Birth

This is the tale of the Montagnard woman and the breech birth and the death of the baby, their presence and their exit from my life.

The 4th Medical Battalion was the Brigade medical service. Actually, it was the division medical service. The tents that were in the Oasis were the 3rd Brigade's portion of the medical service.

On the afternoon of a day that has no other distinction, I was there with Clary and the other doctors doing nothing more than the little one did while wasting time to prevent the drudge of the day from taking too much of a toll. An enlisted man came to the tent and asked us to come and see a Montagnard woman at one of the villages; she had been in labor for many days.

It was plain on examination why this woman had suffered with this prolonged and now arrested labor. The child was a breech presentation with a single foot presentation.

She was a Montagnard woman, a mountain woman since that is the meaning of the French word. They are different racially from the Vietnamese. In general, the two groups were hostile to one another and, for us, we inherited whatever the goodwill that the French had developed among these people to the extent that they were friendly and kind to us. This is in contrast to the Vietnamese who would use every opportunity to take advantage of the Americans to directly steal from them or try to pander to them the remarkable eternally virgin sisters.

With this lady were some members of the family, the husband in the fragmented shirt of a military uniform, the hat, and the standard loincloth.

We labored to deliver the child with all the effort and the skill that we could muster. Since not one of us was an obstetrician, our level of skill was not great. The patient tolerated this whole effort that must have been painful without a cry or yell. She lay there with her husband next to her head while these white men in the green tried to deliver their child. Finally, we did. The child took an agonal breath from the limp body and then no more. The attempts at reviving the child were frantic and fruitless. The baby was dead. In the moments that followed, there was no rancor. There was no crying. There was nothing but the parents carefully wrapping their newly born and newly dead baby in a cloth. The woman carried the child in her arms, and the last I saw of them was they were silhouetted again the afternoon sun and framed by the flap of the tent.

Whatever good or ill we were able to do that afternoon, I was forever cured of the notion that Asiatics treated life carelessly. To them, as to us, the lives of those that we love are profoundly dear, and that dignity is not on the backs of those who wear the finest but in the soul of those who behave that way under the greatest of trials.

Dan Martus, Nashville, TN
Company D, 1st Battalion, 22nd Infantry Regiment

Following a Tradition

Walking across the tarmac at Cam Ranh Bay, trying to adjust my eyes to the blinding light and heat waves reflecting off the concrete and sand, I remember looking at the guys who were walking in the opposite direction. They had already served their twelve-month tour and were on their way home. They were quiet, subdued, and there was heaviness about their face and eyes. For me, it was a stark realization that the tour that lay ahead for me would be long, painful, and lonely.

The knot in the pit of my stomach had actually begun forming halfway across the Pacific during my flight to the Republic of Vietnam. As I gazed out the airplane window and reflected upon the journey that I was embarking on, I thought about my own particular reasons and feelings about going to Vietnam. Both my parents served in the Navy in World War II: my father as a radio technician, and my mother as an ensign who taught navigation to pilots. My Uncle Bern was in the army (infantry) and was at the invasion of Normandy beach on D-Day. There were several from my high school and neighborhood who served in Vietnam; some were wounded and some never made it home. All selflessly and courageously gave of themselves to protect the freedoms that most Americans come to expect and take for granted.

For me, even though I did not want to go, I knew that I should. Therefore, with reluctance, pride, fear, and a sense of duty, I followed the traditions of my family and community and left for this strange unknown land called Vietnam.

Each day I waited for my orders with anticipation. Some left for "The Big Red One," some went to the 25th Infantry Division, others went to the Americal.

Almost a week went by, and my orders finally came through. PFC Daniel J. Martus was assigned to 1st Battalion, 22nd Infantry Regiment, 4th Infantry Division, Pleiku. I later learned that Pleiku was in the central highlands where the jungle was thick and the terrain was hilly. The guys that had been there a while said that this was NVA territory where the enemy were veteran fighters and well armed. They also said that the 4th Infantry Division was notorious for long stays in the field, requiring heavy rucksacks, and a lot of humping through the jungle. Oh well, let the journey begin.

We were somewhat in formation as we offloaded from the truck at the base camp in Pleiku. A sergeant stood before us, looking tattered and torn, as he was assigning us to our units. He said that one of the companies had just been in a serious firefight and needed replacements. He asked us if we had a weapons preference. Some said the M-16, some said the M-79.

I just said, "Give me the biggest thing that you got."

I was assigned to Gary Hurl's gun team as an ammo bearer, and that's how my apprenticeship as a M-60 gunner began with Delta Company, third platoon, a FNG grunt.

Dan Martus, Nashville, TN
Company D, 1st Battalion, 22nd Infantry Regiment

Rucksack Packing—An Art Form

Remember that first trip out to the bush? You were young, you felt strong and tough, fresh out of infantry training. You were issued a mountain of stuff: clothes, bedding, mess kit, canteens, weapon(s), ammo, hand grenades, claymores, a machete, C4, C-rations, and so on. Were we really supposed to carry all this stuff? The old timers' packs seemed so compact and neat while the new guys looked like they were carrying sheds. Adding to the burden, the new guy had to carry the D-handle shovel.

Even though I was probably one of the bigger guys in my platoon, I still continually looked for ways to streamline my pack. And also, by someone else's misfortune, I learned that an incorrectly packed or fitted rucksack could adversely impact your overall center of gravity which would, more than likely, result in disaster.

While coming down a steep hill, I heard a lot of noise coming from behind me. There were clattering thuds, "Oooff-Ooofff...awww sh-t!" A soldier was tumbling head over heels down the trail. Rucksack, legs, arms, weapons, steel pot—all in a cartwheel motion. After what seemed like an eternity, the soldier finally stopped at the bottom of the hill, sprawled out on his back, his rucksack had flipped around to his chest, and his steel pot was covering his face. This "center of gravity" lesson gave all but the man himself a nice moment of comic relief.

Humping through the jungles of the mountainous central highlands was physically difficult and not for the weak of heart, to say the least. Some of the unwritten rules for the veteran grunts were: Never breathe hard when passing a new guy on the trail, always use your neck towel to wipe the sweat off your face before passing a FNG (Funny New Guy), never break stride when humping up a steep hill, and never warn a FNG of the "wait-a-minute" vines. A final unwritten rule was, when at the top, stay standing with your rucksack on, do not drink water, smile and breathe easily as you watch the FNGs struggle with their huge rucksacks up the hill.

After a few months in the bush, and no longer a FNG, my pack was trimmed down to a manageable size. I was now able to keep stride with the rest of the veteran grunts and take my turn at showing up the FNGs.

It was amazing how we found little ways to entertain ourselves while out in the jungle.

Greg Rollinger, Rosemount, MN
Company A, 1st Battalion, 8th Infantry Regiment

A Game of Hearts

In March 1969, the entire 1st Brigade of the 4th Infantry Division, made up of the 1st Battalion, 8th Infantry Regiment; 3rd Battalion, 8th Infantry Regiment; and 3rd Battalion, 12th Infantry Regiment, was part of an operation code named "Wayne Grey." This operation was conducted near the Vietnam-Cambodia border in and around the Plei Trap Valley of Vietnam. The 24th and 66th NVA regiments were known to be there in force and we were sent in to block and destroy their transportation routes, which linked them to the Ho Chi Minh Trail.

I was an M-60 machine gunner in second squad of Company A, 1st Battalion, 8th Infantry Regiment's third platoon. I had been in country for three months by then and had yet to see any major action. Company A had been moving around the countryside from Dak To, to Pleiku, to Blackhawk, to VC Valley, and now to the Cambodian border area. We had been humping all over the central highlands looking for the enemy with limited success. We didn't have that problem in the Plei Trap.

At the beginning of March, Company A was in pretty good shape as to the number of men in the field. At least I know we were in second squad and third platoon. We had ten guys in second squad and had a good complement of guys who were experienced, along with guys like me who were replacements and were still learning. We had an E-7 acting platoon leader, Sergeant First Class Don White, who was on his second tour and kept us straight. Overall, it was a good bunch of guys who got along well together.

On March 2, Company A combat assaulted into LZ Turkey. It was on the banks of the Dak Hondrai River and in the midst of many footpaths, truck roads, and river crossings, all heavily used by the NVA. As we began patrol operations out of this LZ, it was clear that the NVA were in control of the area and intent upon keeping it. Just about every patrol made contact with the enemy, and, once engaged, the NVA were staying around for a fight.

I remember sitting on top of a bunker, right on the river bank, pulling guard duty for guys who were in the river taking a bath when I saw several NVA cross the river upstream from our position and wave at us. I don't know if they thought we were NVA or if they were just that brazen, but the bullets from my M-60, which started going their way probably enlightened them as to who we were and what we were there for.

There was another time when a patrol from another platoon across the river made contact with several NVA. Some "fast movers" (air force jets) were in the area. They came in with napalm bombs, which they dropped on the fleeing enemy. I have a vivid recollection of watching all of this from the LZ—the jets coming in low and releasing the bombs, the bombs tumbling towards the ground, and the fiery explosion when they hit. I was glad they were on our side after watching this lethal show. After the jets had expended their ordinance, our platoon was sent across the river to the contact area to do an assessment. We found several NVA bodies, burned by the napalm, lying on a wide trail. They were fully equipped NVA soldiers with khaki uniforms and brand new AK-50 rifles. You could tell they had been running, as their legs and arms were frozen forever in running positions.

For the first two weeks of the operation, things seemed to be going well for Company A. We had the highest enemy body count in the battalion, and third platoon had the highest in the company. We were kicking ass! We were getting experience under fire, and we were surviving. The third platoon was so far unscathed. That was soon to change.

On March 10 we dismantled LZ Turkey and moved out to do a BDA (bomb damage assessment) of an area where a B-52 "arc light" had been conducted. It was thought to have a large concentration of NVA in the area, thus warranting the B-52 strike. We were going to find out if they were still there. On March 12 three platoons and the company HQ, approximately seventy-five men in all, reached the bomb impact area. As we walked into the area, it was hard to imagine how anyone could have survived the carnage. Huge trees were down and splintered, craters twenty of thirty feet across had been blown out of the jungle floor, and debris was strewn everywhere. Somehow, the enemy had survived. What was later estimated to be an NVA regiment, six hundred to eight hundred men, was dug in guarding a hospital complex and was waiting for us.

Fourth platoon was on point, with third platoon next in line. As we approached the first set of bunkers, the NVA sprang their ambush. All hell broke loose up front, so those of us in third platoon dropped our rucks and ran forward to reinforce the fourth platoon. This left about one hundred yards between the forward two platoons and the rest of the company.

The enemy was everywhere. This was one time that they were going to stay and fight. They had laid out their personal possessions in front of them in preparation for dying. They had us outnumbered, and it was their intent to wipe us out. They had snipers who tied themselves into the trees above us. Their bunkers were linked together, and, as one NVA was killed in a bunker, another would pop up and take his place. They got in behind the point platoons and had both parts of the company completely surrounded. These were fully equipped NVA with pith helmets and web gear across their chests that held three banana clip magazines for their AKs. They were using B-40 rockets, RPGs, grenades, and automatic weapons against us.

Shortly after the fight began, the lieutenant for fourth platoon was wounded along with our third platoon leader, Sergeant First Class White. It was then that Specialist Fourth Class Jerry Loucks from third squad, third platoon, took over command of the point element, and with his leadership, we were able to link up with the rest of the company and bring all of the wounded with us. It took us about eight hours to fight our way about one hundred yards, even with the help of artillery, gunships, jets and everything else we could bring on line to support us.

After we had established a single perimeter for the company, a dust-off was called in to take out our wounded. As the first Huey made its approach into the LZ that had been hacked out of the jungle, the NVA opened up and drove it off. The chopper pilot, Mike Rinehart, called our CO and told him he was coming back in and we should open up around the perimeter to suppress the enemy fire. The word was passed around and as the dust-off came in, we had our "mad minute" to try to keep the NVA heads down.

Following is Mike Rinehart's recollection of that mission.

"To get in, we had to hover under the canopy and into a hillside, and pretty much had to mow our way in, clearing some small stuff out with the main rotor. I remember, I think, there had been a forest fire because the underbrush had been burned. It was still smoking, and we were blowing black soot everywhere. Your guys got loaded in a hurry, and when I hovered backwards out of the hole you were in and turned around, a damn LOH was blocking my flight path out of the jungle canopy. I figured, "What the hell? He's providing cover for us." Instead, he was in the way and caused us to slow down to a crawl. By the time I yelled at him on the emergency frequency (I didn't know what frequency he was on) to get the hell out of the way, I heard and felt the rounds impacting us from the left. Hell, even I knew we were too tempting a target. My armored seat took two hits (felt like a sledgehammer), and the ceramic flaked off on the inside giving me a purple butt—and a subsequent Purple Heart. I heard the rounds hitting back where the wounded were, and some zinging through. Everyone was yelling—except you guys. You were as scared as we were, but at least you were wide-eyed quiet about it.

"The pilot thought I'd been hit and tried to take the controls. We had a yelling match that didn't last but a second. I finally got him to watch the instruments and call a May Day. We were getting ready to crash, but the damn thing surprised me and kept flying, despite the best efforts of the NVA, the LOH, the pilot and me.

"When we landed (as I said, I can't remember where; I just know I got you guys to the nearest doctors), I do remember getting out and helping unload. I helped pull two or three out, and when I saw the guy in the 'hellhole,' the open hole in the center of the helicopter used for winching up casualties, I personally got him out and on a stretcher. I remember looking back when he first got on the aircraft, holding his arm, and smiling. I remember thinking, 'This guy's got the million dollar wound, and he knows he's going home.' When I saw him slumped over in the hellhole, it was the first time I almost lost it. I think he was dead then. I still dream about the guy's eyes…open, unblinking, and dusted in sand. While trying to look for wounds and bleeding, for some stupid reason, I tried also to get the sand out of his eyes. I still dream about that one.

"The second chopper you mention was, I think, me, too. After getting you guys and the others out to 'Mary Lou' or to the 71st Evac, we found there were lots of holes, but nothing of any major significance damaged, so we took off and continued pulling missions. We returned to the same place, or close by, once or twice more and pulled another ten or so out of there. I remember thinking, the whole company is doomed."

Greg Rollinger picks back up with the story.

After getting all the wounded and the bodies of the KIA (killed in action) out and getting a resupply of ammunition, we tried to dig fighting positions as night approached. The ground was so hard and we were so exhausted from the day's events, the most we could manage was getting a shallow fighting position carved out of the ground. We spent the night at one hundred percent alert waiting for the ground attack that luckily, didn't materialize.

The next morning we sent out a patrol to link up with the remaining members of a Company E recon patrol that had been involved in the same fight the day before. We also retrieved our rucksacks and other gear that had been left behind. We heard the thump of enemy mortar rounds leaving their tubes, but they landed outside our perimeter and didn't cause any damage.

Believing that a ground attack was soon to follow, and having lost about one third of the company either killed or wounded, our CO got permission to withdraw from the area instead of going back into the bunker complex, as the battalion commander had desired. We left the same way we went in, with the rear element engaging the NVA as they attacked our position. We suffered several more casualties as we moved three or four clicks to the location where Company C, 1st Battalion, 8th Infantry was set up.

Such was my baptism under fire. I had survived this major initial battle, as had the rest of my second squad. The same could not be said for the rest of the platoon or for the company. We had lost our E-7 platoon leader, and several guys from third squad who were severely wounded. The company had taken so many casualties that we were combined with the remnants of Company C, which had also taken casualties in separate engagements, to form Task Force Alpha under the command of a major.

For the next two weeks we continued to patrol in the Plei Trap. We engaged in several more firefights, including another major ambush on March 19 and 20. There we engaged the NVA in another bunker complex alongside a road being used to truck supplies in from Cambodia. During this firefight, third platoon was decimated, with many WIAs, including another E-7 acting platoon leader, and one killed in action from first squad. It was at this time that our company became ineffective as a field unit, having lost about half the company during the past several weeks. The company was choppered out of the field and taken to Firebase 20, where, along with Company C, we provided perimeter security for the battalion commander and a battery of 105mm howitzers.

FSB 20 was on a hilltop within sight of the Cambodian border. It was a wellestablished firebase with sleeping bunkers with lots of overhead cover. It had fighting positions with trenches linking them all together, a cleared field of fire with concertina wire ringing the perimeter, plus many claymores and trip flares to establish a good defensive line. The fire base encompassed two hilltops with a saddle in between, which is where the LZ was located. A separate perimeter was surrounding each hilltop. Third platoon was responsible for a portion of the main hilltop perimeter, from the LZ to the northwest on the Cambodia border side of the hill.

The firebase was used for a staging point for resupply of the rest of the 1st Battalion, 8th Infantry companies operating in the area. C-rations, water, mail, personnel, and whatever else that was going out to the companies would be first brought out to our LZ, and then, when the companies were in position to be resupplied, put back on the Hueys and taken to that company's LZ.

In addition to the battalion TOC and artillery battery, there was a mess tent, which provided us the luxury of hot meals once or twice a day. After what we had been through the past few weeks, we were happy that we had been given a chance to rest and rebuild before getting sent back out to the field.

The NVA had an artillery forward observer positioned where he could monitor activity on the firebase. We would get incoming artillery rounds shot at us from Cambodia when we were lined up for meals, or if there was lots of activity down on the LZ. This was occurring at least two or three times each day. When we heard the guns fire across the Cambodia border, everyone would dive into their bunkers and wait it out. The 105mm howitzer battery on the firebase would try to get a read on where the enemy guns were located and return fire. At first, we were all pretty scared, since, for most of us, this was the first time that we had been on the receiving end of artillery. But after a few days, we became complacent and used the time to drink beer or soda and to play cards until the "all clear" was sounded.

On March 26, 1969, the daily afternoon barrage started. Second squad was waiting it out in a bunker right next to the path leading down to the LZ. Danny Hinkel, Bugs Moran, Harold Proctor, and I were drinking soda and playing "hearts." After a half dozen rounds had landed without hitting anything, there was a lull in the activity, but no "all clear" had been given. Suddenly, Posey, who was acting squad leader at the time, came running into the bunker saying he needed a volunteer. Apparently the battalion commander had decided to retrieve the C-rations which were destined for the companies out in the field and bring them up the hill so they wouldn't be blown up. Posey was going, and he needed volunteers from each of the squads to help. Danny said he would go, so he put down his cards, put on his helmet, and ran out with Posey. The rest of us waited, cards in hand, for Danny to return so that we could finish the hand.

They had been gone for a few minutes when we heard the sound of the enemy guns firing once again. Within a few seconds the incoming rounds landed, and this time it was close by. We wondered if our guys were safe.

Then, Posey burst into the bunker, with a terrified look on his face, and stated, "Danny's dead."

We just looked at each other, not wanting to believe what he said. Apparently Danny had taken almost a direct hit from one of the enemy rounds. A large piece of shrapnel went through the back of his steel pot and killed him. His body was loaded on a helicopter and we never saw him again. He was the first to be killed in action in our squad. We had been right in the middle of the major firefights the company engaged in during the past month and had survived. The harsh reality of our vulnerability had now been thrown in our faces. It was strictly the luck of the draw who lived and who died, who won or who lost. Much like a game of hearts.

In a few days Operation Wayne Grey was terminated, and FSB 20 was dismantled. Our company was down to thirty-eight guys in the field, less than half of what we had started with just thirty days before. None of the platoons had made it through March without any casualties. What was left of Company A, 1st Battalion, 8th Infantry, was taken to An Khe where we pulled bridge guard duty on Highway 19 until the company was rebuilt.

According to the Brigade Commander's analysis of Operation Wayne Grey, its purpose was accomplished, as evidenced by the lack of major enemy post-Tet offensive action near Kontum City. The initial combat assaults into the Plei Trap Valley surprised the enemy and caused him to deal with an unexpected threat to his rear. With an American battalion astride the NVA's principal line of communication, further offensive action endangered their maneuverability and disrupted their timetable for a post-Tet offensive. The NVA were forced back to their sanctuary in Cambodia.

For the infantrymen, Operation Wayne Grey was a nightmare. Those of us who survived will never be the same. Those who didn't will live forever in our hearts and in our thoughts.

Thomas O'Connor, East Amherst, NY
Battalion Surgeon, 1st Squadron, 10th Cavalry Regiment

The Oasis—Mother's Day 1969

It was Saturday, May 10, the day before Mother's Day 1969. A sign hung on the cabinet door: "O'Connor's Quality Sandbag Construction." My medics had put it there, and the effect pleased me greatly, particularly as the beer flowed and the warmth from the glow of these men I had known for eight months filled the bunker.

Although we had been here at the Oasis earlier in the year and labored in the heat to raise a bunker, we moved from it when we went to the Michelin Rubber plantation. By the time we came back, our bunker was someone else's. Now, we had the 1st Squadron, 69th Armor bunker, but it was not the same as the one we had built. To be fair, the 1st Squadron did a better job than we did, but it was still not the same. They obviously had the help of the engineers. We had only our own sweat and effort. Sheraton and me, Flaherty and all the others had labored in the red clay and heat of the central highlands. Now I was leaving them and this place that had become home for another place and other people. This was my farewell party.

We had beer, we had stories and we had one another's company. It was all there was, and it was all I could have asked. We sang and laughed. I was to go to another post in Saigon. Sexton, my executive officer, was also leaving and the loss to me was getting larger. My last days were here and they laid heavily on me. My replacement, Ben Pope, was already present and already named Gentle Ben by the Chaplain. I had no qualm about leaving him, since I never thought what I had done was so very important or consequential and in truth, it wasn't. Somewhere around 2200 hours or so the party broke up and the troops made their ways to their tents or their bunkers. The guards had long been posted in the line of the bunkers on the perimeter.

Captain Tarrant had made all the troops take down their weapons and clean them and test fire them just a day earlier, a routine act of a good officer, and it saved the lives of many of us. The artillery behind us fired their H&Is over our tents, but I fell asleep from the beer and the night's excitement.

In the midst of a far-away dream, I could hear the guns shooting. Insistently, urgently and frequently they fired, and I woke up. I lay there for a moment until I heard the word out of my dream, the sound of the nightmare: the last seconds of your life are here.

"Incoming! Incoming! Incoming!"

The aim of Vietnamese and the targets they chose would randomly distinguish the living from the dead and wounded. From the distant reaches of my dream I clawed into reality and climbed into my fatigues. The mortars hit again. I put my boots on. The mortars hit again, and the sound of the shrapnel tore into the sandbags and the tent above me; instinctively I ducked. I grabbed my .45 caliber pistol, forgot my helmet and ran out the front of the tent for the command bunker. Within the first steps, the mortars hit to my left with a muffled crump and a burst of orange fire, producing shell fragments that whined around my head and passed into the night. Not more than two minutes had gone, but I was alive and not hurt.

One of the first people I saw was the Squadron Sergeant Major clad in his drawers and tee shirt, helmet and boots, pistol belt and sidearm. He was funny and he knew it. He even used his obviously humorous appearance to help with the tension of the moment.

There was a lot of automatic weapons fire among the sounds of the explosions. It was to our left, but close enough to distinguish the sound of the M-60s and the AK-47s. An AK-47 cut through the darkness like a scythe. It was an eerie sound—a long, purposeful, intended sweep of bullets. I knew people were dying at that very instant.

I jumped up from my seat on the tailgate of the APC, went to the CO, Lieutenant Colonel Renick, and asked permission to go to the medical bunker. He refused. He told me there was nothing I could do. I left him and sat down for a minute and the call came—we had serious casualties. I went to the CO repeatedly, and again he refused. It did not occur to me that I was refusing to obey a direct order. I had to go. I had casualties, and I was one hundred yards away and doing nothing for them. They needed me, and I needed to be with them.

My .45 was without an ammunition clip, so I borrowed one from Ben Pope. I also borrowed his flashlight. The shelling seemed to be lessening as I left the command bunker and ran along the path until I came to a sharp right turn. I fell over a tent stake and cut my leg. I could feel the cut, but it didn't hurt. I was barely able to see the path for twenty feet before a sharp left turn into a gully that separated the artillery from an open place behind the bunkers. The raised mound of earth to my right shielded me from the grazing machine gun fire. The artillery was quiet. I went along this path until I came to the level of the motor pool bunker, and I crossed the mound behind its protection.

The motor pool bunker had been built as a medical bunker. It was tall enough to easily allow ten people inside, standing upright. There were two bunks against the wall on the right and on the back wall at the lower corner there was an opening placed by the original doctor so he would have a rapid exit to the rear. He had a great fear of being trapped with no way out. The reason for the opening was gone (the fear of the Doc's of being trapped), but the opening was still there. A man could get through the opening only by squatting down or going on hands or knees. When the first mortars hit, the troops in the adjacent tents ran for the first overhead cover. Twenty or more ran to the motor pool bunker. Several ran through the front; others entered through the rear opening. They were a crowded mass of bodies, under cover to avoid the plunging mortar fire. Simultaneously with the first mortars the sappers rocketed two adjacent bunkers on the perimeter with B-40 rockets killing several people, including Jules. He was a black kid with a good heart and sense of humor. With the two bunkers destroyed, the sappers and the riflemen came across the PSP runway and were in the compound. They were headed for the guns, but in their haste they failed to see or to appreciate a large engine that growled in the middle of the compound.

It was a large generator the warrant officer in charge of the section had filched, borrowed, scrounged from the Air Force in exchange for some bauble. It was an oversized generator that gave all the light for the compound. It lit the light bulbs in the command bunker and the lights that hung from the ceiling in the motor pool bunker. It illuminated and showed the sweat and relief of the men who now were under the cover of the reinforced roof. This same light must have silhouetted the men getting into the bunker from the rear and attracted the attention of one of the infiltrators. He ran up behind the bunker and squatted down at the opening as the Vietnamese do daily. He saw all the legs of American soldiers milling together in this crowded room. He stuck the AK-47 through the opening and fired. He had to have squinted from the flashes, and the cordite must have burned his eyes, but a deep sense of pleasure must have filled his heart as the bullets tore through Calhoun's thighs and the thighs and the genitals of Sergeant Sundee.

It must have filled the empty coffers of his revenge when the bullets tore through the head of Sergeant Slaughter while Private First Class Weeden was cut down at his legs, and then the bullets smashed through his face. The light went out as desperate hands tore at the bulb that a moment before had brought solace and now aided the destruction. The firing stopped when the magazine went empty and a body fell across the opening. The darkness became complete.

The sounds of death, the rattles of breath through bloodfilled pipes, the screams and the groans saturated the darkness. The terror of the wounded and the near wounded mingled with the smell of blood and the tissue that lay on the floor and plastered the walls. Sergeant Shelton and Turnbow dragged the wounded to the medical bunker twenty-five feet away. The rest helped, and everyone fled to the medical bunker.

I could see the outline of the bunker. I climbed the incline and tried to get into the motor pool bunker, but I could not get into the small opening in the rear. Something blocked the opening. It was heavy and soft. I went around the side of the bunker and shined the flashlight at the two GIs by the blast shield so they would not shoot at me. I went into the bunker through the front, slipped on the floor, and fell getting myself wet with the slimy surface. I shined the light and saw Slaughter's body, his skull largely gone. When I last had seen him alive it was on patrol in the sunlight; now he was on his knees and dead. Another man lay on the floor.

The floor was a mess of coagulating blood, brains and tissues glistening in the flashlight's beam. At the far wall, blocking the opening to the back, was another torn body. The darkness shielded me from the sight when I turned off the flashlight. I went back outside and stayed low behind the blast shield with two GIs. I told them I was going to the medical bunker thirty or forty feet away.

The medical bunker was a very large structure with multiple rooms and had been used as the command bunker before we arrived. The walls were telephone poles and the ceiling eight-by-eight planks of wood all painted green. Each room was separated from the other by walls of two-by-six planks. A small room was on the left. This was where Lieutenant Sexton slept and where I had done my calculus homework by a small desk light. On the right was a much larger room used as the medical treatment area. There were three more rooms: two opposite one another off this common hallway and the final large room in the back, crossing the hallway.

Running the last few feet, I sidestepped two bodies laid out along the front wall against the sandbags. The blast shield in front of the medical bunker was partially torn apart since it obstructed entrance to anyone carrying a stretcher, but still protected a few armed GIs who were crouched holding their weapons and peering into the darkness. I went past them and into the medical room on the right, took my weapon off and gave the flashlight to one of the men. It was very crowded with excited people. I saw Sexton and told him to identify and count the dead and report it to the CO. He told me the most seriously injured were in the back, and I ought to see them. There were lights still on, which allowed us to see and evaluate the wounded.

In the large room in the back Sergeant Sundee was hollering, "They got me in the dick! They got me in the dick!"

He was right although his penile laceration across the glans was minor, but painful and likely resulting from a bone fragment in the compound fracture of the left femur produced by the bullet. When I checked his feet,

I could feel pulses. The blood vessels were intact. The wound although large was not bleeding any longer, and there was no danger to him. Morphine plus some antibiotics were needed along with the stabilization of his leg. In the room to the right lay Steven Calhoun. Both of his thighs were torn apart and fractured. The blood kept oozing from the depths of his wound; there were no pulses and no identifiable bleeders. Pressure on the wound saturated the gauze and he continued to bleed. His right hand was also torn badly as the bullet or a fragment had cut into the bone and the tendon. There was no bleeding from this. We started an IV in his arm to replace his plasma volume. There was no blood available to us. He complained of the heat, his blood pressure barely present, but he was conscious. I knew Calhoun well. He was a kid from New York City and we always talked whenever we'd see each other.

"How are you doing, Doc? Didn't mean to get you out on a night like this." Calmer now than I had ever been in my life, my sense of order had been created, the wounded were all seen, all the tags identifying the wounds were filled out and attached. The shells still hit the bunker, but the sound was muffled by the thousands of sandbags. We waited. My energy was so great I saw the wounded repeatedly.

Shortly after I had come in and some chaos had quieted, I saw a soldier violently shaking and holding an AK-47 tightly in his hands. I stopped and asked what was going on. When the mortar fire came in, he ran to the bunker but forgot his rifle. He ran back to the tent to get it but it was so dark he couldn't see. He squatted down on his haunches so he could feel around under his bunk for his M-16. As he rummaged and the mortars landed, a Vietnamese walked in the other side of the tent and addressed him in Vietnamese. The Vietnamese thought he was a comrade because of the squatting and came closer. When he was close enough, the American jumped him.

He told me, "I hit him up along side the head and grabbed his weapon. He ran that way, and I ran the other."

I could not pry the AK-47 from his grip.

The acrid smell of tear gas began to burn our eyes and noses as it spread around the compound from the supplies of tear gas contained in the CONEX boxes and struck by mortars. Now this tear gas agent was torturing the very people who might have used it to defend themselves.

Calhoun was getting sicker. He wandered in and out of consciousness with an occasional comment. The choppers could not come until light and it was still dark. He had stopped bleeding. There was no more blood to bleed. In the first gray of morning, the first of the choppers came and took away Calhoun, Sundee, and the others who were badly hurt. The rest were taken by jeep or truck to the 4th Medical Battalion and evacuated from there.

The route to and from the 4th Medical Battalion went through the still acrid air from the residual tear gas, and when I came back, GIs on the PSP runway were gawking at the enemy dead. There were six or seven bodies, it was hard to know, since the bodies had been terribly destroyed from the impact of the bullets and the explosions of the satchel charges they had carried. One body lay there with its bowels out onto the runway; several had large pieces of their chests gone. One had his arm torn from his body, and the arm lay there separate from the rest of him. A stray dog, ordinarily food for the Vietnamese, was eating the disembodied Vietnamese arm, while GIs stood about taking pictures. I kicked at the dog and missed, I raged at the soldiers, and they left. The graves registration people came and scooped the bodies unceremoniously up into body bags. In a few hours there were only holes in the tents, in the bunkers and the dried blood and brain on the floor and PSP.

One of the GIs told me he had killed a Vietnamese on the perimeter. He had killed him with a machine gun.

"Good shooting," I said. I felt words hang in the air, so blasphemous and empty, so devoid of meaning. The sound of them in my mind's ear still embarrasses me.

A patrol was mounted to go out beyond the wire and find the enemy: a lieutenant leading, closely followed by twenty men. They had gone less than fifty meters when they were bracketed by mortar fire. The lieutenant was hit in the elbow and was the only casualty.

The planes, F-100s, came bombing and strafing, and then the "Smoky" gun ships and the Cobra gunships shot up the ridge to our front. There was no return fire. A short time later I returned to the area of the motor pool bunker when a single shell landed outside the perimeter. Perhaps it was a shell or just a grenade or a booby trap. I jumped into the motor pool bunker; the bodies were all gone. All the cries were buried in the sand.

I met Sergeant Major Tadashi Mori, a Nisei, from the 442nd Regiment from World War II. He told me to avoid the CO since he was angry with me for disobeying orders. The chaplain had suggested me for a decoration. The sergeant major said more likely there would be a court martial. To avoid it all, he suggested I get on the convoy and leave at the first opportunity.

I packed my gear and wasted the rest of the day until the convoy was ready to go. I climbed aboard and went back to Camp Enari. The next day, Sexton and I went to the 91st Evacuation Hospital at the Pleiku Air Force Base to see Calhoun and check on the other wounded. He was still alive, wrapped in blood soaked plaster and bandages. I was sure he would live through it, but he didn't. He died on May 18, 1969. Sergeant Sundee would lose his leg after two years in the hospital. Sergeant Shelton received a Silver Star, his second in his second war. Turnbow won a Silver Star, as did Captain Tarrant. It was the last time I saw these people except for Sexton and him not for many years. I have found Shelton and Sundee after thirty years of wondering. Calhoun, Jules, and Slaughter are on the Wall in Washington. Three guys at the listening post were captured and returned after the war. I thought they had been killed. Eleven men were killed and twenty-five wounded according to the after-action reports. There were forty-five dead Vietnamese.

Ashley Harrington, Macon, GA
Company C, 3rd Battalion, 12th Infantry Regiment

A Man on the Moon

Assigned to listening post duty thirty to forty meters outside the perimeter during the summer of 1969, I was one of four nervous GIs. As part of Charlie Company, 3rd Battalion, 12th Infantry Regiment, I had been in Vietnam for seven months, having arrived at Long Binh in January of 1969. The nearest they would tell us about our location was that we were thirty miles from Pleiku City, in the central highlands. My hometown of Macon, Georgia, in the heart of the South, was a million miles away for this twenty-one-year-old boy. Now it was July, and we were chasing a NVA regiment through the triple canopy jungle. When night fell, we hurried to set up a perimeter. On this particular night, July 20, I was one of the "lucky ones" to draw listening post duty. Four of us picked what we hoped was a "safe" location and set up for the night. While three of us slept, one man was giving situation reports over the radio every fifteen minutes to the command post in the center of the perimeter. During the night, one of our group was taking his turn and struggling to stay awake.

Suddenly, the command post called and said, "Lima Papa One! This is Charlie Six. They are walking around!"

The GI, scared to death, was immediately alert. He quickly awakened the other three of us with the news of the transmission. When we heard that they were "walking around," we knew that we were surrounded by the NVA. I knew we were in deep trouble. Already being in several firefights, and having been wounded the previous March, I listened with dread to his message.

All this time, the command post continued to transmit, "Lima Papa One! This is Charlie Six, over. They are walking around!"

I just sat and waited for the next transmission and thought of the fight that would come. Now they were saying, "There are two of them walking around!"

At this point, our man asked them, "What part of the perimeter are they walking around?"

Charlie Six replied, "They're walking around the moon!"

I knew this couldn't be true. Here I was in the middle of Vietnam, and there was no way the United States could have landed a man on the moon. But to our relief, it was true. It was July 20, 1969. Millions of Americans were safe at home glued to their TV sets, and there I was in a steamy, hostile jungle.

We were all sharing the same experience, looking at the moon, knowing that we had won the race to put a man on the moon. The only difference was that I was a GI who had not had a bath for three months, was homesick, and scared to death. But that July night, the comment, "They're walking around!" had made us all proud to be Americans.

Gerry Howard, Birmingham, AL
Company A, 1st Battalion, 8th Infantry Regiment

A Long Night on FSB Larry

As October approached in 1969, my tour as a "Shake and Bake" or "instant" NCO had been relatively uneventful. My company, Alpha Company of the 1st Battalion, 8th Infantry Regiments "Bullets," had managed to find a scrap or two and even managed to spring a few ambushes and just generally make life exciting in our AO.

When I arrived in May and did "in-country" training, it became painfully apparent to me that my training as an 11-Charlie mortar NCO wouldn't be used much, and I was right. From May to September, my platoon and I had humped the boonies almost all the time. We did get some time during the summer guarding the bridges on Highway 19 between An Khe and the deep-water port at Qui Nhon. In fact, I turned twenty-one on a bridge on Highway 19 on July 4, 1969. And yes, I did shoot a few star clusters that night. I was the oldest man in the platoon.

Shortly after that, Company A was named Brigade Reaction Force, and life became a little more complicated. We had all kinds of missions and most everybody ended up with multiple air medals as we would some days make several CAs

(Combat Assaults). In September my platoon was up for "first bird" duty at a place to be called FSB Larry. And although I never heard any rounds, the after action report stated that my Huey B model and the two after me carrying the rest of my platoon took numerous AK-47 hits.

Anyway, Company A proceeded to build a fire support base and were we ever happy to get our 81mm mortars. I've got to tell you, my guys were great. We were all draftees, but built 81mm mortar pits and ammo bunkers that anyone would be proud of. And did we practice! Our gunners could put out "scunion" in firepower. Scunion is what my FDC Chief, Guy Lapan called it when asked for maximum firepower from First Lieutenant Gerry Gold, the CO, or some small unit needing support. Scunion was twice the max, and my guys were absolutely magnificent producing it. Guys like Pee Wee Pelican and Haywood Faison—all of them made me proud.

But, as fate would have it, and in army tradition, as soon as we got everything just the way we wanted it—all dug in and enough overhead protection to feel almost comfortable—boom, we were ordered off the hill on an extended hump.

I never had an officer in my platoon the whole time, and only one career NCO who was unable to hump, so for all intents and purposes, I was the platoon leader all this time. First Sergeant Camacho and Lieutenant Gold always treated me with great respect, knowing I was a draftee and instant NCO. Therefore, when a platoon leader had to go to the rear to sign for the SOI codebooks, I always got my turn. What that meant was that a platoon leader There I was, on a firebase I had helped build but surrounded by troops I didn't know.

Every two or three weeks would get a night at Camp Radcliff with hot food, clean clothes, etc. when picking up the new codes. On October 5 it was my turn. We had been humping for about three weeks, and I was excited about going in.

The chopper I was on hadn't been airborne more than thirty seconds after picking me up in a clearing one hundred clicks from nowhere when it was diverted for use as a dustoff. They landed at FSB Larry and put me off late in the afternoon.

I had no idea what company had taken over FSB Larry, which we had built. We had been told that the battalion commander, Lieutenant Colonel Bill Haas had moved a half battery of 105mm howitzers and his tactical operations center to FSB Larry to go with the engineer platoon and infantry company with my 81s.

There I was, on a firebase I had helped build but surrounded by troops I didn't know. It was a strange feeling knowing that all this firepower here meant that this place had regularly been probed, sniped at and mortared because it was too far away for support other than from gunships.

By dark, I had located a small bunker the engineers had built into the side of a 105mm howitzer emplacement and right by one of the 81mm pits we had built. A young private named Michael Raglin and I got up a card game that night by the light of a three-watt bulb we had patched into an artillery generator. It was a moonless, dismal night with heavy mist covering the hill.

About midnight the staff sergeant from the 105mm howitzer unit asked us to step outside because the half battery (three guns) was going to fire some H&I fires at charge six, and he was afraid the little bunker would cave in on us from the concussion.

We had just gone back in the bunker after the 105 fire mission when we heard all kinds of firing from across the perimeter. Heck, we just thought it was a mad minute until small explosions started tracking their way toward us.

In a matter a seconds the 105 ammo box serving as the only window in our bunker exploded into splinters—someone was shooting in at us. The three-watt bulb must have made us an interesting target. This was scary and funny all at the same time. Neither of us could move to where our rifles were because of the fire coming down on us from above. Finally, Raglin got an angle on the light hanging up on the tree trunk center-support for the bunker, and broke it. Later, I wrote him up for—and he got—a Bronze Star for this. It quite probably saved our lives the first time they were saved that night.

The firing down at us immediately stopped, but we could hear footsteps and cursing in Vietnamese headed around to the door of the little bunker. What to do? Too late. This NVA sapper pulled back the poncho covering the bunker entrance, and threw a satchel charge with the fuse burning—guess where?—in my lap.

Well, my momma didn't raise a fool. The fuse had about two inches left. As he ran away, I followed him and, at what I thought was just the right time, I threw it and hit him in the back. The wet heavy weather caused the explosion to be small, I guess. Almost a dud. It didn't kill him or me but it sure ruined my night. Funny and comical.

One of the AK rounds had broken a catsup bottle above Raglin's head, and he really believed he had been shot. We laughed a lot about it later.

After the small satchel charge explosion, I found myself in the 81mm mortar pit. I found an illumination round and twisted the fuse as close to zero as I dared and dropped it in the tube. When it lit up FSB Larry, all I could see across the base was NVA running and shooting into our bunkers. I still hadn't found my rifle so I pointed both index fingers at them in true cowboy style and shouted, "Bang! Bang! Bang!" Funny again, but it seemed to work. They all left! Not my finger going "bang, bang," but probably the illumination round saved our lives for the second time that night.

We were bloody and scared and wet, but better off than the rest of the place. One artilleryman was killed sitting on the field latrine and one 105mm howitzer crewman, who must have been in hand-to-hand combat with them. The engineer officer, whom we had told numerous times not to sleep in the trailer he had on the hill, had been stitched by AK fire. As luck would have it, the battalion surgeon was out there and, after being blown out of his tent by a satchel charge, was able to save the lieutenant's life. About thirty-one others were wounded, and although we found many blood trails and I shot all the mortar ammo on the hill—gunships worked out until dawn—not a single enemy body was found.

At the debriefing about 0800 hours, Lieutenant Colonel Haas said we had been probed by a few VC sappers. That was as close as I came to abusing an officer. At my suggestion, the entire command group looked around them. As far as they could see were hundreds of AK casings and dozens of unexploded satchel charges and chicom grenades.

I was just happy to be alive and anxious to get back to my guys where I would be safe. For sure, I never wanted to spend another long night on FSB Larry.

The rest of my tour was not uneventful, but it was painful due to the ringing in my ears. Not from the satchel charge, but from the AK fire from the window. We did manage to get significant body count that winter, and Company A had plenty to do. Finally, in March 1970, my early discharge for school came through and I went back to "the world."

John Lurski, Averill Park, NY
Company C, 1st Battalion, 22nd Infantry Regiment

The Simple Joys

Everything in life is relative, and probably nowhere was this truer than in the life of a grunt in Vietnam. The simplest of pleasures (absence of misery) became the utmost of joys—like taking a five-minute break on the trail and being able to drop that heavy rucksack. Like spending an entire day at one location, though this joy was usually ruined by being sent out on LP that night, in the rain. Like being in an area secure enough to take those wet boots off at night. Like being sent out on LP before it was pitch black. (It seems that most times when I went out on LP we couldn't see our hands in front of our face and we had to feel our way out about one hundred meters.) Like setting up at night before it rained. Like not crossing a waist-deep stream a half hour before dark. Like pulling guard duty on a firebase. (Fire base living was luxury after a month or more in the boonies; you would even occasionally eat something besides C-rations or those freeze dried LRRP rations usually supplied during the dry season when water was hard to find). Like being resupplied on time. Like not having to carry the D-handle. Like walking on flat ground. Like finding an LZ that didn't require six hours of chopping with machetes to get resupplied. Like waking up in the middle of the night and not finding a slimy leach attached to your neck.

The list is probably endless, but these were a few of the simple joys that made my year as a grunt bearable.

John Lurski, Averill Park, NY
Company C, 1st Battalion, 22nd Infantry Regiment

Persistent Sniper

This probably happened in late 1969. This area of the central highlands was characterized by tall mountains, steep hillsides, and deep valleys (this probably describes most of the central highlands). After an extended period out in the boonies, it was my company's turn to come in to guard the firebase. Being on top of a tall mountain, this firebase seemed like a secure place to be. One day while I was lounging on top of a bunker, a sniper opened up from a hillside across from a steep valley. Probably because the battalion commander was located there, the sniper attracted an incredible amount of attention. It seemed that everything we had on that mountain blasted away at the side of that hill, but as soon as the smoke cleared, the sniper popped off a couple more rounds to let us know that we missed. It must have been a slow day for the air force, because they sent out a couple of F-4s to hit the hillside with a few of their heavy bombs. The ground shook as those jets dived in and unloaded their payload, but again, when the smoke cleared, the sniper popped off a couple more rounds to let us know we'd missed. Fortunately for us, the sniper also missed, and we never heard from him again during my short stay at that firebase. He must have figured that it just wasn't worth it.

John Lurski, Averill Park, NY
Company C, 1st Battalion, 22nd Infantry Regiment

The Combat Assault

The first combat assault is something that probably sticks in every grunt's mind forever. I still remember mine as if it happened yesterday. Seeing the old-timers relaxed and taking it in stride didn't help me. I was still scared—terrified is probably a better description. It was mid-September 1969. The LZ was a mountaintop north of An Khe. My chopper landed, I jumped off and got about fifty feet down the side when I heard an awful noise behind me. The chopper behind mine either took a hit or just crashed, but I can still see the blades whacking the dirt and tree stumps as it rolled over in a big cloud of dust and splinters. Incredibly, no one was hurt, and the chopper crew was out in record time and on the next chopper out. We spent the night on the hilltop, securing the downed chopper.

The next morning, after the downed chopper was hauled out, we moved out down the side of the hill. Now that my adrenalin had returned to near normal levels, the weight of the rucksack became quite noticeable. I knew right then that this wasn't going to be a fun year. The next day I had my first contact as my platoon was opened up at from a hooch we were approaching. This was terrifying. The shooting didn't last long, but we had one killed and one wounded. At this point, I wasn't too optimistic about my chances of lasting a year, but luckily, during my year I wasn't involved in too many firefights, and they generally didn't last too long. I realize how fortunate I was not to have gone through the horror of some of the larger battles that the earlier grunts endured.

January—December 1970

Highlights of 1970 include turning over Camp Enari to the ARVN on April 15 with the 4th Infantry Division relocating to Camp Radcliff at An Khe. In late April, the 3rd Brigade left Vietnam and returned to control of the 25th Infantry Division in Hawaii. In May, the Cambodian sanctuaries of the North Vietnamese Army were attacked. Major General Glenn D. Walker, who had fought with the 4th Infantry Division in World War II, commanded the division from November 1969 until July 1970. Major General William A. Burke served as commander from July 1970 until the division returned to the States. On December 7, 1970, the 4th Infantry Division Colors were relocated from Vietnam to Fort Carson, Colorado. The last 4th Infantry Division soldier killed in hostile action was Specialist 4th Class Francis X. Bunk who was killed on Veteran's Day, November 11, 1970. Total killed in 1970 from hostile and non-hostile causes was 221, with a total of 2,497 who paid the ultimate price while serving with the 4th Infantry Division in Vietnam between July 1966 and December 1970. The division earned eleven campaign streamers, two Republic of Vietnam Crosses of Gallantry with Palm, and the Republic of Vietnam Civil Action Honor Medal, First Class. There were sixteen Presidential Unit Citations, twenty-three Valorous Unit Awards, and twenty Meritorious Unit Citations awarded for actions in Vietnam.

Daniel Boelens, Grand Rapids, MI
4th Battalion, 42nd Field Artillery

Bad Day in the Punchbowl

On January 7 or 8, 1970, elements of the division made a move. It was quite a convoy. Stretching as far back as you could see, coming down the highway, were trucks carrying troops and material of the 4th Infantry Division.

First, a little background. I was one of those guys who enlisted right out of high school. I could not wait to get to Vietnam. My MOS was tanker. The "Nam" needed no tankers at this time. I was sent to the 4th Battalion, 42nd Field Artillery, in the central highlands around the end of November 1968. I was getting bored with no action and wanted to get into it. Here I sat on mountaintops, and sometimes lowlands, setting up firebases, digging holes, and filling sandbags. We fired a lot for the 1st Battalion, 12th Infantry Regiment, but I wanted to see more than that. So when the time came to move, I was all for it. My fellow FNGs all thought I was crazy because I wanted to do some fighting, or at least see it.

On January 8 our battery with the 1st of the 12th Infantry broke off from the main convoy and headed for what I think now was southwest of Pleiku, out near the Chu Pong Massif mountain range. The convoy was led by a tank and a couple of armored cavalry vehicles. We came to one intersection where we saw a burned out ARVN jeep. It appeared to have hit a land mine. Very exciting, I thought. Farther down the road that day, we came across a water buffalo that had stepped on a mine in the road. It must have been thrown about fifty feet from where the mine had gone off. A little later, the lead tank ran over a mine. I could hear the pop of the fuse, but the mine itself never blew, which was damn good for that tank crew. After that, the infantry decided to unload from the trucks and flank the road to foil any ambush that might be there. I was excited at that time, thinking that I was finally seeing what I had come to Vietnam to see.

That night we pulled in next to the road, "circled our wagons," and laid out a perimeter for our 105mm howitzers. The infantry sent out patrols and set up their positions on the outside of us. During the night we fired a few times for the infantry. The next day we fired some more. I am not sure what the calls for fire were all about.

On the morning of January 10 the battery, along with the infantry battalion, was being airlifted to a new landing zone. The infantry was going to send in an advance party to check out the LZ. After that, our artillery battery sent in an advance party to back up the infantry and to start laying out where the battery was going to go, along with setting up a little security.

The CH-47 picked up the advance party that I was on. The advance party from the infantry was Company E. It was in another CH-47, about fifteen minutes in front of us. My heart was going into overtime as I finally was getting to do what I came here for. My position on the chopper was around the opening in the floor. It was, as I think back, about four feet by four feet square. For the whole ride leaned into the open space to see what was going on below us, not wanting to miss anything. When we approached the LZ, I could see F-4 jet airplanes from my perch, dropping bombs in the surrounding hills and around the LZ itself. We then got the call that our assault had been called off. The CH-47 turned around and went back.

We were told when we got back that the insertion had been called off because one of the infantry guys had stepped on a land mine in the LZ (I think this was Specialist Fourth Class James Boone with Echo Company). His foot had been blown off.

When I got off the chopper I headed over to where my equipment had been left. It had been blown all over the place by a flying "crane" that had been picking up some 105s for LZ Punchbowl. I never did find all of my personal gear. The day was not starting off well.

That afternoon around 1530 hours we were again sent back into the LZ; this time there were no problems. We landed, the infantry set up a perimeter, and then we started marking where the 105mm howitzers were going to be set in. During this time the CH-47s and the cranes flew just about non-stop bringing out our equipment. The crane carrying my section's 105 came in, set it down, and left. I went over to the "A-22," which was a tarp with forty rounds of 105 artillery shells in it forming four walls and a bottom. Inside this was placed gear. The A-22 sling was secured under the 105mm howitzer and the chopper picked this all up at once. When I went to retrieve my duffel bag from the top of the A-22 where I had placed it earlier in the day for transport, it was gone. It had fallen out into the jungle en route to LZ Punchbowl. My day still was going wrong. During the drop of the 105 by the Crane, I think it had blown my new flak vest into the ranks of the infantry, so now I had lost that also. Maybe they had just stolen it; I don't know, but it was gone. What else could happen that day?

Around 1930 hours, as some of the guys in the section were digging in and filling sandbags, I was cleaning the breech on the 105. It was out of the gun and could not fire. As I recall, all but one of the 105mm howitzers were torn down for cleaning. I will now remind you that LZ Punchbowl was located in a valley and all around were hills, close hills. The enemy had even mined it after it had been abandoned the last time. I thought the name had been given to it by the troops because we all felt like it was a fishbowl and we were a bunch of sitting ducks. I had only been in country now for six weeks and I would never have used this for a firebase because of the location, so why would higher commanders set us down here to build one? No common sense, maybe, Or maybe, who cares? They did not have to live or try to survive out there.

It was getting dark, but the work did not stop. The enemy opened fire on our ill-prepared firebase. The rounds came directly over my head. The first one hit about one hundred yards to the rear of me. I did not know it at the time, but later we determined that the enemy with their 75mm recoilless rifle had bore-sighted on the flame from one of the stoves in the mess tent. It was located behind me, where the first round hit. On each round after that, they must have cranked the recoilless down a notch or two. The next rounds that went over my head were getting closer and closer to me. After that first round, it did not take me long to know that the action I wanted was now upon me. I was scared. I jumped for the bunker the guys had been digging. It was about three feet by four feet and I was the last one to try and scratch my way in, so I ended up on the top. The noise the enemy rounds made, only a couple of feet overhead, was something else. They made a noise like "wup, wup, wup" and each round was noisier, the "wup" was closer, and I was more scared, praying just like everyone else.

I lay there after the first round—the next round came just to the right of my hole, about twenty feet in the air. It hit just on the other side of the mess trailer. The next round came in about the same place, around fifteen feet overhead. This round hit the mess trailer and paper plates fell like snow, adding to the confusion. The next was ten feet off the ground and hit ten yards between the mess and us. The next round was on the way. I knew it because the blast from the recoilless flashed over our LZ—that is how close the Punchbowl was to the hills that surrounded it. It was like "flash, bang (wup wup wup), flash, bang" as it hit. Then you heard the whining sound of shrapnel spinning through the air. At one point it seemed as if my mind told me that my legs were out of the bunker too far. But I am sure that I had already been hit by then.

The round that got me also hit our A-22, igniting our 105 rounds. So now, besides the recoilless itself, shrapnel from our ammo was also spinning into the air looking for a place to rest. The piece that got me went into my right calf, dipped in, and came back out again. Later, when I looked at it, you could see that there was still a bridge of flesh from one side to the other over the wound. The piece of shrapnel that hit me was so hot that there was no bleeding. My section members and I all jumped up and ran. One of them ran off screaming and was stopped at the perimeter by the infantry. He had been wounded about a year earlier on LZ Mile High.

I crawled towards some other guys that I had come to the unit with. I knew they had been setting up a little ways from me. By this time, the recoilless rifles had stopped firing (I think that there were two). Flares were popping overhead, and the enemy opened up with machine guns, possibly to keep our heads down as they withdrew with the recoilless. I could see a large hole in my fatigue pants where I had been hit. I kept crawling towards friends. I started to get mad that no one seemed to be firing back at the enemy. Maybe they were, but as I recall, they were not. Then I was mad at myself for leaving my M-16 where we had been digging in. I wanted to go back, get it, and fire back.

As I got to within a few yards of my friends (their bunker, I could see, was not much better than ours had been), one of them pointed his rifle and yelled something at me. Thinking I was going to be shot by them, I yelled out my name and that I had been hit. They dragged me in and one said to me, "Well, Boelens. You wanted it, now you got it."

At this time, I was so scared but at the same time very excited. I could think of nothing more than getting back to get my M-16. I left them after a couple of minutes. One of our 105mm howitzers started shooting beehive rounds at the enemy, much too late, I'm sure. I finally made it back to where I was hit. My section sergeant, Sergeant Roberts, and our CO, Captain Hill, were trying to put out the fire that had been our ammo. I assisted them in putting the fire out. I then grabbed my M-16 and a bandoleer of ammo.

"Puff The Magic Dragon," or "Spooky," also came on the scene and fired up the area outside our perimeter, keeping whatever enemy was there well away from us. Never have I been so impressed with a weapon or so happy to see one like this come "on scene" to help.

Things started to calm down. The first sergeant yelled for anyone wounded and someone told him that I had been hit. It's sort of funny— out of about five hundred men at this landing zone, I was the only one who got hit. One other buddy, "Buzznuts," had a small stone fly up and hit him in the face, giving him a small cut.

I was not medivaced out until later that night since my wound was not life threatening. When I did get medivaced out, it was because Company D, 1st Battalion, 12th Infantry Regiment, made contact in the hills, or had some type of small probe on their perimeter. Our battery was asked to fire for them. I was told that we had fired too close and hit a trooper of Company D. I think it was Theodore Clark. He was hit through the right elbow with a piece of shrapnel. So after picking him up, they swung in and got me. I remember looking down at him in the chopper; the elbow did not look so good. Then I turned my attention back to the door and the jungle, M-16 in hand now, and ready (no one knew that I got on with it—Ha!). The way they were handing out Bronze Stars, I thought for sure I had one for this, but they told me later that they had lost the paperwork and Captain Hill, my CO, was gone. I was content with my Purple Heart. To this day, it hangs in my office on the wall, framed along with an article from the Grand Rapids Press of my being wounded and sent to Japan. After spending three months in Japan mending, I pulled some strings and got back to Vietnam, but that's another story.

Roger R. Dufek, Manitowoc, WI
Company A, 3rd Battalion, 12th Infantry Regiment

Lost Ambush Patrol

I was drafted into the army in 1969 and went to Vietnam in January 1970. I served with Company A, 3rd Battalion, 12th Infantry, as a rifleman for about seven months.

The thing that I hated the most was going out on ambushes. I liked security in numbers back in the main perimeter. Every third night, you had ambush duty, usually five or six people. We would go out and set up just before sundown, usually along a well-traveled trail. One night we had just moved into our night location when we heard on the radio that one of our ambushes was lost. That's not very comforting for the ambush because they would have no help if they ran into trouble.

My squad was set in six-foot-tall elephant grass about fifteen yards off of a trail when we saw people coming down the trail. All we could see were the tops of some helmets, and right away, we knew it was the lost ambush. Those guys were pretty scared, and the CO had told them just to get off the trail and sit tight for the night, that we would find them in the morning.

They set up about twenty-five yards away from us, but we didn't let them know right away that we were there. One of the guys in my ambush thought it would be funny to throw a rock over their heads to make some noise, so he did. These guys heard it and called in that they had movement and wanted to know what to do. They sounded pretty scared on the radio, but our captain assured them that if they didn't spring the ambush, they had nothing to fear. After about three or four more rocks in the next few minutes and listening to them on the radio, we thought it was time to let them know that it was us causing the noise. They were a little upset at first but also happy to know that we were nearby and we knew our location. The night was uneventful, and we got together in the morning to go back to the company.

John Lurski, Averill Park, NY
Company C, 1st Battalion, 22nd Infantry Regiment

Walking Point

I don't think many grunts enjoyed walking point. As for me, I absolutely dreaded it. It was probably around February 1970, somewhere in the jungle-covered mountains of the central highlands. After we set up for the night the lieutenant informed me that I would be walking point the next day. Needless to say, I didn't sleep very well that night. The next morning, to make matters worse, the lieutenant informed me that we would be following a heavily used trail. There were no civilians within twenty miles, so a heavily used trail meant there probably were NVA nearby. I'm not ashamed to admit that there were times that day that my knees were shaking as I carefully and quietly moved down that trail. But I did as all of us grunts did, just kept putting one foot in front of the other.

After moving about a click down the trail, I heard a loud explosion behind my right foot. I fell to the ground, rolled a few feet down the side of the hill, took a look at my feet, and was greatly relieved to notice they were both still where they were supposed to be—attached to my legs. I thought I had stepped on a mine, but what had happened was that the second man (who shall remain nameless) was carrying a grenade launcher with a shotgun round. He tripped and fired the round, which blew a hole in the trail right behind my foot. He must have apologized fifty times. I was just looking at my feet and feeling very happy seeing that they were still there.

After traveling a few more clicks down the trail, I heard a noise up ahead, so I stopped and dropped my rucksack. My friend with the grenade launcher and I slowly and quietly moved up to get a better look. Down the side of the hill, a bunch of orangutans were swinging in the trees. What a relief—observing orangutans in their native habitat is much preferred to a firefight.

It sure felt good when we set up that night, knowing how lucky I was to have walked point all day on a heavily used trail and not run into any NVA. To this day, those times that I walked point rank right up there as some of the most stressful days of my life. Back then, the fear of walking into an ambush was one of the leading causes of stress in my life.

James W. Henderson, Grand Prairie, TX
Company B, 1st Battalion, 22nd Infantry Regiment

The D-Handle Shovel

I don't know if it was standard practice everywhere in the 4th Infantry Division, but in my company, we never humped military issue entrenching tools. Instead, we carried a full-sized D-Handle shovel (henceforth referred to simply as the "D-Handle"). Due to the high-performance power of this larger shovel, it was only necessary to carry one D-Handle per squad, with each member taking turns transporting it. When humping the D-Handle up and down the mountain trails, it was a common practice to tie it to the top of your rucksack—handle side up and business end dangling down—with ever-present extra bootlaces. This way it tended to swing free and instead of getting caught on limbs and wait-a-minute vines, it would simply rotate and fall free.

When it was your turn, it was your turn, combat assault or not. No one liked having their turn fall during a combat assault. There was no scientific (or graceful) method to get off the chopper with the D-Handle and all the other gear, plus your weapon. Probably, the most often used method was to make sure you were sitting in the door of the chopper and as it touched down, simply chuck the D-Handle as far as you could (assuming no one was in front of you) and then retrieve it after you got yourself off the chopper.

In April 1970 I was serving with Company B, 1st Battalion, 22nd Infantry Regiment, somewhere in the central highlands in the Binh Dinh Province, north of An Khe. My company was being combat assaulted into a new AO. The landing zone was not "hot," but it was unsecured, and we were on one of the first few choppers in. I was carrying the D-Handle.

Well, "Mr. Brain Surgeon" here decides he has a way to build a better mousetrap. (Mind you, at the time, I weighed probably 130 pounds. I'm sure my fullyloaded ruck sack weighed at least ninety or so pounds). I decided, why not tie the D-Handle to my ruck to start with and not even have to think about it during the CA, just jump out with it tied behind me and let it follow me out?

Our pilot skillfully came in fast and touched down completely, a feat always greatly appreciated by overloaded grunts not wishing to jump even a few inches— much less a few feet, as was sometimes the case. We all began to jump out. As I heaved myself out the door of the chopper, it felt as though an invisible hand was pulling me back. Of course, during the ride, you tended to lean back so the weight of your pack was resting on the floor and you, in turn, were resting on your pack. I think I must have underestimated the weight of my ruck, so I gave an even stronger heave-ho and tried to clear the deck and get off the chopper. Again, the invisible hand yanked me back into the chopper. This time, I looked back and saw a frantic door gunner reaching madly, coming up just short, trying to get my attention with one hand while slapping wildly with the other to get his helmet off. It seemed the top of the D-handle had the intercom wiring leading from his helmet to the pilot wrapped around it. Each time I tried to leap out of the chopper, I was nearly ripping his helmet off, with his head still in it! I lurched, he jerked; I lurched, he jerked; the hapless guy couldn't get away from me.

I finally got us unhooked and got off the chopper. No one else was aware of the little drama that had unfolded except the gunner and me. I was immediately overwhelmed by the hilarity of the scene and by the time I reached my fellow squad members, I was cracking up with laughter. Everyone else was still a little apprehensive and on edge about setting up a perimeter on the unsecured LZ and couldn't figure out what was so funny.

I guess you had to have been me or the door gunner to get the full effect, but I described it to them as best I could. I've often wondered if the door gunner thought it was as funny as I did, or if when he retold the story he called me "this crazy grunt," or something more descriptive, who tried to rip his head off. Who knows? Maybe he'll see this story and recognize himself in it. Sometimes the strangest things could lighten an otherwise tense situation.

Dan Martus, Nashville, TN
Company D, 1st Battalion, 22nd Infantry Regiment

Cambodia

One of the pleasures of being a grunt was flying in a helicopter, just above treetop level, with your feet hanging out the door. You felt so alive. There was the enjoyment of the cool breezes on 90-plus degree days, amazement with the beauty of a lush green, mountainous jungle, and a moment to reflect on the unknown that waited ahead, the possibility of a hot LZ. We had just left the air force base in Pleiku, en route to the jungles of Cambodia near the Ho Chi Minh Trail. President Nixon had given approval for this mission. Our mission was to hit the Ho Chi Minh Trail in an effort to cut off supply routes and demoralize the enemy.

The night before, at the air force base in Pleiku, was festive. We had fun with the "Zoomies" (Air Force pilots), and they had fun partying with us. Many of them had never seen real grunts and were amazed with our gear, weapons, quirks, lingo, irreverence, and other habits. We were a culture unto our own, much different from theirs. And for us, we could not believe that anyone in the military actually lived like they did—football field, swimming pool, paved streets with curbs, night clubs, huge stereos in their rooms—it was like a campus back home. One of the Zoomies got a kick out of putting on my rucksack and lugging around my M-60. (I made sure I took the starter belt of ammo out of the gun first.)

We were headed for Cambodia, so we were freshly resupplied with all the ammo and other gear that we needed: hand grenades, claymores, thousands of rounds of M-60 ammo, and so on. They couldn't believe that we carried all that.

We had heard that things might be hot in Cambodia, so most of us were quiet and somber as we cruised above the treetops. My mind drifted to my upcoming R&R. I'd heard stories about Sydney, Australia, and I couldn't wait to go.

But I couldn't help but think, Would I make it back from Cambodia in one piece? Would I even get to see Sydney?

I had that old familiar sinking feeling in my gut, that feeling that we would be going through some tough times.

We were prepared to hit a hot LZ. We knew the drill. Evacuate the Huey quickly, head for cover, and form a perimeter around the LZ. We all unloaded safely and began our trek into the jungle. This jungle seemed so familiar, but yet it felt so different. There was an odd feeling about this place. We were invading an area that the VC and NVA had occupied freely for many years. In the jungles of Vietnam, I knew that we patrolled through many areas where GIs had been before and had even fought battles there. Not so with Cambodia. It was all new to us.

We picked a spot where our company would set up a perimeter for the night. We definitely would need to dig in and prepare for the worst. We had just dropped our rucksacks when we heard that bone chilling "pop-pop-pop" of small arms fire. It was AK-47 and M-16. A squad had ventured out around the perimeter to scout out the area and had walked into an ambush. Like most firefights, it was over quickly. But not before our lieutenant was shot and killed, and one other man wounded. There was that sinking feeling again. We medivaced the wounded along with the lieutenant's body and then regrouped under the CO's direction.

He knew he had to get our heads back on straight, and he did a good job of calming us down. Tonight might be a long and fierce night. Once again, we were fortunate to have a forward observer with us. He was the best at knowing our exact location and calling in artillery. We all felt safe when he was with us. That night he spotted artillery all around our perimeter, closer than ever. We pulled our steel pots down tight as we hunkered down in our foxholes. The hot shrapnel whizzed through the tree branches above our heads—the closer the better. For us, even though we were tense with the anticipation of an attack, the night was uneventful. For another company a couple of clicks away, things were pretty hairy. We heard small arms fire, grenades, and claymores off and on throughout the night. Most of us got very little sleep that night, but while lying down, I allowed myself the luxury of dreaming about Sydney. I pictured myself walking through the city with a lovely "round-eyed" girl at my side. For a moment, the tension eased a bit.

Most of us got very little sleep that night, but while lying down, I allowed myself the luxury of dreaming about Sydney. I pictured myself walking through the city with a lovely "round-eyed" girl at my side.

The next afternoon we were amazed to see Bud come back to the field. He had been wounded the previous day but insisted that he be allowed to go back to the field with his fellow grunts. That spirit of selfless camaraderie that combat soldiers exemplify is rarely seen in any other walk of life. No recognition was asked for, no medals asked for; Bud just wanted to be there to help his fellow grunts. In my days since, I have yet to experience the depth and power of this bond, the camaraderie of the combat infantry soldier. Little did Bud know how this one act of selflessness would inspire his friends.

A couple of days later, our platoon actually went on patrol down the Ho Chi Minh trail. I never thought I would see the day when we would actually hump down such a well-used trail. It was almost a road, about fifteen feet wide, surfaced with hard packed clay, and almost totally covered by the jungle overhead. We had one point man, but the trail was so wide, we needed a volunteer for a second point man. The CO wanted it to be a machine gunner. Without much hesitation, I volunteered to take a turn at it. And after almost nine months in country, this was my first and only experience walking point.

The patrol, even though tense, was uneventful. After a few more days, our mission was over and we headed back into the more familiar jungles of Vietnam. I felt great. I was now on the home stretch of my tour and would soon be headed to Sydney for my R&R.

Bill Babcock, Narragansett, RI
Company A, 3rd Battalion, 8th Infantry Regiment

Battle Analysis

During the months of April, May, and June of 1970, the United States Army, together with forces of the Republic of South Vietnam, conducted operations, which came to be known as the Cambodian Incursion or Cambodian Invasion. U.S. News and World Report reported that by June

5, 1970, 331 Americans had been killed during this operation. One-sixth of those 331 men were members of Company A, 3rd Battalion, 8th Infantry Regiment, 1st Brigade, 4th Infantry Division.

Cambodia had long been used by the North Vietnam Army and Viet Cong as sanctuaries. Supplies from North Vietnam came down the Ho Chi Minh Trail to the local VC and NVA units who used the area along the Cambodia/South Vietnam border as staging areas to launch attacks against South Vietnam. Up until the spring of 1970, the United States had respected the wishes of the Cambodian government and had not crossed the border in pursuit of the NVA and VC. The enemy was free to come and go as he wished.

In March of 1970 the Cambodian Government was internally overthrown, and President Richard Nixon took the opportunity caused by the political and military turmoil in Cambodia to attack those sanctuaries. On April 28, South Vietnamese Army forces pushed into Cambodia in an area known as the Parrot's Beak. On May 1, U.S. forces followed into the Parrot's Beak and farther north into the "Fish Hook." On May 6, the 1st Brigade of the 4th Infantry Division, commanded by Major General Glenn D. Walker, began operation "Binh Tay," a series of assaults planned against enemy base areas designated as 701, 702, and 740. The 3rd of the 8th Infantry moved on base 702, fifty miles west of Pleiku.

On May 6, Charlie Company, the lead company of the battalion, attempted to air assault into the suspected enemy sanctuary area. Their first two attempts were met by hot LZs. The third attempt to land was initially successful and about half of an artillery battery and half of the infantry company landed. As the remainder of the company attempted to land, an ambush was sprung by an unknown sized enemy force. Two helicopters were shot down, and the remainder of Charlie Company aborted the landing. Early the next morning, as the rest of the battalion was preparing to join Company C, an NVA squad attacked the command group of

Charlie Company and killed the First Sergeant and the Company commander, Lieutenant Robert Phillips.

On May 7 the remainder of the battalion landed at LZ Phillips. The LZ, soon to be a fire support base, was unofficially named by the men of Charlie Company for their slain commander.

As was the usual pattern, one company remained on the firebase as security while the other companies moved off to begin their missions. The mission was to find caches of enemy supplies and locate a reported enemy (battalion-sized) hospital complex somewhere in the battalion's area of operations.

Alpha Company was composed of three rifle platoons and the command group, a total of about one hundred men. Some of the men in the rifle platoons had been taken from rear area jobs as cooks and other non-infantry qualified positions to increase the size of the company for this particular mission. Consequently, these men lacked the skills and experience needed to fight effectively in this type of environment. Other men were new to the company and combat due to the constant turnover in personnel created by the one-year tour of duty, which was standard in Vietnam.

The leadership of Alpha Company consisted of the commanding officer and three platoon leaders. A 22-year-old OCS graduate who had about two months experience in the field as a commander, but none as a platoon leader, commanded the company. He had never been in combat. Leadership of the first platoon came from Staff Sergeant Mull, a platoon sergeant with six months' experience in the field. The third platoon was led by Lieutenant Virgil Judah, a twenty-six-year-old OCS graduate with five months field time. I was the second platoon leader, a twenty-three-year-old ROTC graduate with eight months experience in the field.

The company also had a sniper team consisting of a soldier who had spent one week at an in-country sniper school and three men who provided security for him. Although he had been to school, the sniper had no actual experience before this mission and did not know a lot about his weapon. This was evident when he was observed removing the sniper scope from the rifle to clean it. Once this weapon had been sighted, the scope should not have been removed. This inexperience and lack of training proved very costly later in the mission.

After landing on LZ Phillips, Company A moved off to the west to begin its search for the enemy. Movement was slow through thick, triple-canopy jungle that blocked out much of the sunlight that filtered through the trees.

The company moved all afternoon, calling in the location, direction and size of any trails that were discovered. As we began to set up our night defensive perimeter about 1700 hours, a burst of M-16 fire caused everyone to duck for cover. A lone enemy soldier had decided to surrender and had simply walked into the perimeter. One of our men had taken a shot at him before realizing he was giving up. The prisoner was questioned by the CO. He told us he was just a rice farmer recruited by the NVA and forced to work for them. He just wanted to be out of any fight that might develop. He was either unable or unwilling to tell us anything else. The rest of the night passed without any contact.

Early on the morning of May 8, my second platoon was sent on a patrol to the southwest, while Lieutenant Judah's third platoon swept southeast. The first platoon secured the CP group. My platoon soon discovered a large trail junction. The trail was well used and had bicycle tracks on it. A small thatched hut sat in the middle of the trail junction. It was obviously part of the Ho Chi Minh Trail complex and probably a major intersection, with the hut acting as a checkpoint direction center. I set my platoon in an ambush position covering the trail junction and waited.

The sniper fired at a range of fifty to one hundred meters, missed, and was wounded by the NVA, who then ran back down the trail and escaped.

At 1330 hours the CO called and told me to abandon the ambush site and return to the CP. He then sent the four-man sniper team to the same site to ambush the trail. Instead of concentrating his limited firepower on the center of the intersection, the team leader placed one man on each avenue of the junction. An hour later, three NVA walked down the east trail. The sniper fired at a range of fifty to one hundred meters, missed, and was wounded by the NVA, who then ran back down the trail and escaped.

At the same time that the sniper team made contact, my platoon was searching a cache site about a thousand meters to the north of the company CP. Upon returning from the ambush site, I had been sent to aid the first platoon, which had discovered the cache. The third platoon now secured the CP.

Staff Sergeant Mull had already called in Cobra gunships on several hooches before moving into the cache site. As both platoons searched, a lone enemy soldier jumped up and began firing on us. One of Sergeant Mull's men returned fire and the wounded VC ran off down a trail.

The CO called and told me to have the first and second platoons set up for the night where we were, and join him in the morning. I pointed out to him that higher headquarters had advised all commanders not to split up at night since the enemy strength was unknown. He did not change his order.

At 1730 hours the headquarters RTO called to tell me that the CO and two other men were missing in action. The captain had decided to recon a possible ambush site for Lieutenant Judah's platoon. He took Lieutenant Judah and three men from the third platoon and headed off down the trail that the three NVA had followed earlier that day. Lieutenant Judah pointed out that they should take a radio, but the CO said there was no need since they were only going a short distance.

The five men had moved about two or three hundred meters down the trail when they came upon several hooches with bunkers under them. Instead of going back or sending back for help, the CO had the five men get on line and started to sweep into the enemy complex. Firing broke out from the direction of the hooches, and one man was killed instantly. The

CO and two men were now out of Lieutenant Judah's sight, and someone called for a medic. Lieutenant Judah lowcrawled out of the kill zone and went back to the CP location for help. He returned to the contact area and was immediately pinned down by enemy fire. A second man was killed and one other wounded. No more was heard from the CO and the two men with him.

As the senior officer I assumed command of Company A and moved the first and second platoons back to the CP. I then moved forward with a small element of about six men to the contact area. I felt it best not to take the whole company forward until I could determine the situation and estimate the enemy strength. I found Lieutenant Judah, and he explained what had happened. Since it was quickly becoming dark and we could do nothing for the three missing men, I decided to pull everyone back into the CP area and form a perimeter for the night. Using smoke grenades to hide us from view and the M-60 machine gun fire to suppress the enemy position, I had Lieutenant Judah withdraw his men as I went out and got the wounded man to my front. I remained behind with my RTO and M-60 team to provide covering fire for the dustoff evacuation helicopter as it took out the wounded man. Under the cover of darkness, my team and I returned to the company perimeter.

The next day we got ready to move back into the enemy complex. I sent Lieutenant Judah's platoon back the way we went the first day and Staff Sergeant Mull's platoon around what we thought was the left flank. I was with the second platoon, ready to move in either direction depending on what happened. Staff Sergeant Mull made contact first. Firing began even before he reached the left flank, and he was immediately pinned down. Bullets flew overhead and around any man who tried to advance into the complex. I called Lieutenant Judah, who had the company's forward observer, with him and had him call artillery fire in front of Sergeant Mull's position. As the artillery impacted, setting fire to the hooches, Lieutenant Judah called me saying that the forward observer had been shot from behind and he, too, was under fire. He could not tell where the fire was coming from. I decided to pull back again and abandon the attempt to penetrate the enemy position.

Back in the perimeter, the battalion commander called to say a new captain was being sent out to take command. It turned out to be Company A's old commander, Captain Hunt. Captain Hunt decided to go back in again.

I moved my platoon up to the front of the enemy complex, just behind where we had left two of our dead the day before. My mission was to support Captain Hunt and the other two platoons as they tried to flank from the left. We were also to try to recover our dead, who lay out in an open area between the enemy and us. As Captain Hunt moved in, he was fired on and was unable to move. One of my men, Specialist McCarthy, crawled out to try to recover one of the bodies in front of us. As he started to pull the body back, a single shot rang out and McCarthy was mortally wounded by a bullet in the head. Another man ran out, picked him up, and carried him back to our position. Captain Hunt decided to pull back once again.

At this point it was obvious that the enemy was well dug-in with plenty of overhead cover. Artillery had little effect on them. Captain Hunt asked for an air strike on the complex but was turned down by the battalion commander. He felt there might still be a chance the CO and the others were alive and did not want to risk killing them with the air strike. Since it was quickly becoming dark, Captain Hunt decided to wait until morning to try again.

Early on the morning of May 10, Captain Hunt requested an aerial recon of the enemy position to get a better fix on what we were up against. A helicopter hunter-killer team reported we were on the edge of what appeared to be a battalion-sized enemy complex with a trench line and overhead cover going all around it. Smaller trenches ran out to its front, which gave the enemy flanking shots on anyone approaching the main trench. The complex appeared deserted.

Captain Hunt decided to have the entire company sweep on line into the complex from the left flank. As we prepared to move out, we heard three single shots come from the direction of the complex. I led the second platoon up the left flank of the complex followed by the first platoon, the CP group, and the third platoon. We got on line and started in together, burning hooches and dropping grenades into bunkers as we went. No fire came from the enemy positions. They were gone. Fifteen minutes into the assault, Captain Hunt called and told me to halt my platoon and move to his location. They had found the CO and the others. The three men were lying face down in a trench, hands tied behind their backs, shot in the back of the head. They had been captured the first day of the contact. The three shots we heard in the morning had been their execution by the retreating NVA.

During the three days of contact, six men of Alpha Company died. Six more were seriously wounded by the enemy, and eight more received minor wounds from friendly artillery and gunships called in dangerously close to support men on the ground.

The principal source for this battle analysis was my own recollection of events that took place eighteen years ago (analysis written in 1988). Exact locations and exact times have escaped my memory; however, the events reported here will never be forgotten.

Michael Belis, Carencro, LA
Company C, 1st Battalion, 22nd Infantry Regiment

Monkey in the Foxhole

Charlie Company, 1st Battalion, 22nd Infantry Regiment was in the jungle between Kontum and An Khe in September and October 1970. Mostly, we humped all day long, stopping at around 1600 or 1700 hours to set up a NDP (Night Defensive Position) where we would stay the night. We would ring the perimeter with foxholes, three guys to a hole. Not far behind the hole, we would snap two ponchos together and stretch them over branches to make a tent with a third poncho as ground cover. Each guy would take his turn in the hole on guard duty, usually two or four hours at a time, then crawl back to the hooch to wake up the next one for his turn.

It was pitch black in the jungle at night—so dark you couldn't see your hand in front of your face. Guard duty consisted of listening for sounds. I was awakened by Lewis about 0200 hours for my next turn, and as we moved by each other he whispered in my ear, "There's a monkey in the foxhole."

I managed a groggy, "What?" but he was already in the hooch and asleep. I took my position sitting on the edge of the hole with my legs inside the hole itself. We would punch holes in our empty C-ration cans and toss them down into the bottom of the foxholes, so that when we moved out in the morning and filled in the holes, the litter we left behind would be buried. We didn't want the NVA to use any of it.

About fifteen minutes after starting my turn, there came a noise from my left, the sound of metal clinking. It scared the hell out of me when I realized it came from the end of the foxhole I was sitting in. Then I remembered what Lewis had said. I was sharing the hole with a monkey three feet or so away from me. It was too dark to see him, but from the sounds he was making, I could tell that he was going through our empty food cans and eating the scraps and remnants.

It was kind of neat at first to have the little fella there, but he was sure making a lot of noise as he would go through the cans. And, when he was finished with a can, he would throw it down in the hole, hitting other cans and making more noise. To me, it seemed like he was making as much noise as a full brass band and was giving away my exact position to the entire North Vietnamese Army. For an instant, I thought of shooting him, but I couldn't even see him, and for all I knew, I might hit the guys in the next hole instead. Besides, I'd be telling the NVA exactly where everybody was. I scooped up a handful of dirt and threw it in the monkey's direction. He made little pitter patter sounds as he scurried out of the hole. All was quiet for about five minutes, and then he was back going through the cans again.

This went on for the rest of my turn and at one point, he threw down a can and hit me square in the leg. I had to calm down, knowing that even if I managed to jump on the little SOB in the dark and strangle him, they don't give Purple Hearts for being torn up by a monkey. When it was time, I crawled back to the hooch and woke up "Utah" for his turn at guard. I felt his shoulder, got close, and whispered to him, "There's a monkey in the foxhole." In three seconds, I was asleep and out like a light.

The next afternoon as we were setting up our next NDP, the three of us all talked about the monkey, and how he had scared, aggravated and angered us, one by one, throughout the night.

Michael Belis, Carencro, LA
Company C, 1st Battalion, 22nd Infantry Regiment

The Sniper

Company C, 1st Battalion, 22nd Infantry Regiment, stayed in the jungle between An Khe and Kontum for over two months in late 1970. We humped everything on our backs, finding or making a clearing every four or five days for resupply by chopper. High in the mountains we took water from the streams, adding purification tablets and lots of Kool Aid. At times, we would come across nothing but water too foul to use or no water at all. Then, the slicks would sling huge black rubber blivets with potable water and bring them with the resupply.

At one LZ on the top of a ridgeline, a couple of hours after we had received our resupply, another soldier we called "Utah" and I were detailed to fill the canteens for our squad. The LZ had been cut by hand and blown with C-4 by us and engineers who had been flown out to help. The blivet was at one end of the LZ next to a large pile of cut-down limbs and branches and tree trunks. As we were filling canteens, a sniper in the opposite tree line fired a shot that literally went right between Utah and me. We dived into the pile of limbs just as his second shot cracked overhead. His third shot smacked into the limbs and made us burrow deeper into the tangle of branches, nearer to the ground.

The guys in the tree line on our side of the LZ yelled out to stay put. (We weren't going anywhere.) We each had a rifle and a bandoleer of ammo, a pack of cigarettes, all the water we wanted, and were behind excellent cover. We figured we could stay there all day, no problem.

About twenty minutes to half an hour later, we heard brush breaking in the jungle at our end of the LZ halfway to the sniper's tree line. Then we heard a lot of brush breaking, and even chopping and hacking, followed by a whole lot of shouted curses. It was the unmistakable voice of Livingston, our squad leader for the first squad. He was a southern boy, and we southern boys have a knack for colorful language, but Livingston was teaching us all a few new things in the stuff he was yelling. "Utah" and I laughed until we cried, for we knew what had happened. Livingston had led the rest of the squad around the LZ to go get the sniper, but had run into growth so thick they couldn't get through it. It really upset him to not be able to get that NVA.

After things quieted down the sniper popped off another round just to let us know he was still there. Half an hour or so after that, the guys yelled out to us to get ready to run toward our side of the LZ. They were calling in artillery on the opposite tree line, and would lay down covering fire with M-60s for us. They would hold fire long enough for us to make it to the safety of the trees. Four M-60 machine guns opened up and when they stopped, the guys started yelling, but we were already up and running. The last twenty feet I flew through the air, landing on my stomach next to a gunner from the second platoon who had resumed firing before I hit the ground. Not but a few seconds later, the artillery began impacting on the far side of the LZ. Sometime after it finished, a lieutenant led a patrol but found neither hide nor hair of the sniper.

Livingston was something else. He had once run right up to a dink in a spider hole and shot the man in the head from only a few feet away. Only a couple of months before the sniper at the LZ, Livingston had taken a hit in the arm from a claymore booby trap, and a few weeks later was back humping the bush again. I still smile when I remember how frustrated he was not being able to get through that brush and get that sniper.

Chuck Boyle, Baton Rouge, LA
Companies A & C, 3rd Battalion, 22nd Infantry Regiment

Absolution

As a Vietnam Veteran I am honored—flattered—to have been asked to write something in summary regarding the awesome war experiences you've read in this book. As a writer, and as the editor for Utah Beach to Pleiku, I am intimately familiar with all of the stories in this book, World War II and Vietnam. Thus, Bob Babcock afforded me this opportunity to comment and I eagerly accepted.

He said, "Speak for your guys, the Vietnam veteran."

I can only speak to the Vietnam veteran through the body of all of you veterans who have experienced war and who have read this book—most particularly you World War II veterans. It was through your model of patriotism—your heroics—that made me a soldier. My being in uniform in Vietnam, was directly connected to your noble sacrifice. Let me explain.

I was born in Conemaugh, Pennsylvania. It was a sleepy, sooty, coal-mining town in the 1940s, but even as a small boy, I realized that the major event of the day was World War II.

I remember the mood well: War, sacrifice, and pride. To be a soldier was an honorable and a wonderful thing to be.

One afternoon, in the summer of 1945, when I was barely five years old, I stood on our creaky wooden porch to watch a parade of soldiers march through town. Sirens screamed and drums beat. There were flashing lights and little flags waving. The parade was led by our only fire truck, a military jeep, and old Mr. Lehman, riding on his motorcycle. They may have been veterans of the European theater, the Pacific, or they may have been young men preparing for war, but there they were, row after row of handsome uniformed men, passing by in step, carrying their rifles at "right shoulder."

As they passed in front of our house I danced with glee, and my mother told me it was "VJ Day."

"The war is over! Peace has come at last!" she cried.

So excited was I that I broke free from her grasp, dashed from the porch and joined the parade of victorious men, falling in behind them. And yes, tramp, tramp, tramp, we boys went marching. I believe I even had a little wooden stick and I, too, carried it at "right shoulder."

I followed them through town until they finally halted and dispersed at a local veterans' hall—the American Legion, perhaps. The afternoon turned into evening, and I became lost. I did not panic, for I held the trusty hand of a soldier. Although I was just a boy, I knew that I had frightened my mother and that I was in a heap of trouble back up there on Oak Street where she waited. Instinctively, however, I knew that somehow these soldiers would cover for me, make everything all right.

I remember a tall, strong, soldier picking me up, putting me astride his shoulders and carrying me back to my mother. I didn't care about the scolding I was going to get. I was so thrilled to be in the company of a soldier. I still am.

I remember the soldier explaining my predicament with a smile. He stood up for me, and my mother accepted his polite tale.

The years passed and it seemed that I was always in the company of soldiers. From my father I learned of his "doughboy" years in France. (General "Blackjack" Pershing had signed his discharge in 1918, writing that, "Johnny Boyle was a good horseman."

The brother of Charles Strank, our neighbor, told me how Chuck and some other fellows raised the flag on Iwo Jima and he got the Congressional Medal of Honor for it.

Korea came along and I remember my older brother Jack, his high school friends and many others, so splendid in their Marine Corp uniforms, teaching all of us kids how to sing the "Halls of Montezuma."

From the cradle to my teenage years, it was always one big patriotic event after another. We whitewashed veterans tombstones and we placed flags on veterans graves. We picnicked next to their resting places on the Fourth of July, and prayed over them on Memorial Day. So it was only natural, based on that kind of upbringing, that kind of tradition—that one should love their country; even fight and die for it—that I too, joined the ranks. Just like so many of you did, for the same reasons.

In 1967, I found myself on a jungle floor in Vietnam, an infantryman in the 3rd Battalion, 22nd Infantry, "The Regulars."

The tragedy and excesses of that war have been well documented by authors much more qualified than I. I cannot explain that war. I cannot speak for the men in high places who made that war—for whatever reasons: Greed perhaps or a misplaced idea about what America should be, or her role in the world. But, I can tell you about the Vietnam veteran, the men... soldiers.

They were as wholesome in their beliefs about America as any soldier who has ever passed before them. They were as patriotic as you would have them be—as their parents and teachers would have wanted them to be. They were as strong and handsome and charitable as that soldier who picked me up and put me on his shoulders and carried me home to my mother so long ago.

They were as eager in their desire to serve their country, to save the people of Southeast Asia from the clutches of Communism as the World War II soldiers were to save Europe and Asia.

At least, that is what we believed was our purpose at the time. So we marched off to Vietnam—honorably motivated—to serve our country as our fathers and brothers and uncles had done before us.

It is no secret that the war became a quagmire of political ineptitude here at home. My God—young college kids getting killed by our own soldiers at Kent State University. Do you remember that? Do you remember the assassinations of Dr. Martin Luther King Jr., and Bobby Kennedy? Were you out on patrol the night Dr. King died with a squad or platoon of black and white men with whom you entrusted everything, even your soul? Did you shrug it off and keep digging dirt and filling sandbags so that you might survive the jungle night?

How about the "Chicago Seven?" You remember all that, too, I'm sure.

It was a time of social upheaval at home and it became a tragedy on the battlefield. Young people circled the White House, chanting, "Hey, hey, LBJ. How many kids did you kill today?" American flags were burned in protest to the war we were fighting. Draft cards were torn up, and some were publicly soaked in pigs' blood.

This revolution at home and the failure of the war effort in Vietnam sucked the morale right out of me, and I suppose it might have done the same to you. Yet, you fought on... bravely and honorably.

The level of despair over Vietnam—the disenchantment with our leaders—the guilt; it was somehow transferred to the shoulders of our soldiers—the only symbol of government that people could see on the streets in America. Some in our society turned against their sons, and you boys felt it deep within your hearts and souls— and some still feel guilty about having been there. Many of our men quickly changed from their uniforms to civilian clothes as they made their way home after their tour of duty, unable to speak honestly to their loved ones and families about their experiences.

Heck, America as a whole was violently against the war by the time you got home. Few veterans felt like bragging about their service in the face of such an anti-war mood. Most of us stripped off our uniforms and went back to work, quietly. But what the hell, there wasn't any parade to go to anyway, was there?

Yes, we shut up about it—many of us even denying that we had ever served in Vietnam. Still the agony of our hell—our battles, our friends dying right beside us— it boiled inside our bellies, screaming to be released.

The ultimate indignity of it all occurred when Vietnam was handed over to the Communists by even more spineless men in high places. You boys had won the battles, but the nation's leaders would not allow you to savor a peace. All American units were out of Vietnam two years before the Saigon government collapsed and the Communists seized control of South Vietnam.

It became fashionable among the media, even common and trite, to say, "The only war 'we' ever lost."

Yes, the war was lost, and yes, "they" did lose the war.

But you men, those of you who fought it... you never lost a damn thing! Hear me... You didn't lose anything!

Oh, yeah, you might have lost an arm or a leg or an eye—maybe some muscle tissue. Even worse, you might have lost your best friend, but you didn't lose the war! I knew, felt in my heart, that someday, our absolution, our exoneration from guilt, our release from this silent and very personal agony would come. Some think that our vindication is that great Wall down there in Washington, D.C. Remember that parade... Finally?

For me, my absolution came at a reunion of World War II, Cold War, and Vietnam veterans of the 22nd Infantry Regiment at Gettysburg, PA, in October 1998. At about 0820 hours, a tall, handsome World War II soldier stood before the membership and welcomed us Vietnam Veterans into their own brotherhood of heroes.

He said, "To all you Vietnam Vets... welcome home. We welcome you to our ranks and we are proud of you. We extend to you the challenge of keeping our 22nd Infantry Regiment Society alive... and I know you will do it!"

And then, you know what happened? All of the World War II veterans stood and clapped for us. It felt good, being accepted by those who count the most: Our brothers, our uncles, and our fathers. I felt proud to stand beside the soldiers of World War II and share the memories of war. I know that you never abandoned us. I know that you knew we were following your soldierly example. I know that you know what we tried to do for America and for the people of South Vietnam. It is sufficient reward for me, that you, the greatest generation, recognize and honor our service on the battlefield.

I speak for all 4th Infantry Division Vietnam veterans, the living and the dead. We accept the torch of leadership that you have passed to us. We are steadfast and loyal, as always.

I daresay that soldier who picked me up and carried me home would be mighty proud of this book and of the men and women who wrote it.

Note: Charles J. "Chuck" Boyle is the author of Absolution, Charlie Company, 3rd Battalion, 22nd Infantry. ISBN 1-887901-30-2—Sergeant Kirkland's Press, 1999. Bob Babcock, Marietta, GA—Company B, 1st Battalion, 22nd Infantry Regiment

Final Thoughts on 4th Infantry Division in Vietnam

The 4th Infantry Division's participation in World War II was marked with a beginning—the invasion of Utah Beach on D-Day—and an end—VE day on May 8, 1945. Our Cold War participation spanned several decades but was marked with the dissolution of the Soviet Union and the tearing down of the Berlin Wall.

No specific beginning or end events can be pointed to for the 4th Infantry Division's experience in Vietnam. But, rather than just leaving our Vietnam War involvement hanging, let me try to give some final thoughts and perspective on the 4th Infantry Division's successes in Vietnam.

When we arrived in Vietnam in the summer of 1966, we started disrupting the NVA and Viet Cong influence in our areas of operation. I personally recall one of the first patrols my platoon and I were on. It was a mission to provide security for an engineer unit clearing a road of mines for the first time since the French left Vietnam in 1954. The division's movement to the Cambodian border and their long period of search and destroy missions on the Ho Chi Minh trail badly disrupted the NVA flow of men and materials into the south.

In 1969, the American policy of "Vietnamization" was begun. We gradually turned over our areas of operations and bases to the Army of South Vietnam (ARVN). Camp Enari and the central highlands responsibility was turned over to the ARVN 22nd Infantry Division on April 15, 1970. The 4th moved farther east to Camp Radcliff, near An Khe, which had been established in 1965 by the 1st Cavalry Division (Airmobile). On April 26, 1970, the 3rd Brigade, 4th Infantry Division left Vietnam and returned to their former parent unit, the 25th Infantry Division, elements of which had returned to Hawaii. The incursion into Cambodia in May 1970 marked the last major operation for the 4th Infantry Division. Patrols secured the area around An Khe for the next several months. In November 1970, the 1st Battalion, 22nd Infantry Regiment; 1st Squadron, 10th Cavalry Regiment; and 5th Battalion, 16th Field Artillery Regiment were assigned to other commands in Vietnam for further action. The 4th Infantry Division colors were finally returned to the United States and their new post at Fort Carson, Colorado, on December 7, 1970. There they combined resources with the 5th Infantry Division to become a mechanized division, which they are today.

It was almost eighteen months later, in the spring and summer of 1972, that the NVA were successful in entrenching themselves in the rugged terrain around Kontum. It wasn't until the final NVA offensive in early 1975, over four full years after the 4th Infantry Division had returned home, that Pleiku and the central highlands fell into communist hands. On April 30, 1975, Saigon and the government of South Vietnam fell to the NVA.

Why do I explain what happened after the 4th Infantry Division left the central highlands and their base south of Pleiku? As so many of us Vietnam veterans like to say, "We were winning when I left."

For those who did not serve in Vietnam, it is important that you understand the significance of the 4th Infantry Division's experience between 1966 and 1970. At no time did the 4th Infantry Division soldiers fail to accomplish their mission.

On the contrary, the soldiers of the 4th Infantry Division fought in some of the toughest battles of the Vietnam war, in some of the hardest terrain that an American army has ever fought in, and came out with their heads held high. Our missions, as they were given to us, were accomplished.

The stories of the soldiers of the Vietnam War are no different from those of our predecessors from previous wars—it is the story of common men doing the uncommon things that their country asked them to do. I know that I went to Vietnam to fight communism in Southeast Asia rather than to have to fight it in the United States. And, I believe my fellow soldiers and I were successful in accomplishing that mission. No one can say what our world would be like today if we had not done our duty in Vietnam in 1966-1970.

The American press and entertainment industry has stereotyped the Vietnam veteran as a dope addict, a baby killer, and a loser. That is wrong. The vast majority of Vietnam veterans are true American patriots, just like their fathers and grandfathers who answered our country's call to service in World War I, World War II, and the Cold War. And, as that great American philosopher Forrest Gump said, "That's all I'm going to say about that."